Brief Encounters

Previous Publications

JUDITH KITCHEN

ESSAYS
The Circus Train
Half in Shade
Distance and Direction
Only the Dance

NOVEL
The House on Eccles Road

ANTHOLOGIES
Short Takes
In Brief
In Short
The Poets Guide to the Birds

DINAH LENNEY

MEMOIR AND ESSAYS
Bigger than Life: A Murder, a Memoir
The Object Parade

CRAFT
Acting for Young Actors

Brief Encounters

A Collection of Contemporary Nonfiction

EDITED BY

Judith Kitchen and Dinah Lenney

W. W. Norton & Company

Independent Publishers Since 1923

NEW YORK • LONDON

For information about special discounts for bulk
purchases, please contact W. W. Norton Special Sales
at specialsales@wwnorton.com or 800-233-4830

Manufacturing by RR Donnelly Westford
Book design by Faern de Vicq
Production manager: Louise Mattarelliano

ISBN: 978-0-393-35099-9 (pbk.)

W. W. Norton & Company, Inc.
500 Fifth Avenue, New York, N.Y. 10110
www.wwnorton.com

W. W. Norton & Company Ltd.
Castle House, 75/76 Wells Street, London W1T 3QT

1 2 3 4 5 6 7 8 9 0

Do we want to dedicate this book, and to whom? Ideas?
What color cover jacket would you like?
　　　　　　　　　　　—Judith Kitchen, October 4, 2014

Are you there? Can you hear what I have to
tell you? Our lives are finite—and yet . . . Look
at the way they preserve themselves.
　　　　　　　　　　　—Judith Kitchen, *The Circus Train*

For Judith

Acknowledgments

I'm grateful to Fred Mills for cheering me up—
and to Stanley Rubin for cheering me on—
and to Amy Cherry and her colleagues at W. W. Norton for making a beautiful book.

Thanks also and especially to the writers gathered here— and to the readers wherever they are.

—*Dinah Lenney*
December 2014

Contents

Brief Encounters

Introduction

I'VE BEEN THINKING about an exhibit I saw a few years ago at the Metropolitan Museum of Art. "Rooms with a View," it was called—and if I hadn't had any other reason to fly across the country, it would have been enough: four galleries, beautifully curated, and each piece (there were more than fifty) featured a window. I loved it—loved the idea, loved its execution—the frame within the frame in every single painting, that was why I had to see; that was the hook, the angle that caught and held my imagination—the possibilities within and beyond the life of each canvas, the narrative opening in ways mysterious and provocative and ongoing, and those ongoing mysteries and provocations essential to its depth and truth. My mother-the-designer—who lives in New York, who had seen the show on her own—had other ideas: when she and I compared notes, we discovered we'd had different experiences, hers perhaps more in line with the curator's intentions than mine. The paintings weren't about the windows, said she. They'd been selected for their subject matter—for how each interior evoked the culture of the time, the values and habits of the people who had lived and worked in those rooms. She was right, of course. But so was I. A curator can lead the way, after all; she can even offer a headset and a guided tour—but, "Everything that is worthwhile is to some extent subjective," wrote Nabokov in "Good Readers and Good Writers," and therefore, deserves a subjective response.

Recently, with this intro in mind, I went back to the *New York Times* review that caught my eye in the first place, where critic Roberta Smith wrote, "The works here determinedly say no to established authoritative statements: formal portraiture and large-scale history painting"; under the circumstances, as applied to this collection of prose, how perfectly apt.

Although, as befits the genre (personal essay), I'm compelled to *confess*: I don't actually remember the paintings in order. I couldn't tell you which I saw first, or last, or how they were arranged on the walls. Nor do I suppose that the ones that struck me at the time would strike me today. Maybe some of them would. Undoubtedly others would spark for me as well. What I will insist is that they worked together; something for everyone and each piece worthy in and of itself, of course; but placed side by side, or across from each other—how this view mirrored that! How these lines, this shading, these curtains, this blue, this figure of a woman, this man in his topcoat, echoed, answered, or resolved an image I'd seen only moments before. There were some canvases I came back to again and again, and each time they looked different to me. Because that's how it is with art, or how it should be—and also because, as a collection, they engaged to inform each other and my experience of them; and would do so, I'm certain, all over again.

Brief Encounters, I hope, is much the same sort of deal. Actually, I wish we could retitle it *Meaningful Encounter* (singular) or *Continuous Encounter* (ditto). My point? Think of this book as a gallery: no large-scale portraits or formal histories here, but by virtue of collecting these "shorts," we mean to appeal to your readerly desire for resonance and depth.

Therefore I invite you to read the whole thing at once. Read it today, tonight, starting here, starting now, cover to cover. Or no. No, don't do that—linger, savor, take your time. Revel in each piece (we did)—and maybe share the excitement we felt as they began to accumulate; to talk to each other; to commiserate, contradict, enrich, color and shade, take on new properties and dimensions having everything to do with proximity and the way they fell into order.

Collections of anything speak to abiding appreciation as opposed to short attention spans. So we offer this one—which contains multitudes, by the way: multiple collections within the collection. In some cases we've placed them just so, back to back, as with Glazner and Wilson on sport, or Montemarano and Nadelson on pets. In others we've got them in dialogue on the level of the sentence or the subject: that is, where one writer ends, another begins, as with Cooley and Kothari, Parms and Geyer. Woven all the way through, to keep you situated and as if we'd planned it, notions about place and displacement—see Lopate, Schwartz, Ulin, Boylan, Daum, Talbot, Martone, and Weschler (among so many others); and as prevalent as is geography as a theme, so is getting from here to there, as contemplated by Birkerts, Borich, Iyer, and Gay; which inevitably brings up the ties that continue to bind and confound us: with our mothers (Wickersham and Berne), and fathers (Goldberg and Wilson), and brothers and sisters (Hurd, Anastas)—and partners (Houston, Miller, Shumaker)—and friends (Sukrungruang, Bonomo, Daugherty).

Brief Encounters is not meant as a response, or concession—or capitulation!—to these distracted times. Just as those paintings in "Rooms with a View" were chosen for themselves, so it was with each of the essays here: it's we who are better for having brought them together: happier, sadder, wiser, more aware of the ways we're connected to each other and the world.

*

Recently, I came across a book called *What We See When We Read*, by Peter Mendelsund, a designer and art director at Knopf. Again and again, Mendelsund reminds his readers that no two of us experience a book in exactly the same way. That every reader comes to the text with his or her singular imagination (and baggage), and thus makes it his or her own.

And about the reader—about ourselves as readers—he writes:

> *We perform a book—we perform a reading of a book.*
> *We perform a book, and we attend the performance.*
>
> *(As readers, we are both the conductor and the orchestra, as well as the audience.)*

That's to say it's up to you now: this is your collection—your encounters to do with as you please. Read—read any way you like, for as long as you like: start at the start, at the end, in the middle. Discover your own perfect order, as we discovered ours. As we will, no doubt, on rereading, perceive yet another. Perform this book—enjoy the performance.

—*Dinah Lenney, 2014*

AROUND TWENTY YEARS ago, when I first began work on this series of anthologies, nonfiction writers had begun turning to a shorter unit of text, and the "short" was just coming into its own. My co-editor and I scoured books and journals and found several examples; often they were segments of longer pieces. Then began the endless round of, yes, photocopying letters, stuffing envelopes, hand-writing addresses, licking stamps, and waiting for the replies. Even ten years ago—when it was possible to find many more shorts in many more places—contacting authors and publishers still took considerable time.

Technology has caught up with us (still more content to choose from!)—for this project we not only went to books and journals and newspapers, but also to online magazines (complete with illustrations and hyperlinks), blogs, and often the authors themselves. Email made for rapid and easy turnaround and we were amazed at how quickly we were able to put together a collection of work by contemporary and emerging writers. We even have an entry from a particularly penetrating and lyrical blog. As always, one of the main sources was Dinty W. Moore's *Brevity* magazine, a top-quality online journal that prints essays of 750 words and under. Since our limit remains a maximum of 2,000 words, we were happy to find that many new magazines were printing outstanding short (but not too short) pieces.

Not surprisingly, many of these selections take advantage of today's technology by incorporating the language of the Internet, Google, and Facebook, and, although the reading experience is different in a book, we have tried to include some that are, in some form or other, interactive. For example, some list links, and several pieces refer to—and include—photographs, now easily incorporated as part of the text.

Although technology breeds innovation, it can also erode tradition. As Dani Shapiro said in an article in the *New Yorker*, "Facebook is, after all, a way of staying connected in an increasingly busy and disconnected world—but it can also feel thin and undigested, a skimming over of data rather than a deep sink into the specificity and emotional reality of human experience." We, too, worry about this trend, and we've seen some evidence that with so much online activity, writers—and readers—may be settling for work that has what we would call "a one-read shelf [substitute 'click'] life." Too much instant drama without the necessary reflection. What intrigues us is a traditional essay—writ small, and with a distinctive voice. So we've tried to select a broad cross-section of human experience in addition to some more whimsical experiments. Throughout, we have scattered pieces that contain commentary on art, music, literature, and a smattering of political observation that might not become dated by the time of next month's new conference. The result is a mixture of memoir and critique, article and meditation, slice-of-life and conjecture, fragment and contemplation.

There is often something in the air—something that writers seem to tap into. This collection contains less love and more violence. What does that mean? Less landscape and more town- or cityscape. Less nature and more regret. Less lyric and more narrative. Is this just coincidence? And more diversity—witness the proliferation of Spanish words. As always, there is an enduring emphasis on family, childhood, and the central role of memory. There's fun in noting trends, and this time we found an uncanny number of pieces on sleeping, dreaming, and waking—enough that we decided to weave those nighttime pieces into an ongoing "theme." There's more than one Schwinn bicycle circling the block here, more than one sewing pattern, along with a few sets of high-thread-count sheets. All the fast-fading ephemera: cigarettes, catalogs, train sets, road maps, lottery tickets. Certain words made their way from essay to essay, establishing themselves as common concerns: *water, cloud, rain, photograph, listen*. "Listen," they say, as though all the noises in our environment—Muzak at the gas station, cell phones in the airport—are endangering the close attention it takes to hear what someone is compelled to say. "Listen," they command, as they call our shortened attention spans to the larger world and its vast physical pleasures.

—*Judith Kitchen, 2014*

James Richardson

Aphorisms & Ten-Second Essays

THE ROAD REACHES every place, the shortcut only one.

Wind does not blow the wind away, nor water wash away the water.

Patience is not very different from courage. It just takes longer.

Listen. But not too carefully, since what I'm saying is not exactly what I mean.

There is a moment falling asleep when you can't tell whether voices are in the room or in your head. Wide awake, you may be embarrassed or cross if your imaginary conversation with someone is interrupted by the person himself, as if he might have heard. Our thinking about our lives is dramatic: scenes and scripts and voices. I'm surprised that multiple personalities are so much less common in reality than in fiction: what a little disorder it would take, a distraction, a sleep, for one of our minor characters to imagine *he* was the star, to speak out for everyone else. And that's what it would be, a change of billing, not of authorship. For you do not write your play—you are just the character in it called *The Playwright*. The real writer, you never meet.

More dangerous than the worst is the pretty good you can no longer tell from the best.

That the bookstores divide into romance and mystery suggests that the two most powerful fantasies are someone to love and someone to blame.

In the long run, the single sin is less of a problem than the good reasons for it.

Decades later, I dream long dreams of my brother alive. Or I am still in my first marriage, and childless: none of what I now call my life has been thought of. Does this mean that news travels slowly, that there are still great strata of the brain waiting to feel shocks we thought had reached our cores? More likely, the stories we tell ourselves of the past and the present, the possible and the fantastic, exist in the mind separately from the secondary characteristics no longer and not real. How lightly, closing my eyes, that connection between the image and its status is deranged. I realize more and more that some idea or love or scene I have only thought of all these years has become as important as what actually happened, realer.

By looking for the origins of things we deceive ourselves about their inevitability. Things that did not happen also have origins.

Theories of happiness are somehow less troubled by the misfortunes of the deserving than by all those people who are happy and couldn't possibly be.

So many times I've made myself stupid with the fear of being outsmarted.

All but the most durable books serve us simply by opening a window on all we wanted to say and feel and think about. We may not even notice that they have not said it themselves till we go back to them years later and do not find what we loved in them. You cannot keep the view by taking the window with you.

I say nothing works anymore, but I get up and it's tomorrow.

Success is whatever humiliation everyone has agreed to compete for.

Things fall of their own weightlessness.

I don't know what is meant by Know Thyself, which seems to ask a window to look at a window. I aspire to know when best to walk or eat, which music I need, and how to keep myself sitting as I am now, stubbornly enraptured with doing next to nothing. These are likely the things people learn who have to start persnickety cars in the cold, or get the most out of exhausted fields.

I say I have no self-knowledge, but I know which things I will never tell you.

If you want to know how they could forget you, wait till you forget them.

I keep glimpsing the loneliness I want, my thoughts without me.

When a jet flies overhead, every glass in the cupboard sings. Feelings are like that: choral, not single; mixed, never pure. The sentimentalist may want to deny the sadness or boredom in his happiness, or the freedom that lightens even the worst loss. The moralist will resist his faint complicity. The sophisticate, dreading to be found naïve, will exclaim upon the traces of vanity or lust in any motive, as if they were the whole. Each is selling himself simplicity; each is weakened with his fear of weakness.

Why should the whole lake have the same name?

There are silences harder to take back than words.

Singing is a way of remembering to breathe.

This sentence is headed into the future, and past it, into the past.

Martha Cooley

What I Hear

THE SOUNDS VARY.

There's always a low-pitched thrumming in the background, comparable to the sound of an engine room. Of some sort of equipment running all the time. Not loud but steady, though with slight intermittent variations—as I imagine an engine room might sound if one were standing at a distance from it and its door were opened briefly, then closed. There are yawnings as the low thrum is amplified, then suppressed. At times there's something like a pulse, too, which might be called a ringing in my ears. As though a very large bell has been rung, and what I'm hearing is the lapping of sound-waves after the noise made by the clapper has died away.

Then there are the high-pitched sounds. They aren't consistent, though they're continuous. Sometimes I hear a shrill whistling, sometimes a keen needling, sometimes the slightly lower-toned sound of a violin string being bowed, sometimes the classic fingernails-on-blackboard sound. Now and then, something like crickets in summertime. There are ascents and dips in these varied high-pitched sounds: they swoop around the walls of the chamber that is my head—one sound arising and resolving into another, another, another . . .

If I manage to consider this nonstop, inescapable aural experience not as a condition known as tinnitus but as a performance, I can convince myself I'm listening to a concert by a composer who insists on continuous contrasts. A composer who needs the depth of the underlying *basso* and the heights of trillings and shrillings all at once, all the time. But if I'm unable to avail myself of this metaphor—unable to think of what's happening in my head as a musical event I happen not to have purchased tickets for, but must attend nonetheless—then I'm left feeling as though I'm in a torture chamber. One from which I cannot escape: it's my head, after all. I'm listening to *me*, hearing the sound of *myself*.

IF, WHILE WRITING the *Inferno*, Dante had considered the perfect *contrappasso* for narcissists—the punishment that would perfectly and eternally fit their sin—I'm sure he'd have come up with tinnitus.

Ceaseless sounds in one's head are arguably the ultimate torment of self-consciousness. They seat the noisy self front-and-center, elbowing aside any other sound-makers. I cannot listen to music at low volume, for my tinnitus interferes. Even forceful music can be overridden by what goes on in my head. And I have no idea what people are talking about when they talk about silence; it doesn't exist for me.

Perhaps it never did—not for me, nor for Dante's sinners or anyone else. Perhaps all people experience at least a very mild form of tinnitus. Silence is an abstraction, after all; it can never be a reality. Go to a very quiet place and you'll invariably discover it's not quiet after all; tiny noise-makers thrive all around you. And who can assert exactly where to draw the line between noises outside and inside one's head?

Certainly people who've worked around loud machinery, or played in loud bands, or turned their headsets up too loud for too long, are at risk of experiencing a self-generated din. But then there are people who didn't injure their ears yet are still subject to this condition, if that's the right word for it. This existential challenge. This tester of sanity, this bane of self-awareness.

The sound of the self's echo-chamber, I sometimes think of it as. The sound of solipsism.

I can terrify myself, focusing on what I hear in my head. I wonder if I'm suffocating, not from lack of air but from lack of noiselessness. What does it mean, that my self cannot shut the hell up?

Certain things worsen my tinnitus: stress, fatigue, strong emotion. I can ignore it, to some degree. There are stretches of time during each day—sometimes a moment or two, sometimes longer, a few hours—when I'm barely conscious of the soundtrack in the background, the aural accompaniment to my daily doings. I can choose not to pay any attention, even try to pretend, for a little while, that it's not there.

But I don't ever kid myself that it's going away. That ain't happening till I die.

EVER SINCE I was a child, I've had the experience of falling asleep and then awakening, now and then, to a peculiar sense of deracination. As if whatever normally roots me just isn't there; as if the tether has snapped. I can feel my self scrambling for a purchase on coherence, and as I wait for it to do so, I hear it playing its usual music.

Usual, that is, in the sense of familiar, ever-present. But not usual as in repetitive, for my tinnitus is improvisational; it never repeats itself. Are its sounds therefore aleatory, composed purely by chance? Or do they represent something going on in my autonomous nervous system? Or in my psyche, soul, whatever one wants to call it?

I don't know. That's one of the teachings of tinnitus, in fact. Each day it sings to me: *You don't have a clue, do you?*

IN MY HEAD there's an orchestra, conductor-less but animated. Going nonstop.

The instruments don't have players; they play themselves. The music they make is true to my discords and excitements, fears and thrills, questions and uncertainties. It's their natural accompaniment, this music. It offers my inner life an ever-changing set of sound-shapes that form and disperse like clouds, uncanny yet familiar.

Oh be quiet, I tell the instruments now and then, you're never quiet, what's wrong with you!

They pay no attention, of course. Uncensored, immune to judgment, they simply keep going.

The instruments are playing me to myself. What can I do but listen?

Geeta Kothari

Listen

MY FATHER TAUGHT my sister and me every action mattered. Not because of karma or reincarnation. Not because of dharma or right actions.

If we placed our shoes the wrong way in the closet—let them flip over, facedown—our mother would die. If we swung our legs while sitting—our mother would die. If we bought leather on a Saturday—our mother would die. I asked, maybe once, maybe a second or third time, definitely not a fourth time, "Why?" and my father, sounding pained, said, "Must you ask such questions?" So I believed, as did my sister, that when I bought my shoes, how I placed them in the closet or on the floor of the living room, where my father would trip on them, mattered. And as long as I followed these rules—no leather on Saturday, no swinging my legs with careless abandon—my mother would live.

There were other rules: the no-traveling-on-Tuesday-or-Saturday rule; the no-cutting-nails-after-sunset rule; the no-vacuuming-after-dark rule. If you traveled on a Tuesday or Saturday, you wouldn't reach your destination. If you vacuumed after dark, you'd lose your money (or never make any). I have no memory of the consequences of cutting your nails after sunset. When I was child, nail-cutting—finger-and-toenails—happened on the weekend. We sat on the parquet floor of my parents' bedroom in a patch of sunlight, with newspaper under our feet. After we were done, my mother wrapped up the newspaper and tossed it into the incinerator in the hallway. Keeping cut nails in the apartment was bad luck.

As was asking anyone where he or she was going. Leaving the apartment with four suitcases, bound for India, my father would warn my sister and me not to talk to anyone. He avoided looking at anyone else who boarded the elevator and discouraged all conversation with monosyllabic answers.

"Going on a trip?"

"Yes." Or sometimes, "Maybe."

In the awkward silence that followed, he would stare at the indicator or, worse, turn to one of us—my mother, my sister, or me—and start speaking in Hindi, desperate to avoid further conversation about his trip. For if someone asked where we were going, we'd never get to India. Our journey would stall or we'd be diverted. We'd be delayed in traffic and miss our flight. Luggage would end up on the other side of the world.

Bad things would happen.

LEAVING HOME wasn't easy. If I sneezed as my father was leaving the apartment—and because I had allergies, this happened all the time—my father would shut the door and look at me.

Sneeze again, he'd say.

I can't, I'd say.

Oh boy, he'd sigh, and then he'd take a seat at the dining table, situated in the foyer.

The second sneeze canceled the first. But when it became clear

I couldn't control my sneezes, my father instituted a new procedure. If I sneezed, he would point to the sugar.

Take a pinch, he said.

Why?

Geeta, he said. Don't argue.

We had three words for sugar in our house—*shakkar*, *cheeni*, and *khaand*—and I understood all of them. What I did not understand was how a pinch of sugar could cancel out a sneeze.

Why don't you listen to me? he said.

I took a pinch of sugar. I didn't ask where he was going. I kept my shoes neatly lined up in my closet. I believed my actions would keep my parents alive forever.

I listened.

I LEFT HOME. I moved to another state, and sometimes I wonder, if I hadn't given my parents my address, would they have asked for it?

I have my own house now. When my husband leaves, I ask, "When will you be back?" or "Going to the gym?" We remove our shoes at the front door, and by the end of the week, they've piled up, and it takes a while to put a pair together. One day, searching through the mess, I flipped one of my felt slippers over. It lay face down on the floor as I sifted through the shoes, late for work and irritable.

I stuffed my feet into my boots and ignored the slipper. My parents were both dead. I could buy leather any day of the week. I could sneeze before leaving the house. I could sneeze when my husband left the house.

I had one word for sugar. Despite my best efforts, the people who understood the other words were gone.

Why don't you listen to me?

But my husband's mother was still alive. What would happen to her if I left that slipper flipped over? She was my mother-in-law, not my mother. Canadian, not Indian. Raised Mennonite, on a farm in Manitoba, she would never let a sneeze prevent her from leaving the house. She bought leather purses and shoes any day of the week.

I stared at the grooved rubber sole of my slipper.

And then I turned it over.

Patrick Madden

Dispatch from Montevideo

In which the Madden family flies to Uruguay and plays the lottery

I AM A DOTING FATHER, sufficiently hardworking, eager to sing and wrestle with my children, but I must admit that there are times when I question the sanity of bringing six of them into this world. Just recently, for instance, we made our way diagonally across most of the United States, from the Rockies to the Everglades, then south across the equator and the seasons in a day-long journey to Montevideo, Uruguay. Delays and frustrations of the kind we experienced are trying enough when all one faces is boredom and discomfort, but they're increased substantially when one is responsible for the boredom and discomfort of younger others who've no compunctions about running amok shouting their dissatisfactions. And when the planned trip will last four months, and we're carting all sorts of hand-me-downs for the cousins and school supplies for the at-risk kids my sister-in-law teaches, and the airlines have cut back their allowed checked bags from two to one and from seventy pounds to fifty, then we Maddens are a scene worth scoffing at: laden with backpacks and duffel bags, bulging roller bags in tow, carrying the two wriggling little ones, we struggled through security, exasperated, from gate to gate. Did I mention that the domestic legs of our flight were canceled?

We were placed on other flights, but our carefully reserved block of seats was lost, even from Miami to Montevideo, and we were planted all over the planes. After an hour-and-a-half on hold I was told that I'd have to take it up with the counter agent at the airport, or else ask kind strangers to switch seats once we were on board.

Ah, but what an adventure! More adventurous for the half dozen half-pints we'd brought.

> *An adventure is only an inconvenience rightly considered.*
> —G. K. Chesterton, "On Running After One's Hat"

And really, the success of a journey like this can be determined by answering one simple question: Did we get there in one piece? Yes, we did, and mostly in seats next to or near one another. When we arrived, finally, a little later than scheduled, a bit ragged and sweaty, with unbrushed teeth and morning breath, we gasped through yawns at the long-loved beauties of late-winter Montevideo: palms among pines, sun shining from the north, celestial blue sky dotted by puffs of cloud, a general buzz of motor activity, and (even unexpected things) a brand-new airport terminal with all the latest technologies and amenities.

Having taken our time gathering all our belongings, we had deplaned behind the throng headed for immigration. When we found our fellow travelers, they were snaked into a long line waiting for their interviews and rubber stamps, so we braced for one more delay, but the airport staff took pity and shuffled us into a line for flight crews and the handicapped. I tried to avoid eye contact with the folks in the queue as we were called almost immediately to the glass booth.

As she made her way pleasantly-methodically through our passports, calling us one by one and thumping her stamp from inkpad to book in staccato trochee, our official stopped and smiled. "Who's Sara?"

Sara raised her hand and eyebrows.

"My namesake!" the official beamed.

I glanced at her name tag, though I never really doubted.

"No way!" she sang as she studied Sara's vitals. "She was born on the tenth of March?"

"Yes," Karina replied.

"That's my birthday, too! I can't believe it. Not even if I'd wanted a coincidence." She rummaged through her purse to show us her ID. Sure enough, she was "from the tenth of March," as she said again; 1962, I noted surreptitiously.

We all raised our eyebrows and smiled, commenting on the rarity of it all, as she flipped to another passport, Marcos's. "September fifteenth!" she cried. "That's my son's birthday!" Much excitement followed as we played along. "And January twenty-eighth!?" She had found James's. "That's when my father was born. No; I mean, *no*. This is just too much!" We carried on our accompaniment, but really, there was nowhere else to go. We'd already reached maximum excitement.

She hadn't been paying attention to dates before she noted Sara's, so she quickly ran through the rest of the family's, saying aloud each birth date, but she came up empty. So that was it, then: three same birthdays between our family and hers, with the double correspondence: the two Saras born on the same day of March. From the three days she had 10, 15, and 28. To round out her cosmic lucky numbers, she asked Karina and me for our ages: 35 and 41. "Perfect," she said. "I'll play them in the *Cinco de Oro*. The jackpot's up to forty-five million pesos."

"That's a good idea," said Karina, happy with the happenstance.

"And if I win, I'll track you down and give you half."

"Well, then, I hope you win."

"I hope I win, yes. I mean, how wouldn't I win? I swear, with all the people I've passed through immigration, this has never happened before. What a day!"

Call it a fluke or call it fate, the law of large numbers or the sporadic alignment of chance in a vast chaotic system. Work at immigration long enough, and you're bound to meet a doppelgänger, if only in name and birthday. A kid with your name crosses your path once a week, maybe, depending on how common your name is; once a day if your name is Sara. The question is whether you recognize what you're seeing, hear a mother calling or see a document. And the statistical probability that a specific other shares your very birthday is 0.27 percent, very low. But gather a random sampling of people and ask them when they were born. Despite what your intuition might tell you—that shared birthdays are rare—with only twenty-three people, you've got a better than 50 percent chance that two will have been born on the same day of the same month. Increase the number of people to thirty, and the probability grows to over 70 percent. With only fifty-seven people, at least two will share a birthday 99 percent of the time. Among the conveniently estimated three hundred sixty-seven people milling about the immigration checkpoint of José Carrasco International Airport around 10:40 a.m. on Tuesday, August 28, a shared birthday was an absolute certainty. That the sharers would find each other in the crowd, well . . . discerning that probability requires a different algebra.

We are a pattern-finding species, perhaps none of us more so than the essayists, whose job it is to corral bits of raw experience into meaning without inventing rounded scenarios and uncanny coincidences. Our imaginations don't supply the materials, but they make the connections.

> *Men observe when things hit, and not when they miss; and commit to memory the one, and forget and pass over the other.*
>
> —Francis Bacon, *Sylva Sylvarum*

The next day, once we'd mostly unpacked and some of us had showered and all of us had eaten our favorite Olympic sandwiches and pascualina and salami and cheese, Karina and her mother ran off to throw away forty pesos on a lottery ticket. We were sated, after all, surrounded by family, feasting and laughing and sharing memories and stories. The air veritably buzzed with the chaotic hum of all those children asking questions and making observations, pouring themselves soda from the refrigerator without asking, leaving the door open when they took their leave or made an entrance, doling out the kisses to grandparents and aunts and uncles and cousins, bouncing off the walls. If 10-15-28-35-41 weren't our lucky numbers, then so what? So blessed were we in that moment that a donation to the void seemed a fitting sacrifice, a symbolic payment for the hubbub of joy, an investment in just a bit more, please.

Sven Birkerts

One Long Sentence

ONE LONG SENTENCE is what it felt like, the day's travel, emphasis falling first on *long*, for all the obvious reasons, but also on *sentence*, for reasons almost equally obvious, except "sentence" here used in the sense of a task, a punishment not to be commuted, though play could be made with that word as well, since what I'm talking about is travel, going to the airport so as to get from one city to another, the directionality of that process almost grammatical, starting with what I'll call the beginning of the sentence, my arriving through the big automatic doors as through the wide mouth of a funnel and being from that moment on led by a kind of syntactical logic from one point to another, each point representing the next narrowing increment of that funnel—from the ticket counter into the line for document and security check, then to the divestiture of belt and shoes and coins and keys, all preliminary to the frisk-position indignity of having the nethers irradiated and inspected, after which the re-vestiture and humping down the long corridor, that being the equivalent in this analogy to the narrower aperture of the funnel, my forward motion conspicuously against the tide of the oncoming throngs, all those who have debarked, who are already carrying the air of the un-pent, whereas

heading to the waiting area I am feeling ever more pent, subjected
to the diktat of the vast systems and schedules and inadvertencies
over which one has no control whatsoever, all agency surrendered,
nothing someone like me can do upon setting down my bags
and subsiding into the waiting area seat but attend the garbled
announcements and heed, or try *not* to heed, the screens everywhere, the maps and talking heads on the weather feed, finding
myself either way braced against some item of breaking news that
might yet affect my trajectory, the storm system developing over
the Rockies, or the unsettled air-mass moving down from Canada; nothing for me to do but wait for the first indications that
boarding is imminent, those indications comprising not only the
posted notice on the screen at the gate, but also the peripherally
noted movements of my fellow passengers, who for some occult
reason *always* know better than I do what is happening—witness
the unprompted massing that begins there by the far wall, a gathering that, like every gathering of bodies the world over, manifests
almost instantly that agitated jockeying, with the undisguised
suspicion directed by everyone standing at everyone else, all of it
somehow making it unthinkable that I would simply wait in my
seat and not myself join the tense commotion; so of course I do—
how not?—whereupon ensues that most uncomfortable inter-
val of shifting from foot to foot while nudging my bag forward,
guarding with elbows and posture-cues that little area I have
claimed through tenancy, a discomfort matched some time later
by the jerky forward snaking of what has mysteriously become a
line of sorts, and the whole business merely shifts into a different
key when we all begin inching down the aisle of the plane, with
everyone's (certainly my) cold-blooded calculations about getting
their bag into a free bin space (should such still exist), and then the
bodily origami exertions of folding the oversized body into the
undersized seat, right next to the big guy who will for sure turn

out to be the captain of his college lacrosse team, the only recom-
pense for all this then being able to study from below the slow
parade of those who were behind me filing past and making the
identical eye and body movements that I just made myself; and
then, of course, come the myriad departure preparations, the seal-
ing of the doors, the sub-abdominal rumble of the engines and
the fast sharp clicks as the cabin attendant moves front to back
securing the overhead bins, and then comes the ultimate token
jolt of our collective fates being sealed as the craft jerks away from
the gangway and begins the taxi-queue, at which point there is
nothing for me to do but stare out the rubber-glazed porthole at
the tarmac panorama, the criss-cross movements of carts and fuel
trucks, the intermittent glimpse of the tall fin of the plane right in
front, nothing to do but breathe in and out calmly and calculate
how well my row position sets me up for drink service, no task
but to mark my place in what has been a very long sentence and
which will be longer still, that being the nature of the complex-
compound entity that is the traveler's day, which has its first origins in the unsettled sleep of the night before and keeps unfolding
through its innumerable preliminaries, acquiring renewed impe-
tus as the plane builds its shuddering velocity on the ground and
then, with what feels like the magical shift of a change of state,
suddenly breaks with the ground and lifts, and lifts and lifts, and
if the time is right and we are favored by the weather, there comes
the second transformation, which is the beautiful rise from the
clouded-over ground atmosphere into that acetylene blue, the blue
so pure when it first strikes the eye that it would seem there *is*
redemption, there *is* freedom—though this time it is too late in
the day, the blue is gone, there is, instead, a kind of bruised mauve
lying over the cloud mass that extends on and on, that incredible uniformity, darkening ever so gradually as we move forward,
though in truth it feels that we are suspended without motion, and

it is not until I am well into the second of my distressingly small
screw-top merlots that the window square has become fully dark,
nothing to be seen then, not for the next hour, nothing below, the
sentence having become truly interminable, all my thoughts now
moving away from this tedious moment, in which my fellow passengers are either reading or doing things with their laptops—or,
like my lacrosse captain, sleeping—forward to the idea of arrival,
the imagery of it suddenly available, the happy practical business
of life on the ground, from my first debarking the plane to my
later riffling through the mail waiting on the kitchen counter, all
of it within reach, nearly so, nearly so—except that like a worthy
sentence, at least any sentence I would aspire to write, this one
takes its unforeseen turn, figurative *and* literal, as the pilot, who
has been steadily lowering our altitude for some minutes, quite
suddenly banks left, a full-body tilt, and as he does we either cut
through the cloud mass, or else it has ended when I wasn't looking; in any case, the plane veers sharply left and down and as I put
my face to the window I see what looks like a vast spill of sugar,
only brighter, harder, really more like some display in a museum
kept under glass so that children won't reach down to touch, and
as I now push in past the window reflections, to try to really *see*,
I feel it, in the part of the body that knows: this is me, all of us,
hanging in parenthesis outside of ourselves, here out in space in
the night, but at the same time homing in on script and schedule,
our long room tipping lightly side to side, the lights below coming
closer in small jumps, the first murky definition of buildings and
houses, the arterial sprawl of roads, fields, and parks marked by
boundary lights, the abrupt grinding whine of the landing gear,
and the feeling, we all have it (I'm sure), everyone on alert, sitting
up, that very soon this will be brought to a close, our plane will be
touching down on what is still, on the pilot's radar screen, the size
of a punctuation mark, a period.

Pico Iyer

Why I Travel

"WHAT AM I AFRAID OF?" I asked myself not long ago. Not many things. A traveler can't afford to carry fears with him, leaping into the unknown on every trip. The only things I could think of were snakes, which sometimes fill my dreams—and heights, which induce in me a mad impulse to take a running jump. And the previous year I'd been involved in a near-fatal car crash in Bolivia, my taxi almost plunging off a ravine, at twelve thousand feet, as it rolled and rolled after being driven into a mountain at high speed, all its passengers (but me) ending up in the hospital. I'd been wary of narrow and unpaved roads ever since.

Five days later, I was being driven—at very high speed—on the wrong side of a two-lane road, bicycles and blaring trucks and overfull buses and children coming at us, towards a sheer rock face in the center of Sri Lanka. Sigiriya is reached by thirteen hundred steps, straight up, it seems, and my guidebook had told me that the ascent of the great rise was "not for the faint-hearted," perhaps better appreciated from the ground. Halfway up the rock face, climbing a vertiginous spiral staircase—bought, I later learned, from the London Underground in the 1930s—I looked down and saw nothing but air. A three- or four-hundred-foot drop at my feet, if I slipped, and jungle all around.

"Are there accidents here?" I asked my guide, fumbling along the guardrail, and wondering why my job demanded such trips of me.

"Oh, too many," he said. "So many people are so crazy."

We climbed up and up, passing some half-sensible travelers who had decided to climb partway, but not ascend further, through a staircase set between a sculpted lion's paws. Signs everywhere warned against what my guide told me were swarms of "killer bees." At the top of our ascent, he said, it was mostly snakes.

"Snakes?"

"Only pythons, sir. No problem."

Chameleons turned red and white and green in the sun at the top of the rock face. Huge lizards who might have been iguanas—"land monitors," someone said—breathed evilly among the outcroppings. A man with a small wicker basket looked at me and said, "You want see cobra?"

It could have been a compendium of my nightmares. "Leopards, wild elephants," my driver had said, listing the occupants of the jungle we were driving through. "Also guerrillas, Tamil guerrillas, very close. You see the trucks? They always drive together, too close, because of the wild elephants."

Ten months before, when I'd volunteered to take the trip (to an editor who had offered me the chance to go anywhere from Iran to Mongolia), a cease-fire had been in place in Sri Lanka and it had lasted three years. A tsunami had swept through the ill-starred island less than two years before, but that, in my crazy logic, meant that the odds were against any other calamity visiting. Westerners were buying up property in the walled fort in Galle and deluxe six-star hotels were opening up everywhere.

Almost the minute I chose Sri Lanka as my dream destination, and began making plans to go there, a new hard-line government came into power, after elections, and fighting resumed with new intensity. My editor wrote to me excitedly that war made our story more vibrant and topical than ever; I, not knowing where to turn, and with a sinking and unfamiliar feeling in my stomach, went to a chapel high in the hills two days before I left California and prayed for something and then, the next day, went again, as if for insurance.

Never, in a lifetime of travel, had I felt so uneasy about leaving the certainties of home behind; something, I was sure, was telling me not to go.

At this point, on the road next to the place where the guerrillas and elephants were said to lurk, our vehicle broke down. Then the car was started up again, by a wild-looking mechanic dressed in nothing but a sarong and an explosion of frizzy hair, and the driver started going faster, into the path of oncoming cars, swerving and then veering off at the last minute. "No problem," he said. "I have never had accident."

But—I didn't need to remind him—it didn't matter if he was a flawless driver himself. If anyone else on the road, many of them driving without licenses, or while drunk, made a mistake, we would be history, and if we hit anyone else, the blame would fall on us. The sensation of rolling and rolling in the car, ever closer to the precipice in Bolivia, came back to me with unwanted intensity.

"You have brothers and sisters?" I said, to distract myself.

"One sister, sir. But she died, fifteen years old. Driver, too many drinking, hit her on the road."

Then the car gave out again. Night began to fall over the jungle. The people riding bicycles began to fade away. We were alone in the chattering darkness.

For twenty years now, I'd taken great pains not to visit Sri Lanka, paradisal though it was said to be; it was the one spot in the world where I was directly implicated in a savage revolution. My father was a Tamil, after all, from South India; my name, my very face branded me as a member of the group tearing up the island with terrorist attacks. I'd decided, when I made my plans, that such issues were irrelevant: but now, in the weeks since I'd bought my ticket, new outbursts of violence, on both sides of the war, brought Sri Lanka into the headlines every day. A kind Englishwoman who had invited me to look in on her when I visited Colombo—her life had been changed, she said, after she found herself on holiday in Sri Lanka when the tsunami arrived and decided to abandon her job and work on the paradise island—had come down with dengue fever. Indeed, most of the ambassadorial corps in Colombo was said to have contracted the rare and famously horrible disease.

My first day in the country, two days before, the third highest man in the Sri Lankan army had been picked off by a suicide bomber only minutes away from where I was having breakfast. Only weeks before, six sightseers had been shot dead in a national park, and sixty-four more civilians died when their bus ran over a mine. The Temple of the Tooth, the previous day—the holiest shrine in the country—had been more full of soldiers and of guns than of monks.

Now it was pitch-black, and the absence of lights coming from our car matched the absence of lights all around. The leopards, the wild elephants, certainly the guerrillas—all the attributes of what the newspapers called the "teardrop island"—seemed very close indeed. The driver tried to use his cell phone, but all he heard was static.

"You have phone, sir?" he asked.

"On the far side of the world."

The trip that followed—a man had emerged out of the darkness from a barn of rusty spare parts and had done something, after an hour of fumbling, to jump-start the car—never happened, I tell myself now. We were able to drive, so long as we never slowed down and didn't turn our lights on. Through the teeming darkness we careened, like kids on a roller-coaster, into the face of coming trucks, down narrow country roads crowded with bicycles and cows and children walking back from school, around turns, the driver taking both hands off the wheel to demonstrate how he'd slept with the guerrillas, closing his eyes in his delight at his bravery.

Faster and faster, because to slow down meant what sounded to me like death.

The roads grew narrower as we climbed up into the hills around Kandy, the curves grew more frequent. Children, it seemed to me, were everywhere—not least behind the wheel of our car and in the passenger seat. I didn't travel in search of fear, and yet here I was, still unrecovered from my bloody moment in Bolivia.

By the time—somehow—we got back to the hotel, snakes and precipitous heights seemed very far behind me. I had had enough of the teardrop island, though in fact my trip was just beginning, and I had ten days of driving across it still ahead. I wondered why I traveled to such places, except maybe to take myself through my fears and come out the other end.

And then I thought of the driver, risking his life every day on the same roads that had already claimed his teenage sister. I thought of the man in the rusty garage, surrounded in the dark by guerrillas every night. I thought of the children walking along the roads every day, on their way to school or back again, in between cars that never slowed down and had no headlights on. It didn't have anything to do with me and my everyday fears, I thought; travel was the only way I knew to find out what life was like for most of the rest of the human race.

More than six billion neighbors in the global village, and for most of them my day of terrors had been just one more day among ten thousand such.

Leslie Jamison

La Plata Perdida

THIS IS HOW you visit the silver mines of Potosí, the highest city in the world: First take an airplane to El Alto, where some peoples' hearts collapse under the altitude as soon as they step off the plane. El Alto is at 4,061 meters. Potosí is higher. You take a bus to Oruru, and another one from there. You might share your seat with an animal. You might see a movie starring Jean-Claude Van Damme. These are popular on overnights: Van Damme fighting terrorists, killing bad guys, speaking the mouth-awkward language of another dubbed tongue.

When you get off the bus, Potosí will look like other Bolivian towns—old women roasting ears of corn over open flames, sidewalks full of skinny dogs and broken appliances—until it looks different: the pastel walls around its central plaza, the elegant balconies, the stately courtyards. Maybe you think it's beautiful. Maybe you think it's a bit too much, too colonial, a little gauche. Maybe later, the memory of these buildings will make you feel a bit sick in the heart.

People come to Potosí to see the famous silver mines of Cerro

Rico, so you will see them too. Take a tour. Smile politely when the man behind the desk tells you that the miners will get a cut of the money. Tell him, in your beseeching Spanish, that this is very nice. Put on your gear: boots and overalls, a bandanna over your mouth. Take a van to the miners' market. Here, you will find severed goats' heads sharing tables with Che Guevara ski caps. *Viva La Revolución!* There are shiny white skins, unfurled, that are the long stripped interiors of animals' intestines.

But you are here to buy presents for the underground men: bright sodas whose flavors are colors instead of fruits; sticks of dynamite; coca leaves in small blue bags. These are gifts for the miners but really, of course, they are gifts for the givers: you will *give something back*, as they say, and this pleases you. You will cover your subterranean tracks.

Listen carefully to your guide, Favio, an angry man your own age. He is barely twenty-five but he has three brothers in the mines and two young sons who will work here too, someday, unless he can pay their way out. Then he smiles slightly and says *but you did not come to hear about my life*, and you did, of course, always greedy for other peoples' lives, but first you must listen to the rest because listening is a gift too, or this is what you tell yourself: the tentative idea that this knowing can make a difference.

So *oye!* Listen up. They call Cerro Rico the mountain that eats men because it already has, six million so far. Potosí *conquistadores* got rich on its silver and they built all kinds of pretty courtyards in town. But six million, my God. You glance sheepishly at your gifts: your lucky dynamite, your grape soda.

The mountain is full of mouths but you only visit one: a dark hole on a hillside littered with crusty old jeans, long discarded, dirty beer bottles and toilet paper, small mounds of human excrement. Here, you are told, is where the miners eat and drink and shit between back-to-back twelve-hour shifts. *Oh, yes; yes, of course.*

You find the mine shaft bearable at first, a cool dark hallway, until it absolutely isn't: two-ton trolleys barreling down thin infrastructure, steep tunnels full of foul dust, all of them snaking towards the center of an unbelievable heat. Sometimes you have to kneel. Sometimes you have to crawl. Sometimes you pass miners, cheeks bulged with mounds of half-chewed coca, and someone gives them bottles of soda while the guide asks: *How are you?*

Favio gives you the scoop on President Evo. Everybody thought he'd make it better but then he didn't. Evo calls the miners his brothers but still keeps raising their taxes. There have been strikes. There have always been strikes. Things are "under discussion" in La Paz. You nod. You know there must be questions worth asking but what you ask is: *How much longer until we get to Level Three?* You are having a little trouble breathing. Your bandanna is gummed with gray dust.

In Level Three, at the end of the ventilation tubes, you see two men standing at the bottom of a dark hole. *Let me tell you how we get through the day,* Favio says. *We miners, we are always telling jokes. These men were probably telling jokes just before we came.* They have been underground for five hours and they've got another seven left. Do they want some dynamite, as a gift? They do.

On the way out, you pass the statue of a demon. He is called *Tio.* The Uncle-Devil. He's got a cigarette in his mouth, a beer in his hand, and a big wooden erection in his crotch. The miners are mainly Catholic but down here they worship the Devil. Who else could possibly hold sway? They worship until they are thirty-five, or maybe forty, and then they die. They die from accidents or silicosis, a disease one calls "the uniting of dust in the lungs." They leave their sons behind to work a mountain with a little less silver than the one their fathers worked, and their fathers before them.

At the exit, there is sunlight, and clean air. This is something. But you catch sight of yourself in the darkened glass of your minivan—your cheeks black, neck black, lips black—and the truth is you look like a devil too.

Anika Fajardo

What Didn't Happen

I WAS BORN IN COLOMBIA. This is true. I was born in a Spanish-style whitewashed hospital that was later leveled by an earthquake and rebuilt in its likeness. I was born in a small city in the southwestern Colombian mountains, and my father congratulated himself with *tragos* while my mother swore and labored, screamed and pushed.

I began my life in Spanish. This is true. *Zapato* and *leche* were my first words. I crawled on wooden floorboards and encountered tropical insects as big as soup bowls. I teethed on mango seeds, masticating the sweet yellow flesh until my tiny pearls appeared in pink gums. This is true.

And if my mother had never taken me back to the U.S., if my parents had never parted, never fought over me, never fallen out of love, if I would have grown up in that rented house in Colombia, I would have heard the peals of the *iglesia*'s iron bells. When my *amigas* went to mass with their *abuelas*, my hippie parents—a *mezcla* of American progressive values and Colombian pride— would have kept me at home, my mother reading aloud chapters from a dog-eared copy of *Winnie-the-Pooh*.

If we had lived, not in a Minneapolis suburb but in a town in

South America, I would have watched my mother at her wooden loom, slapping the treadle against the warp with a comforting thud and singing the folk songs of Joni Mitchell. She would have played me scratchy records of Peter, Paul and Mary and we would have sung along in two part harmony. These recordings I remember so well from my childhood would have been, had we stayed in Colombia, the only time I would have heard English spoken by anyone other than my parents.

My *abuelitos* would have adored me just as my maternal grandparents did. I would have been, for a time, the only granddaughter, a perfect excuse for spoiling and indulging. *Dulcitas* and *caramelos* and rides on my *abuelo*'s shoulders would have been mine.

I would have worn my mother's hand-sewn clothes embroidered with her original abstract flowers and designs. When my mother taught English I would have stayed with a *primo* or the *vecino* next door. The neighbors would have fed me *café con leche* and taught me to dance the *cumbia*, wanting to mold me into a true *Colombiana*.

The house was at one end of a single-lane bridge where cars and *camionetas* waited for their turn to cross, and, with my father's radicalized ideals and my mother's Midwestern upbringing, we would have lived in a sort of comfortable isolation in our traditional town. I would have been a happy child, pampered and loved.

My parents would not have been happy. The nights my father spent locked in his *taller* would have made my mother silent in loneliness, wishing for her Minnesota parents, her brothers, her American girlfriends. She and I would have tiptoed around the drafty *casa* where she would have scrubbed clothes by hand over a large rough stone until my father emerged, splattered in paint, exhausted and self-congratulatory.

My mother would have flown into an occasional rage that

made her more like her adopted country, and my father and I would have sought refuge in flowers and walks on sun-dappled trails. He would have set up a miniature easel next to his own and we would have painted pastoral scenes side by side until my mother's soprano rendition of "Blowin' in the Wind" would have come floating up into the hills above our house. My father and I would have marched home through the high altitude jungle to kiss and make up, the picture of familial bliss for another couple days.

If I would have lived in Popayán when I was eight, I would have been there when an earthquake hit our town and I would have been with my cousins buying bread in the *panadería*. There would have been a tremble and great rush as if the ocean were suddenly overtaking the coastal mountains. The moment when my *primo* was struck by falling fragments from the ovens would have been repeated over and over in my childhood nightmares. The brick missed his head—*gracias a díos*—but his shoulder would have always been a reminder of the earth moving. My auntie would have rushed us out into the dust-filled *plaza*, and when it was over the equatorial sun would have laughed at the debris nature had left us.

Even though my family would have been the only non-Catholics in the *pueblo*, we would have gone to gawk at the Pope when he came to bless our devastated town. I would have remembered very little of the papal visit, only the crowds and the vendors selling hand-painted plaques in the shape of *el Papa*'s hat. My father wouldn't have bought me one, and, since I would have been unaccustomed to being told no, my hot selfish tears would have made the people around us assume we had lost loved ones in the *terremoto*. My mother would have found this to be another reason she should never have left the United States.

By fifteen, I would have come back from a visit to the U.S. to find that my best friend's *hermano* had been killed by *guerrillas*. The brother would have been just seventeen. He would have saved up for a *motocicleta* and would have taken off on a rosy October morning to drive into the *páramo*. He and his *amigos* would have been young, beautiful boys with short, black buzz cuts who would have started *la universidad* next year. I would have been half in love with one of the *hermano's* friends, although I never would have admitted it. And when all seven boys, mistaken for military, were shot in the knees before being shot dead in the back, I would have imagined them, as I do now, face down on a winding mountain road, the shiny coffee leaves and giant sugarcane shading the bikes that lay abandoned on the gravel, a vicious *guerrilla* killing that would have made no sense to either me or the families in the *pueblo*.

When I went to a big Midwestern university—assuming I even went to college—my accent would have been stilted and cautious. Even though my mother would have spoken English to me had we stayed in Colombia, there would have been holes in my vocabulary, experiences that set me apart. I wouldn't have had a *quinceñera*, but I wouldn't have gone to prom either. I would have earned A's in English class at *la colegia*, but I would have strained to understand the subtitled episodes of *Saved by the Bell* I would have watched, not on a looming color TV in the basement of the house on Edgerton, but on a small black and white *tele* at the foot of my parents' bed.

At home in Colombia, I would have always been viewed as the outsider. My skin would have been lighter than the other *muchachos* in our neighborhood. My German legs and ankles, clearly descended from my mother's Anglo Saxon roots, would have made me self-conscious in front of my Colombian *amigas*—girls with the slender bodies of *Indios*.

And whenever I visited my mother's family in the U.S., I would have found myself even more of an outsider. I would have been pasted with labels: Hispanic, foreigner, Latina, minority. My English would have been grammatically exact, but colloquially forced, and my Spanish wouldn't have been like the more familiar *Mexicanos'* drawn-out rhythm.

If I somehow would have still met my future husband, and if I brought this *gringo* back to Colombia to meet my parents, my father would have given him a Colombian kiss on the cheek and then called him "dude" to show he was a modern man. My mother would have been stand-offish, but secretly relieved that I was marrying an American.

But my newlywed life in the U.S. would have found me as confused as my mismatched parents. I would have pined for the humidity of the valleys and the crisp air of *las montañas*. I would have spent my money on long-distance phone calls to friends in Bogotá, Quito, Cartagena. I would have found myself simultaneously homesick and at home. I would have discovered that my handsome *esposo* didn't always understand my accented English, didn't like the *sancocho* or deathly sweet *café con canela* I prepared for him. We would have had to compromise when the days became endless and *las noches* filled with arguments, fighting, misunderstandings—all those problems that arise from a joining and a clash of two cultures. And, like my mother before me, I would have had to decide which life I wanted.

But this, all this, it isn't what happened—this isn't the life my mother chose. I was born in Colombia. This is true. In a whitewashed hospital that was destroyed by a *terremoto*. In a town with *abuelitos* and *amigitas* and *guerrillas*. In a family that loved me. This is true.

Ira Sukrungruang

Summer Days, 1983

I.

He was Thai, not the strange, pale Chicago Catholic boys I palled
with. Then, I had no Thai friends. Because of this, my parents
loved him, thought he would be a good influence on me, that his
presence would halt America spreading in my veins. It did not
matter that he was years older, a high schooler who lacked high
school friends. What mattered was how he took flight, bike like
an appendage. How he and bike spun and twirled, how he and
bike traversed the world on one wheel. How I was in awe, the
on-looking second grader, the boy watching his first Thai friend,
Thai magician, Thai god.

II.

This is what happened: we lay in suburban grass, staring at the sky,
the contrails of a plane landing at the airport a few miles away.
He said, Easy life. He whistled. Easy everything. Words slipped
out like my neighbor's sprinkler, vowels lingered longer from his
lips. Easy, he said and bumped against my shoulder. Meanwhile,
clouds took animal shapes, ants tickled the underside of my arm.

III.

This is what happened: he stayed the night once, and we unrolled the fold-out couch and lay underneath it—our cave—past bedtime; he was Thai after all and Thais were allowed leniency. My parents succumbed to sleep hours ago, the house dark except for Johnny Carson on TV, his white hair, his white suit, his white teeth, like a lighthouse.

IV.

This is what happened: he pulled down his pants. Johnny Carson swung an imaginary golf club. Ed McMahon's guttural laugh.

V.

This is what happened: he grabbed it tight in his hands and tapped my shoulder.

And this: he pointed at my pajama bottoms.

And this: Let me see yours.

And this: I slid my shorts down to my ankles.

And this: his hushed laughter, lek, small in Thai.

VI.

Years later, when I was in high school, I would see him at a Chicago party, beer in hand, beautiful white girl on his arm. How I envied him again, envied the ease with which he stood and talked to everyone at the party. How he seemed a sun that planets revolved around. How this woman, lips like peppers, touched and traced his cheeks with a red fingernail.

When he saw me, his eyes widened, his smile widened, his sin-

SUMMER DAYS, 1983 | 59

ewy arms widened to embrace me. He said I had grown. Yai, big. Asked if I remembered that summer, those days of bike and sky. You look good, he said. A man.

VII.

I tell my wife the story. We are in bed, the southern Illinois sun filtering through the laced curtains, our dogs lying in patches of light. She tells me it's not normal, but it didn't feel wrong then nor does it now, only a memory without anchor. She says I have stored this memory in a dusty corner of my brain.

Perhaps.

Perhaps, this is what we do, sometimes, to endure. Perhaps, we wish these moments away like an eyelash, like dandelion fuzz.

When he comes back, it is without sentiment, a dropped rock in water, ripples and ripples, spreading and spreading. What remains is a drawing left too long in the rain, the faint lines of chalk, a world empty of grace and color.

Claudia Rankine

Excerpt from **Don't Let Me Be Lonely**

IN A TAXI speeding uptown on the West Side Highway, I let my thoughts drift below the surface of the Hudson until it finally occurs to me that feelings fill the gaps created by the indirectness of experience. Though the experience is social, thoughts carry it into a singular space and it is this that causes the feelings of loneliness; or it is this that collides the feeling with the experience so that what is left is the solitude called loneliness. And from that space of loneliness, I can feel the cab driver watching me in his rearview mirror.

He wants to know if I attend Columbia University.

> Years ago, now I just live in the
> neighborhood.
>
> You seem like a smart lady. What do
> you do for your living?
>
> I write about the liver.

The liver? Really? You are a doctor?

No, no. I write about the liver
because I'm thinking as if trying to weep.

Excuse me? You think the liver
is connected to thoughts?

Well, not exactly.

Anyway, tell me something, you have
lived in this country many years?

Over thirty.

Well yes, then. So tell me this, have you
noticed these white people, they think
they are better than everyone else?

Have I noticed? Are you joking? You're
not joking. Where are you from?

Pakistan.

I see. It's only a few months since 9/11.
They think you're al Qaeda.

I know. But the things they say to me.
They don't know anything.

Be happy you can't read their thoughts, I want to say to him. I
smile into the rearview mirror instead. Why with such a nice
smile are you trying to weep? he asks as we pull up to my building.

Harrison Candelaria Fletcher

White

CREAM

With a cup of strong coffee and five packets of creamer, I can approximate the skin color of the nine members of my mother's family.

MILK

I never see the shadow of the red carton flash, and even when the pint of milk explodes against the head of my wheat-haired friend I'm late to understand what the Chicano boy means when he curses from the sidewalk of my junior high cafeteria, "Shit. Missed that honky."

EGGSHELL

Ricky Sandoval pins me by the throat against a C-building locker, the combination lock spinning beside my head, and slaps me on one cheek, then the other, until my composure cracks, my eyes water, and my face turns red.

"See?" he says. "That's all you need. A little color."

SCAR

The razor is too dull to cut, so I scratch a fingernail on the back of my left hand hoping my big brother will see. He yanks me off the front porch anyway and into the kitchen where he and his father-less friends have found a better way to scar—a curtain pin heated orange on the gas range and pressed to the tender fold between thumb and forefinger, into the shape of a cross, into the symbol of belonging he'd seen on brown Chicano fists. He holds my arm tight against the Formica counter while I close my eyes and still see the blue flame. A vodka shot. A cold water blast. I stand beside him as our matching crucifixes swell with blood. Afterward, we raise vegetable gardens, set pampas plumes alight, and bust phone booths until glass drips from our denim jackets like rain. I pick the scab to keep the scar alive, but my cross fades first, swallowed by pale skin.

FLUORESCENT

Brendon Jefferson is the only black kid in tenth grade PE. He dribbles two basketballs simultaneously, leaps above the rim, dunks them both. I watch from the sidelines, envious.

One morning during wrestling, we sit side by side on the mat with the soccer captain and the driver of a low-slung Monte Carlo, hugging our knees while the coach pairs us into matches. Brendon looks at each of us, then pokes his thigh, the soccer player's thigh, and the low-rider's thigh.

"Check this out," he says. "I'm black. He's yellow. He's brown. And you . . ."

He jabs my skin, bloodless under fluorescent lights.

"You're just white!"

He rolls onto his back, laughing.

We wrestle to a draw.

GHOST

After college I attend a National Association of Hispanic Journalists convention in Dallas. I linger among the beige cubicles while other reporters and editors brush past me with résumés and business cards. When I approach, they study my face, squint at my name tag, and turn away. Several hours into the job fair, with few interviews and even fewer prospects, I duck into a men's room, flip over my badge, and scribble in my mother's maiden name, Candelaria. Back in the main arena, recruiters smile, hands extend, appointments open.

I walk through walls.

LIGHTBULB

"A Chicano," explains the sculptor, the activist, the co-founder of the Denver multicultural arts council, "is someone who is born in the United States but has a blood mixture of Aztec and Spanish. A Chicano is a person with one foot in one culture and one foot in another culture who resists being forced to choose. A Chicano is a person trying to define themselves for themselves. A Chicano is a person seeking their true identity.

"I guess that makes me a Chicano," I say, touching my pale cheek.

"Me, too," she says, laughing. "And I was born in Mexico."

BLANK

Note: Please answer BOTH questions, numbers 7 *and* 8.

7. Are you Spanish/Hispanic/Latino? (Mark the "no" box if not Spanish/Hispanic/Latino)

   ☐ No, not Spanish/Hispanic/Latino

☐ Yes, Puerto Rican
☐ Yes, Cuban
☐ Yes, Mexican, Mexican-American, Chicano
☐ Yes, other Spanish, Hispanic, Latino—Print here:

_____

8. What is your race? Mark one
☐ Black, African-American, Negro
☐ American Indian, Alaskan Native
☐ Pacific Islander, Asian
☐ White
☐ Some other race. Print here: _____

S. L. Wisenberg

Passover Rental Furniture: Houston

WAS IT IN HIGH SCHOOL or college? Before and after Passover I would drive to the rental place and pick up and bring back table-cloths and napkins. My mother rented them for our seders, where we had twenty-five to thirty people. At the rental place, was it one guy or two? I remember one worker who would ask me out, and it was ridiculous, just on the face of it. Our ages, for one. I didn't know him, he didn't know me, he was flirting, heavily, and I was unequipped. My mother had not prepared me for this when she gave directions to the commercial shed where I was to retrieve and return the linens. Do you have a boyfriend? he asked and being honest, I said no. Then why won't you go out with me? I didn't know how to say no without making him think it was because he was black. He was black, yes, and a manual worker, yes, and he was older, and I was in town for only a few days, but mostly he was an obnoxious insistent stranger. He knew he had me, because he was black, and I was polite, and he knew he held the card, he knew I was thinking black/white and because I was thinking it he was thinking it or vice versa. And vice versa. It was the 1970s, and he or the two of them, if there were two, were not Emmett Till, life was not still like that, they knew I would not get a posse to pull him from bed and fit a tire necklace around him and drown him. Thank goodness. So they reveled in my discomfiture and the fact that the stakes were not high. I would not call out the dogs. I was bound by the fear of my own racism and was not yet schooled in pushing men away, those who were dangerous and those who were not. I was still schooled in smiling. If that is the legacy of Till in the New South, then was my experience all bad? My discomfiture as a Southern (off-) white woman was little enough of a sacrifice to, or a by-product of, their sense of freedom, the excesses of their freedom. And let's not forget the irony of our having had black women help prepare and serve the dinner which was set out upon the rented linens. Of course my parents were paying them well. Of course the women were glad to have the extra money. Of course we treated them well. But of course it was hard not to think of them as we read and talked and sang about slavery and freedom, the way their ancestors must have thought of our biblical ancestors as they sang, *Go down, Moses, way down in Egypt's land* . . .

Lia Purpura

Brief Treatise Against Irony

THE OPPOSITE OF irony is nakedness. To be available to the eyes of others. So instead of ironic furnishings—carved coconut earrings or monkeys or mugs for tourists, Aloha, Willkommen, each worse than the next, that's the point—a person buys a painting she can afford and hangs it in her house. Gives it something called "pride of place." In this, the very rich resemble the not-so-rich-at-all: taste displayed according to means. What you see is what they like. Ugly, vapid, tender, exquisite: you're free to judge. Such things in a frame, on a shelf front and center crass/gilded, quiet/frank—are defenseless; sent forth without armor, or veils, or banter.

*

The cure for irony isn't a dose of sincerity. Sincerity can't be applied like a salve, or plaster, or arranged to countervail mockery. Sincerity doesn't take measures to appear to be, or to seem. Asked to prove itself, its voice squeaks. Sincerity walks head first into wind—and suffers the cold. In rough surf, it erodes. In heat, it stains. Its gauges work. It's accurate.

To be an apple tree in fall, to fully enter the realm of gold, to be right up against the end, and no longer green—that gesture can't be conscripted. Sincerity isn't in service of. A tree doesn't will itself to turn, to feel the chill crenellate in leaves, and let go. A tree gives over. That phrase "the promise of Spring?" Trees really believe it.

*

Irony masks. It prepares for, in advance. No one sees its heart adjusting, dimming, tamping. Irony wouldn't admit to *heart* (too messy, percussive). It ducks into corners and drops from eaves. It sniffs for changes in weather, so as to be first to . . . first to what? Whatever there is to be first to deny. Irony's a stick figure in an over-sized coat. It refuses the pleasures of shivering, the anticipation of a warm house after taking out the garbage—in a T-shirt, in an ice storm—that small restoration, minor hardship that stokes gratitude.

*

Irony rules its subjects the way a monarch might—the fiefdom-centric variety, not the Monarch butterfly, hereing and thereing, gathering and bestowing, alighting on ripening buds with gifts, that a new crop might bloom—such delicate work, the scattering of gold.

*

Irony has a wobbly compass at its center. Seasickness from its north star, skidding. Irony references, cites, points to for the sake of having pointed—and in doing so, advances not at all. Each year its finger grows longer and thinner, as pale, slippery, and hollow as a stalactite. Its weather is clammy. Its system low-pressure. It suffers not the exertions of bright sun shining equally on good and evil, the deserving and the not-so.

Irony isn't equipped to navigate rough democracies.

*

Unlike boredom, it has no reserves. Irony sits and stews. If "boredom is a state in which hope is being secretly negotiated" (tacked on my bulletin board, author unknown)—then irony is not fit to negotiate.

(But wait—I looked it up! Attributable to philosopher/psychologist Adam Phillips! Irony would do well to get younger. Be excited—still—about the powers of the Web!)

Irony would do well to hope for . . . *something*. Let disappointment come. Maybe envy. Squirm in frustration. Because none of this—boredom, disappointment, etc.—will kill you. Out of real need, or absence, or tedium, irony could begin to make something—not just lean. Lean into whom, or towards what? *Is this a good angle?* Irony asks. *It shows my good side?* As if someone is always, always looking.

*

Irony is the outward sign of a feeling one's trying not to have. The adult version of yanking your crush's braid on the playground. *See*, it announces, *I'm not at all interested!* The wide-lapel suit, worn not-seriously. The studiously untended mutton chops.

The song "How Deep Is Your Love," though I hated it, was part of the soundtrack of my thirteenth year, and my long stay in the hospital. I did love a boy then, who was undergoing the same back surgery. He was funny and gentle; I missed him terribly when he (or I) was wheeled away for some procedure. His—they lived near, in the South Bronx—brought lots of food when visiting and always shared with my parents. I know we kissed. How would we have managed that, both of us stuck in body casts?

When we left, we exchanged a few letters, but I never saw him again.

I'd never play that song, say, at a dinner party, the table set with wine glasses from Bea's & Roger's (that double possessive the reason for buying) Anniversary Cruise, 1977.

I don't imagine anyone *liked*, for example, the smell of coal trains, blackening the Russian stations of their childhood. But much is returned by way of that scent (admixed with sausages, perfume, cigarettes), held somewhere secretly, then bestowed. The most unlikely song or smell will guard a past and present it whole, when you're least expecting it. Thus a person might find herself in tears, right there in the dentist's chair, under the classic rock speaker. Or when passing a newly tarred street, a whole country, an era, Moskovsky station in winter, steams up in the summer heat.

*

Irony has no sense of time. So what might have been meaningful once (blue Snoopy lunch box, his kind face and gladness at the midday reunion) is wiped away by irony's taking it up again—as a find, an amusing touch. Which of course keeps one from having to face the ragged truth of endings, the breakage, the loss, i.e. one's own finitude. Irony opposes the heirloom, the keepsake. It turns away from good leftovers. Nor will it cook up a fresh thing on a special occasion. A thing that might fail, burn, collapse. Require the guests' good cheer, indulgence, willingness to order last-minute pizza, be part of a wholly disastrous dinner but a great story ever after—i.e. *history*.

*

Irony travels in one direction, around and around an inner circle.

A kids' TV show I used to watch, *Zoom*, ran a skit with a character called "Fannee Doolee." She liked any person, place, thing, or concept with double letters in it, but hated its non-double-lettered equivalent, so "Fannee Doolee likes sweets but hates candy." You could figure out how to play the game if you watched for a while, but it wasn't apparent right away. Tuning in every week, a kid learned to pay attention, be curious, believe in hints. *Something* was there to be decoded. It was a *challenge*. A *riddle*. (In fact, once you solved the mystery, you could send in your own example to be read on TV.) A riddle is an invitation, a game in language, while irony cordons off knowing. Admits only the knowing few. The tickets are invisible. You can't buy them anywhere. In this way, irony both suggests and thwarts travel.

The inside track is a very small circle.

*

Irony is not animal. Animal just *is*—frightened, glad, gentle, vicious: of the moment. Last week, when I was walking my dog in the woods (urban woods with nearby streets), we were set upon by a pack; at first, dog by dog, they were tame, sniffing and romping and chasing Ruby. Then something turned. A mind like a wind blew through the dogs, gathered strength like a wave, from far off. It was slow and elemental as a tide. Once it entered, the conversion was swift. They closed in on my dog, growling and jumping, listening not at all to their walker's shrill whistle. We slipped through a hole in the fence just in time.

The dogs weren't kidding. Nor were they angry. Just subject to a force that turned them deeply into themselves. Which was an amazing thing to watch: instinct finding a vein and entering. As it did for me, bestowing a calm I don't always have. In them was nothing tricky, or cruel. Nothing *taught*; they weren't trained for meanness, as some city dogs are. They made a new shape, an organism that worked as one. It was beautiful and terrifying to see.

*

Irony assumes itself to be *the* mode by which knowingness gets expressed.

Look, I'm from New York. That "we've seen it all" attitude? It's based in fact, not arrogance. If you've seen it all—in the course of a recent hour, two dogs in mink coats (I asked; I *had* to), a guy selling used dentures from a backpack (yes, *really*), if you know the ropes (at a deli during the morning rush, do not ponder the menu, do *not* dig around in your bag for exact change, just order and keep moving)—then irony's passé. And something else overtakes— something older. Brisker. Sharper. Let's call it *the absurd*. The daily surreal. All the infinite, unpredictable ways to be human. Look, it's New York: you can do whatever the bleep you please. Ride your bike in a bikini with a snake as a necklace (it was hot that day, she was en route to the pet sitter, and *he really likes to go for rides*). The closer one is to the absurd, the more irony—a cultivated, intentional thing—looks kind of earnest. All that time put in to make an impression, all that care taken to seem not to care!

But something else, too. Irony's local, homegrown, provincial, though it pretends to worldliness. There's a moment in Nabokov's memoir, *Speak, Memory*, where he gets angry considering the kind of reader who cannot understand the depths of loss an immigrant feels: "The following passage is not for the general reader, but for the particular idiot who, because he lost a fortune in some crash, thinks he understands me. My old (since 1917) quarrel with the Soviet dictatorship is wholly unrelated to any question of property. My contempt for the émigré who 'hates the Reds' because they 'stole' his money and land is complete. The nostalgia I have been cherishing all these years is a hypertrophied sense of lost childhood, not sorrow for lost banknotes . . ." Real exile is enforced distance from one's internal geography. And irony doesn't immigrate. All that *contempt, nostalgia, sorrow*—it's not safe.

Of course irony's all over New York, in so many forms and registers: Jeff Koons' giant, balloon-style, steel bunny sculptures; a more affordable curated collection of vintage Mr. Bubble, Pop Tart, Jetsons T-shirts. Both sort of, kind of make you laugh, but not too much. Not out loud. . . more a mumbly, appraisal-sound. Which I guess you practice behind your hand.

The absurd's both public and shared.

To get the absurd, to really know it, is to understand brevity, longing, how much is thwarted or unmet, or met only partly. To acknowledge the infinite scheme, confirm the stark/tender, sad/sweet whole to which we all belong; to recognize the endless ways to be human—*counter, original, spare, strange*, as Hopkins wrote—and the lightness attending that recognition; the flash of camaraderie the absurd allows (brief glance at seat mate on the bus, eyebrow cocked to passerby): *this* constitutes the ethos I'm talking about. Open to all. Democratic. Abundant in New York, and available in so many versions, tongues, flavors: Puerto Rican. Senegalese. Korean. Etc.

Ironic is no one's country of origin. Oh, I *get* it alright. It's just not interesting. It won't be amazed. It won't admit fear. There isn't a bit of longing in it. No danger. No failure. No dream.

Barbara Hurd

Cocoons

THE SUMMER I was nine, I cut open a chrysalis. They were everywhere in the fields near our neighborhood—small papery things attached to milkweeds and the stalks of nondescript grasses, waiting for the right temperature or humidity, adequate leaf buds, longer days. I grew impatient. The sun was warm, shrubs were green-dotted with buds. I pinched a chrysalis off and set it down on a rock, took out my pocketknife, and pressed hard with the tip, the cover on either side dimpling in, the dark line of the interior growing wider and longer, that sense of inside pressure released at last, as if what was in there had been aching to get out and needed me and my knife to do it. It looked damp, pressed, the wings no more than tiny crescents. It quivered, spasmed, stilled. I took a nearby stalk and tried to pry up its wings which lay matted against its body.

Too soon, too soon, I crooned. I put my finger on its head. I remember that I wasn't appalled. Not even guilty. I studied its shapelessness. I couldn't tell if it was alive. I rolled it in a leaf, scraped a little trough in the ground, and lay it inside, brushed over it a bit of dirt and leaf mold. With a twig, I poked a small breathing hole through its cover for an air-tube. I didn't consider rain or the probing proboscises of predators.

For days I thought of it out there in the woods, under the cover of dirt, the days lengthening and warming, and imagined it finally rising, the only moth in the neighborhood unhindered by the binding silk threads of its cocoon, taking flight straight out of the earth.

I'd killed it, of course. Moths, I learned later, need the pressure of exiting a tight cocoon to finish their metamorphosis. From the inside, they nick a small hole with the tiny saw-like ridge on the top of their heads, and squeeze through the opening, while the tight cincture kneads extraneous fluids, massages the wet body. What I released from the cocoon that day was deformed, unfinished.

Still, it felt good, that cutting open. A deliberate act in defiance of patience, a quick rip, a brutality to undo the months of apathy. I felt alive. Did it matter that my timing was off?

*

"Do you ever wonder," I asked my twin one night as we were falling asleep, "if we were born on time?"

"Huh?" she mumbled.

"What a week more or less in the womb might have done for us?"

She turned over, away from me.

"Maybe your foot would've straightened out. Maybe you wouldn't have been so colicky." Maybe, I didn't say, we would have understood each other better. Or maybe I would've had different eyes, a nose I could trust. Maybe coming a week too soon had left us all stunned and scrambling, our parents unprepared, their hearts slicked down and pressed too tight against their chests, unable to open. Or were we a week late? How else to explain the silent enclosure of this family, this dimness all around, the way I often felt I was talking under water, the sounds muffled, all of us in slow motion, an outstretched arm floating just out of reach, cheeks ballooning with air, hair rising and falling and up there somewhere a different kind of light I kept trying to swim up to.

Across our room, as if on the other side of the continent, the sound of her breathing reached me. It was even, deep. Sometimes everything seemed hopelessly far away to me, the distance uncrossable. I lay awake for hours, listening to her, imagining myself cocoon-wrapped and waiting, imagined all of us with saw-like ridges built into our heads. Or not waiting, but cut loose before our time, helpless in the open air. How does anyone ever know exactly what's too soon or too late, what will wither in the interminable dark or gasp and shrivel in the too-early light? Or transcend its beginning, become beautiful, fly for a while?

Phillip Lopate

Max and Minna

MY FIRST AIRPLANE flight was a transcontinental one, from New York to Los Angeles. I was seventeen, flying with my twenty-year-old brother Lenny to spend the summer with our Red relatives, Uncle Max and Aunt Minna. The flight had been jammed to capacity, with screaming babies, as unglamorous as airline travel would later routinely become, though at least they served us meals. We looked down with wonderment at the reddish Rocky Mountains and the Grand Canyon ("off to your right"). During the descent, I experienced piercing pain, a first indication that I was one of those whose ears would not take kindly to steep landings.

That summer of 1962, I had finished my sophomore year at Columbia, while Lenny, having dropped out of school, was at loose ends. My mother decided to send us away to her older brother Max. It was not the first time she had done this, having packed Lenny off when he was twelve to her brother George's in Brookline, Massachusetts, then sent me to that Boston suburb three summers after. As the poor relation in her large family, a ghetto-dweller to boot, she felt entitled to impose her spawn on her older siblings' kindness. Lenny and I were happy to be gotten off her hands, and the whole notion of California was intensely romantic to us; from our provincial New Yorker standpoint, it was the Antipodes.

We had a day or two to explore Los Angeles on our own, before taking the bus to Auberry, California, where Max and Minna lived. I remember our walking around in a daze under the hot sun, trying to sightsee landmarks like the Brown Derby restaurant, the Hollywood sidewalk of stars and Grauman's Chinese Theatre, and feeling tired, grouchy, and agoraphobic. I can still summon up the sensation of that pounding sinus headache between the eyebrows that resulted from exposure to a glaring sun and too little shadow from low-slung buildings. I was discovering an essential part of my identity, the Pedestrian, and Los Angeles proved too spread-out to investigate easily on foot.

Complicating the mood was that Lenny and I were annoying each other. He kept trying to assert his seniority, making plans for the day or deciding whether to turn left or right, and I kept questioning them. I had been in awe of his three-years-ahead-of-me artistic knowledge and worldly experience, but now I wanted to form my own independent judgments; and having gotten into an Ivy League school while he was a college dropout made me feel superior, if smug. We were an odd couple in any case: he bohemian, messy, and hot-headed; I, more phlegmatic, bookish, and detached. We desperately clung to each other throughout our California adventure, but this very dependency made us snappish.

It was almost with relief that we quit the city and traveled north to the little mountain town of Auberry, though when we got there we found ourselves in the middle of nowhere. It was a small hilly drive-through town of two thousand souls, with one café, one bar, one gas station, one post office, and Max and Minna's dry goods establishment. Their store sold everything from bolts of cloth to novelties and kitchenware. The closest city was Fresno, a salesman's junction and cow town, where we would be driven in by Uncle Max once a week and spend the day roaming around, looking for movie theaters or bookstores, while he stocked up on supplies. The rest of the time we were stuck in Auberry, with Max and Minna our only company.

They had been Communist Party members, and had moved out to California from Brooklyn during the McCarthy era, when things started getting too hot back East. Max, a bald-headed man with a mustache, always struck me as affable but a little dim. He deferred to his wife, two years older and the brains of the outfit. Minna had been born in Russia and I always pictured her when younger as a firebrand, our family's Emma Goldman. By the time we came to visit she was grey-haired, bespectacled, and rotund, with a sharp, querulous manner. I wish I could paint a picture of an idyllic American summer in the country with kind elderly relatives who took in these two skittish boys from the city and smothered them in healthy foods and wisdom and taught them to milk the cows, but such was not the case. Minna was bitter and wary, as she had every right to be. She told us that two F.B.I. men regularly parked a car by the post office, a hundred yards downhill from their store, and checked on their mail and questioned their customers about whether they had seen or heard any suspicious—i.e., unpatriotic—behavior.

In the evening, as we watched television on a modest black-and-white set in their snug living room, barely a show could go by without her commenting on the behavior of someone vis-à-vis HUAC. "That one sang," she would sneer, or "He ratted, spilled his guts out." *Sea Hunt*, one of my favorite shows, starring Lloyd Bridges (father of Beau and Jeff), was regularly interrupted by her disgusted remarks about his informing. "He named names till he was blue in the face."

Minna was proud that they sold to the Native Americans who lived nearby, and had a regular Indian clientele, always treating them with utmost politeness and extending them credit, unlike some of the other businesses in town that discriminated. She could not have been more pleased when they invited her to a pig roast. All four of us crammed into Max's pickup truck and drove to the reservation, where we witnessed the pig half-buried in dirt and slow-burned.

Otherwise, Minna and Max seemed alienated from their neighbors. Minna did not like our going to the bar at the bottom of the hill, because the owner had been involved in some criminal business. When not being a friend of the oppressed, she was rigidly moralistic, a Communist Puritan.

Once a month, some friends of theirs would drive up from Los Angeles with sacks of bagels and smoked salmon. They were about the same age as Max and Minna, and I don't know what solaced our relatives more, the C.P. gossip they brought from L.A. or their fresh bagels. We were shooed from the house: I suspect they were having a meeting, though it was never clear to me whether Max and Minna were still in the Party or had left it or been kicked out. It wasn't the kind of question you could ask directly. One day, snooping through their desk drawer, I found several pages of handwritten notes on yellow scratch paper about the relationship between Marxist-Leninism and Maoism. They were like study notes a dutiful undergraduate might take in a seminar. How poignant—how pathetic—yet no, how admirable, in its way, that these oldsters were still trying to figure out the correct political line, stuck way out in the boondocks.

We would mock her behind her back and sometimes to her

face, smart-alecks that we were. In the early sixties, with JFK in the White House and civil rights marchers in Mississippi, you either bought the whole idealistic "Ask not what your country can do for you" rhetoric or you didn't. I didn't: I was still too far down on the social ladder, too poor to think of helping those less fortunate, and too preoccupied with making myself into a writer to take social injustice that seriously.

Minna disapproved of our cynicism and political indifference, as she did of our laziness. She was shocked that we did not offer to do more chores. Here we were, two able-bodied young men, slinking around rent-free, doing nothing but reading and playing games, while these two elderly folk worked morning to night. In retrospect I can see her point; we *were* lazy, with that bottomless tiredness and self-absorption typical of teenagers. Reluctantly, we agreed to paint the store ceiling, which needed a new coat. During those days of overhead painting, taking turns moving the ladder and the drop cloth, my brother and I settled into bickering like an old married couple. We bickered to pass the time; it meant nothing, though it disturbed Aunt Minna. "Boys, boys, don't argue. Brothers should get along."

Mostly we hid from her noodging, in the little cabin behind their house where we slept. There was barely room for anything besides the two beds, but we turned it into a baseball field, using a rolled pair of socks and a broomstick bat. Epic games of nine innings and sometimes double headers would transpire. Overall, we got along rather well, considering we were incessantly in each other's company. In the morning, we washed up together at the sink in Max and Minna's house. One morning, as Lenny was shaving, I turned the water from hot to cold so that I could splash my face. My brother screamed: "What are you trying to do, kill me?" I had not realized cold water might make a razor blade more slippery. Still, it seemed excessive to accuse me of trying to slit his throat, and I told him so. But a doubt lodged in my mind. *Was* I trying to kill him? I contained multitudes; I would not put anything past me.

The rest of the time we read or wrote. Lenny had become interested in foreign policy, and was reading books by George F. Kennan and Henry Kissinger with an eye toward writing a novel about diplomacy. Many years later, in his capacity as radio interviewer, he would confront Kissinger, pleased at having given Nixon's ex–Secretary of State a hard time. Had he forgotten, or buried deep in his subconscious, the respect he once accorded Kissinger? Of course I remembered that embarrassing detail; what else are younger brothers good for? In any case, he took notes on Kennan and Kissinger and summarized various foreign policy conundrums for me.

I was reading Henry Fielding that summer, *Tom Jones* and *Joseph Andrews*. In part, I was getting a jump on a course in eighteenth century English novels I planned to take that fall; but I was also thoroughly enchanted by Fielding's humorous, rounded sentences, his sensual characters and essayistic prologues—that confident, maximalist fullness. I was to feel increasingly at home in the eighteenth century, around Fielding, Sterne, Johnson, Swift, and Diderot. Six months earlier, in my Dostoyevskian phase, I had tried to kill myself. Rebounding from that attempt, I had suddenly become bored with extremity and anguish: I craved balance, sanity, irony, mischief, worldliness with a touch of optimism. It would all come out well in the end, just as *Tom Jones* closes with a marriage. I was suddenly feeling well-adjusted, perhaps overly so. In two years *I* would find myself married. Meanwhile I wrote several short stories in a Fieldingesque vein. It was a productive summer—my own private Yaddo.

Aunt Minna liked Lenny more than me. I had no problem with that; it intrigued me. I speculated she felt sympathy for him because she saw him as the underdog. I seemed headed for the winner's circle; she had no interest in such types. She kept after him to finish college. I don't think Lenny took her advice that seriously, but in short order he did reapply to college, and finished getting his bachelor's degree and a master's. Minna lived to be ninety-four years old, long past her husband; she died in 1993. Neither my brother nor I ever contacted her in the years after that dry hot summer, either to boast that we had turned out all right or to say thank you. We never saw her or Max again. To do that, we would have had to return to Auberry, which was unthinkable. Not that it had been so hellish; just that it was sequestered in the humiliating, powerless past, sealed off, as it were, on the wrong end of a time machine.

Nicholas Montemarano

No Results Found

ONE WAY WOULD BE to wait, she hasn't been gone a full day, yesterday at this hour she was alive, you felt her breath on your face. Give it time. Emotion recollected in tranquillity, and so on. Wordsworth, of course. Better, maybe, to read what others have written. Google search: "Updike dead dog poems." Or read *Dog Years* or *My Dog Tulip* or *Marley and Me* or *Old Yeller*, for God's sake.

Maybe do some research. All those books, can't remember the titles, about how dogs think, how they feel, how they love, and so on, or maybe keep it light and read that bestselling novel *A Dog's Purpose*, about a dog who keeps getting reincarnated and tries to figure out the meaning of life.

Google search: "dead dogs in literature." Google search: "grief dog died." Google search: "pet loss support groups."

Maybe forget Google and look at your own photos and videos, cry a little, and start writing. Maybe include the questions your four-year-old son asks, such as: "Where is Ralph?" And: "Where did her life go?" And: "Is fur still on her body?" And: "If I listen to your heart, will I hear her?" You could write the piece made up entirely of his questions and omit the answers, or made up entirely of your answers with the questions implied, and maybe it would be less sentimental that way.

The lyric essay, according to *The Seneca Review*, "might move more by association, leaping from one path of thought to another by way of imagery or connotation, advancing by juxtaposition or sidewinding poetic logic."

There's that Lydia Davis story you love called "St. Martin," ostensibly about housesitting but really about—spoiler alert—a dog who goes missing. "We knew he would not have stayed away so long unless he had somehow been stopped from coming back," the narrator writes. Rereading this story might trigger memories from a year ago—though you don't really need help—when Ralph, eleven and near deaf, wandered away in the woods during a family vacation—a herder, she had never wandered away before— and you walked the woods while your wife remained at the cabin with your son, and then your wife walked the woods while you remained at the cabin with your son, and then you walked the same woods again. It was raining, the creek swollen, the storm expected to worsen. Seven hours missing. You believed she was dead, caught in barbed wire or drowned in the creek; you imagined her wounded and alone, frightened of the thunder and lightning. But just before dark a neighbor found her on the other side of the woods—a resurrection, the rest of her life a bonus. You and your wife and son hugged and kissed each other and then hugged and petted Ralph.

David Foster Wallace said or wrote something somewhere, I swear he did, about dead dogs, that writers shouldn't be afraid to write the story of a dog dying, that brave writers needed to get at real sentiment by risking sentimentality, I swear he did, I don't think I'm making this up.

It's well known that David Foster Wallace loved his dogs and cried "like a toddler" when one of his dogs got sick and had to be put down and "would go by the veterinary office and sit outside the freezer where his dog lay."

Maybe take his word for it that there's a freezer, or maybe Google search: "what happens to dog's body between euthanasia and cremation." Or maybe try to forget that and Google search: "feel-good books about dogs" or "feel-good movies about dogs."

Maybe watch *Air Bud* with your son. Or *Air Bud: Golden Receiver.* Or *Air Bud: World Pup.* Or *Air Bud: Seventh Inning Fetch.* Or *Air Bud: Spikes Back.* Or any of the many *Air Buddies* films about Buddy's puppies.

As if lowbrow films or lowbrow word play will change anything.

According to the folks at *The Seneca Review,* "The lyric essay does not expound. It may merely mention."

In that case, you should merely mention that her back legs gave out, she could no longer control her bowels, her bladder, could no longer hear. She was not in pain, which is what made it difficult to decide when. She could no longer walk without scraping and cutting open her back paws, but still enjoyed smelling the world, still enjoyed a steak. And you must write about her last night on the front lawn, fireflies at dusk, and then your wife sleeping on the floor beside her in a sleeping bag and you across the room on the couch, taking turns waking to comfort her, and too quickly: daylight, your son asking why you aren't in bed like every morning, then breakfast, your son driven to soccer camp, back home, only a few hours left, one last walk. "She looks a little better this morning," you tell your wife. Then, through tears: "I wish she'd fall, just so we know we're doing the right thing." Ever obedient, she stumbles and falls. You help her up and walk home. "We should go," your wife says. "But we'll be early," you say. "Isn't she going back into the house one more time?" "We need to go," your wife says. The ride: car windows down, her face in the wind, drivers smiling at the German Shepherd leaning out the window (she could be going to the park, to the creek), and then much too quickly you're there, they've been waiting for you, they lead you to the "comfort room" where you finally see what you've been trying to imagine for the week since you made the appointment: a couch, a chair, the pillowy dog bed on the floor where she will die.

When you type "how" Google suggests "how i met your mother," and when you type "how soon" Google suggests "how soon is now lyrics," and when you type "how soon is too soon" Google suggests "how soon is too soon to get married," and when you type "how soon is too soon to," Google suggests "how soon is too soon to say i love you," and when you type "how soon is too soon to write" Google suggests "how soon is too soon to write a thank you note," and when you type "how soon is too soon to write about dog's death," Google gives you over twenty-five million results in 0.48 seconds.

If someone locates the David Foster Wallace quote, please email me at: nicholas.montemarano@fandm.edu.

There is no other way. You must mention: the vet said it would be a matter of seconds. You and your wife held the dog, petted her, murmured endearments. Be brave and include them. Sweet dog, sweet Ralph, we love you, we're here, it's okay, we're right here, what a good dog you've been, what a good friend, thank you, we love you, we're right here, it's okay, honey, it's okay, we're here. With the injection her eyes closed, her back legs twitched slightly and stiffened, she wheezed twice. We're here, sweet girl, it's okay. The vet said he was sorry, something went wrong. You looked at her chest still rising and falling. The vet left the room and came back with his assistant, who shaved another leg, found another vein. You tried to comfort your wife: She's okay, she's in a deep sleep, don't worry, she's not in pain. Then the second injection, the vet bending with his stethoscope to listen. "I'm sorry," he said, "but her heart's still beating, I'll need to give a little more." You kept saying, "It's okay, we're here," but wanted to knock the needle from his hands and say, "Wait, stop, we've changed our minds, we want another week, another day." And then the third injection, the stethoscope, and finally: "Her heart has stopped. She's gone."

Neruda wrote a poem called "A Dog Has Died" in which he mentions his lack of belief in a heaven for people but his belief in "a heaven for all dogdom." If anyone has proof of such a place or a really convincing argument in its favor, please email me at: nicholas.montemarano@fandm.edu.

I apologize for shifting back and forth between "you" and "I" but I'm not the same person who looked into her eyes when her life went out of them. I keep using "you" because I can't stop talking to myself in these empty rooms.

The Seneca Review again on the lyric essay: "Loyal to that original sense of essay as a test or a quest, an attempt at making sense."

I could make a few more leaps, play with the word "loyal," for example, but there are no literary maneuvers to make this make sense, and so perhaps this is not an essay after all.

Google search: "how long is too long to stay with your dog's body after she is no longer inside the body." Google search: "do dogs have souls."

Mention, not merely, the empty bed, her hair on the front lawn, the chewed tennis ball in the yard, her collar in your wife's hand as she sleeps curled into herself, how she might have slept when a girl, food left in a bowl on the floor, a man crying over the sink as he scrapes cold dog food into the garbage disposal and hesitates before flipping the switch.

"The lyric essay stalks its subject like a quarry but is never content to merely explain or confess."

But I must confess that more than once I was impatient with her during a walk as she sniffed grass and flowers and trees. I was anxious to get back to my desk and work on the novel I was writing in which she was a character, a scene in which she sniffed grass and flowers and trees.

Google search: "female German Shepherd Ralph alive." No results found.

NO RESULTS FOUND | 91

Maybe end with the sound she'd make when settling into a more comfortable position—a cross between a sigh and a satisfied groan.

Or how you and your wife would run in opposite directions at the park, and she'd run back and forth, back and forth, wanting to keep her pack together.

Or how if you and your wife were crying—a fight, let's say— she would sense your sadness and lick your faces.

Or that recurring dream: you, your wife, and Ralph about to be washed out to sea. A gigantic wave is coming. With one hand you clutch your wife's wrist so tightly you could break it, with the other you grab Ralph's collar. You take a deep breath. Here comes the wave. You call out into the wind: "Don't let go—no matter what."

How you'd wake relieved to the sound of Ralph downstairs, lapping water from her bowl.

Scott Nadelson

Parental Pride

THERE WAS THE CAT, the one we called Lady Luck because we'd first found her, six weeks old, running through four lanes of traffic, now jumping and prancing on the back lawn, tossing something into the air and leaping after it, back arched, tail stiff, claws bared. I caught sight of her from an upstairs window when I should have been getting dressed for work and stayed where I was, towel around my waist, underwear in hand. It was a mouse she'd tossed, I could see that now, and it was alive. Or rather, what I really saw was its movement as the cat let it wriggle away, the grass quivering in a curving line toward a flower bed, though it didn't get more than a few feet before she pounced, batting it down with both paws and holding it firm. Then she picked it up again, by its skinny tail, bucked her head so that it flung over her back, and twirled so she could trap it as soon as it landed. I knew the mouse was suffering, terribly, but I couldn't help admiring Lady Luck's hunting skill and taking pleasure in her success. She'd always been a skittish cat, cowering whenever strangers came near, often getting attacked by one of the neighborhood strays, and even though I knew it was ridiculous to project human emotions onto her, I assumed that catching the mouse would provide a necessary boost to her self-confidence. I probably didn't think about it in quite those terms, but I did recall then, or maybe it was later, a fight I'd gotten into as a ten-year-old, the only one I'd ever instigated, though I'd been reluctantly drawn into plenty of others, usually by a sadistic neighbor who liked to beat me over the head with a rubber snake. This was a fight I'd asked for, challenging a kid who'd said something mildly insulting to me on the bus home from school. The kid was undersized like me, maybe a little smaller, a babyfaced redhead with big pink freckles everywhere, even on his lips and knuckles, and whatever insulting thing he'd said had sparked a cool rage I'd never felt before, an indignation that made me abandon the shy, shrinking self I'd always known and call out for everyone on the bus to hear, Zeek Field, four o'clock. Be there. It was one thing for the sadistic neighbor to beat me with a rubber snake or throw dog shit at me—I'd take that as a consequence of being small and badly dressed, an easy target— but I wouldn't let a word pass from the babyfaced redhead, who should have tried to make himself invisible to avoid being harassed, as I did, though it never seemed to do any good. After I told him to meet me at Zeek Field, he should have hidden himself away for a few days and hoped everyone forgot my challenge, but there he was when I arrived, in fresh shorts and T-shirt, bouncing on the balls of his feet as he must have seen boxers do on TV. Half the other kids from the bus had shown up, too, standing around the baseball diamond, already cheering us on as I laid my bike beside the backstop. It hadn't occurred to me to change clothes before coming. I'd just spent the last hour pacing from kitchen to living room, scarfing half a bag of Oreos, and now my mouth was dry, my school clothes stiff. I was probably wearing corduroys and a plaid shirt, or else jeans my mother had ironed like slacks so a white line showed down the middle of each leg. No wonder I got picked on daily. The redhead kept bouncing as I approached, smiling to himself or laughing at something I hadn't heard, and the rest of the kids closed around us, calling out predictable things you'd always hear at a fight like this—kick his ass, show him who's a pussy now—and rooting halfheartedly for one or the other of us, since all they really wanted was blood and pain. Who it belonged to didn't matter. I'm guessing my sadistic neighbor was there, though I can't remember for sure, giddily pounding a fist into a palm. I knew nothing about fighting, how to throw a punch or block one, and at first all I could do was heave a few big roundhouses that nudged the redhead's shoulder and chest. The blows he landed weren't any firmer, and the crowd grew restless, their taunts menacing. If we didn't beat each other, I knew, they'd beat both of us worse. But then the redhead caught my nose with his forearm, hard, and I froze. There was a little trickle of blood onto my lips, and as I wiped it away, that cold rage growing colder, crystallizing, I could see in his face that he realized he'd made a mistake. All at once I knew exactly the right way to throw a punch, straight out from my chest to his jaw. He turned his face away, but I kept punching, the back of his head, his neck, until he went down on his knees. He was crying, I knew he was, but I jumped on him anyway, aware now that he was indeed smaller than I, quite a bit so, but that didn't stop me from shoving his face into the pitcher's mound, grinding cheek and nose into coarse dirt until other kids pulled me away. They carried me on their shoulders, howling in triumph, as if they'd been rooting for me all along. I'd given them more violence than they'd expected, they loved me for it, and if the sadistic neighbor was there, I want to believe I tossed him a look before getting on my bike and pedaling away, one that said, You're next. But my rage had already thawed, or maybe evaporated, it was gone with the first punch, and on my way home I started sobbing. I wished I'd let the redhead's insult pass, wished I'd kept to my shy, shrinking ways, not because I regretted what I'd done, but because I knew news of the fight would soon reach my parents, which it did, a day later. My mother called me aside after dinner to let me know what she'd heard from another boy's mother and ask if it was true that I'd started the fight. I probably relayed whatever insulting thing the redhead had said, blubbering, expecting her to scold me, which she did, but far more gently than I'd anticipated. She said predictable things about ignoring hurtful words, about defending myself only when absolutely necessary. But in her voice I could hear something other than chastisement and disapproval, and I could see it in the edges of her frown, too. There was a burgeoning pride in her undersized son who was so often getting beaten over the head with a rubber snake, whose school clothes were sometimes dotted with dog shit, yes, this little guy had finally found a way to stand up for himself, and not only had he challenged another kid to a fight over a trivial insult, but he'd beaten that babyfaced redhead nose down in the dirt until he was a weeping bundle of freckles begging for mercy. This was what she'd always wanted for her child, a confidence born of independence, of standing strong in a world that tried to knock him down, and if others had to fall for him to feel good about himself, so be it. Wasn't it what I wanted for my own daughter, now three, bossed around by older kids in her preschool class? When I dropped her off or picked her up, I could see already how she assumed the retreating manner of the smallest kid in the room, drifting to the edge of the story circle, the biggest and most aggressive of the others crowding forward and clamoring for the teacher's attention. And all I could do was hope that next year, when she was no longer the smallest, she'd find some new peanut of a child to boss around in turn, and though that other child's self-esteem might suffer, she'd just have to take it out on some kid who followed. As I watched my daughter through the window of her classroom, standing out of the way as bigger kids claimed the best toys and left her with nothing but an armless doll and a handful of faded letter blocks, I told myself that that other child was no concern of mine. And neither was the mouse, though it, of course, would have no such opportunity to take out its suffering on something else. Lady Luck carried it in her jaws now, gently, not wanting to crush it, not yet. She moved to the patio, a place she usually avoided because it was so open and exposed—evidence, I thought, that this game, however cruel, was good for her—and though I was too far away to see, I imagined the mouse's tiny frame trembling against her teeth. What power she must have felt, what fierce giddy unstoppable joy. How could I not want her to feel this way always? How could I not want to feel it myself? She dropped the mouse on the patio's concrete pad, and it scurried away, underneath a fern at its edge. For a moment it seemed that Lady Luck had lost sight of it, and I was already tugging on my underwear, ready to head out and pull aside the fern leaves to show her where it had gone. But her confusion was only a feint: soon enough, her paw shot out and dragged the mouse back into the open. And that was when I remembered, or maybe it was later—damn this associative mind, damn its love of patterns—an article I'd read in the previous Sunday's *Times*, about one of the recent gang rapes in India, a portrait of the perpetrators and the culture that had spawned them. The authors described the vast hopeless slums of Mumbai, the poverty and boredom and feelings of worthlessness that characterized the lives of men who did nothing but play cards and drink all day in concrete shacks with tin roofs, who dubbed young women "prey" and hunted them because they felt they deserved more than what they had and because they had nothing better to do. After the rape, one of the men had gone straight home and told his mother what he'd done, boastfully, as if he knew she'd want to hear it. The article quoted her at length, saying first that what he'd done was wrong, of course it was, but why was that girl here to begin with, everyone knew this part of the city was dangerous after dark, and wasn't she a harlot anyway, didn't she already have her knickers down for some other man, and what was her boy supposed to do when her legs were spread for all the world to see? Her defensiveness hardly masked pride in the son who'd wrestled with the cruel world that kept him on his knees, who'd found a way to make it his own. Why should she care about a girl in skimpy clothes? Remembering her words then or later, I had no doubt that if she'd been with her son in the abandoned factory where he and three other men repeatedly raped the woman, a photojournalist, while her co-worker, tied up with her belt, listened from behind a partially crumbled wall, she would have held those legs apart so her son could squat between them, just as I would have pushed aside fern leaves to help Lady Luck find the mouse. But she didn't need my help now, because there in the middle of the patio, exposed to anyone who wanted to watch, she happily chewed the mouse's head loose from its body.

Chris Daley

Thoughts on Time
After Viewing Christian Marclay's **The Clock**

The Clock *is a twenty-four-hour single-channel montage constructed from thousands of moments of cinema and television history depicting the passage of time. Marclay has excerpted each of these moments from their original contexts and edited them together to create a functioning timepiece synchronized to local time wherever it is viewed—marking the exact time in real time for the viewer for twenty-four consecutive hours.*

—Los Angeles County Museum of Art

12:01. I have given myself an hour in which to write this. An hour used in this way seems an approximate and subjective measurement. If I become caught up in this project, an hour could pass fleetly. I could look up at the corner of my screen and see a :37 when I expected a :14. If I become distracted or prove unable to sever relations to my phone, the hour might drag endlessly.

12:14. There is no way to control time, although for my purposes here, I will chart it. We think that we have it shackled and compartmentalized, but time must find this amusing. We could no more likely shape fire. I was recently with a six-year-old girl who

THOUGHTS ON TIME | 99

said when she grew up she wanted to be a singer, President, and the clouds, so she could block out the sun and make it less hot. Time is equally ambitious and unregulated.

12:19. Because when you sit in a theater watching Christian Marclay's *The Clock*—in my case, at the Los Angeles County Museum of Art—you become aware of what it might look like to manipulate time, to take its temperature, to capture it in small increments and hold it up like a gift.

12:24. A friend thought that *The Clock* was twenty-four hours of clock faces. How dull that would be. And how unlike Marclay's project. Clocks, perhaps the most stiff and uninteresting aspect of time as we experience it, are simply a device for Marclay to use in his exploration of the nature of time, or as time is lived.

12:28. I have seen two sections of *The Clock* on two separate occasions: 3:30–4:10 p.m. and 10:05–11:05 a.m. During both visits, I was viscerally aware of what time of day it was, not in terms of what the clock says, but in terms of what happens at this time of day. This is 3:35 in the afternoon, the film said. Here it is from the angle of a meter expiring as a man runs to the bank. Here it is from the angle of a team of law enforcement officers rushing to a bombsite. (There is much rushing toward bombsites in *The Clock*. Thus is the nature of Hollywood.) Here it is from the angle of some women sitting down to tea in a period drama.

12:33. Here is 10:06 in the morning. Big and Carrie are getting married. A couple is waking up. A woman is not waking up, as Humphrey Bogart leans over her prone and drug-addled body. ("I can vacuum! She takes the pills!" the housekeeper has explained.)

A team of law enforcement officers rushes to a bombsite. Sophia Loren runs sexily to breakfast while Marlon Brando tells her to eat more quickly. ("Yes, sir!" she keeps saying sexily.)

12:38. Because not only is *The Clock* about time—about how expectations of behavior change throughout the minutes, hours, day, about how decisions are made incessantly based on what some lines in a circle dictate—it is about the movies. Thousands of movies that Christian Marclay watched with a singular purpose, for how long? How much time?

12:48. Alarm clocks in movies demonstrate how careless filmmakers can be. In my 10:05–11:05 a.m. visit, alarms were going off willy nilly, as if someone would actually set their alarm for 10:13, 10:37, 10:54 . . .

12:51. Marclay's editing makes clear that certain minutes of the hour are more important than others. As the top of the hour approaches, the drama builds—artificially created by editing sequences, but also intrinsic to our arrangement of and adherence to clock time. Things happen purposefully at 2, at 5, at 8; if something happens at 4:37 or 9:03, it is either by accident or because someone is not, literally and metaphorically, on time.

12:58. One of the strangest sensations of *The Clock* is that, at least once during each of my two visits which were to be followed by other engagements, I felt the need to look at my watch. I was sitting there in the theater, watching time pass, but somehow in my mind, cinema time and real time existed in two separate realms. Realizing that in this one particular instance they do not is startling and magical.

Lynne Sharon Schwartz

The Renaissance

WHEN I WAS THIRTEEN, a year of such adolescent angst that I was sure it would be the worst year of my life, I started ninth grade. On the first day of history class, our teacher, Mr. Feigenbaum, told us about the Renaissance. Mr. Feigenbaum, whom I can still see standing beside his large wooden desk at the front of the classroom—I was short and always had a seat up front—was also fairly short and wore a brown suit. He had dark hair thinning at the top, and glasses with thick dark rims. He wasn't heavy but pear-shaped. There was nothing remarkable about his appearance; he was the sort of person you might not notice on the street. But he became remarkable to me because he was the first person to utter the transformative word, Renaissance, in my presence.

He told us that in the fourteenth and fifteenth centuries in Europe a dazzling phenomenon swept over the land, a reawakening of love for art and beauty, above all the arts and legacy of the ancient worlds of Greece and Rome, along with a burgeoning of new art and thought. It was especially startling because, he told us, it came after a period of some centuries called the Dark Ages, in which all of Europe apparently slept. Under a spell, I thought as he spoke. As in a fairy tale.

I pictured a dim world in which nothing ever happened, shadowy and crepuscular as if trapped in a prolonged, static twilight. Nobody did much of anything besides the daily chores necessary to stay alive, and these they did in the dark and in silence, riddled with ennui. Then all at once burst the dazzling dawn of the Renaissance. Brilliant golden light broke through the clouds, spreading over every obscure corner of Europe, and people woke from their torpor and the Dark Ages were over. Everyone started painting and writing and making sculptures. (I later learned that the Dark Ages were not as dark as I had envisioned: plenty went on, but for the purposes of ninth grade, the Dark Ages did not merit class time.)

I was tremendously excited by this news of the Renaissance, which I'd never had an inkling of. Besides being exciting in itself, the news gave me hope, since I was living through my own Dark Age, mired in boredom and fretfulness, feeling rejected and useless, quite without alluring prospects. I swore to remember for the rest of my life how miserable I'd been that year. Surely I could never feel such misery again.

And in fact I didn't. Naturally I've had far more serious troubles than those typical of adolescence. But I've never again had that unique thirteen-ish feeling. It's nihilistic. You don't know who you are or what you want to do with your life, and you can't bear anything or anyone in it.

It's common knowledge that adolescents become obnoxious, typically towards their parents, and the causes are common knowledge too, though I've always found some of them dubious. One of the ways of being obnoxious, perhaps more frequent in girls, is having contempt for one's mother. In reality, there was nothing contemptible about my mother. She was good-humored, forthright, and had a peaceable nature. She was sociable, indeed charismatic, and often had friends over to play a favorite game of that time, mah-jongg. It must have been all those admirable qualities that I scorned, because I was just the opposite. In my uncertainty about who I was and how I could tolerate living, I must have needed to cling tightly to my ill humor and secrecy and argumentativeness. I longed to flee, but where? How? I knew there was a world beyond my immediate and circumscribed surroundings, indeed right over the bridge in Manhattan, but I didn't know how to get to it. Or rather, I knew how, but was not yet permitted to make the subway trip on my own. If thirteen wasn't the worst year of my life, it was surely a dark time.

I found my mother's limitations intolerable and was often uncivil to her. My brother-in-law, who joined the family when I was ten by marrying my much older sister, and who was calm and even-tempered, a peacemaker like my mother, said to me, "Can't you at least be polite to her? She's your mother, after all. Can't you talk to her?"

"How can I talk to her?" I said. "She doesn't even know what the Renaissance is."

Now, it's true that subjects like the Renaissance were not discussed in my family. But in retrospect, it's likely that my mother had in fact heard of the Renaissance. She completed high school in Brooklyn and went on to secretarial school, though I doubt that the Renaissance appeared on the curriculum there. But they might have covered the Renaissance in her high school. Would it have been in the syllabus? Surely some teachers other than Mr. Feigenbaum knew about it. Even if my mother hadn't heard of it, she might have liked to; I could have told her. But that never occurred to me.

One reason this contempt for my mother feels odd today is that not so long before it began, or emerged—a mere few years—

one of my favorite privileges was helping her prepare for her semi-weekly mah-jongg games when her turn came round to host them. I loved to set up the folding bridge table in the dining room and place the four chairs around it, while my mother busied herself in the kitchen putting candies and nuts in little bowls, a prelude to the coffee and cake that would be served when the game was over.

My mother's mah-jongg set was in a mahogany colored box of a sort of alligator material, longer and narrower than an attaché case. It had two brass levers on the sides that you snapped to open it. Inside, the supplies for the game were neatly stacked in compartments, a niche for every item. I set out racks about twelve inches long for each player, on which they would line up their tiles. At one edge of each rack were four small brass posts, about two and a half inches high, for the hexagonally shaped mah-jongg money, red, green, blue, and yellow for different denominations, each about the size of a nickel, with a hexagonal hole in the middle. I slid the money onto the brass poles through the hexagonal holes. The poles had a joint about halfway up, so they could bend over at a right angle, to keep the money secure. These curious little joints charmed me; I jiggled them over and over, like bending an elbow.

Next I set a mah-jongg card at each of the four places. The cards, a little smaller than postcards, were folded, and opened into three sections with enigmatic lists on each of the six sides. The lists showed the combinations of tiles that made a winning hand. Although I became familiar with the game from watching, circling the table and peering over the women's shoulders, I never understood the hieroglyphics of the cards.

The tiles, a little larger than a pat of butter, were a buttery color, each with a design on one side: dot, crack, bam, and wind. My favorite task was dumping them from the box onto the center of the table and hearing the delicate clinking sounds they made.

Then I had to turn each one face down, hiding their Chinese designs. This I loved to do. It was laborious, but I enjoyed watching my progress—order obliterating chaos. I've always liked repetitive, incremental tasks like that.

Before the women arrived, my mother would check my work to see that I'd done it all correctly, and I was always proud when I had. Then the doorbell began to ring: the players arrived, and after the greetings and some gossip, they would sit down, gather the face-down tiles, and line them up on their racks.

And by some unbidden process, puberty, I suppose, and all that accompanies it, somehow this intimacy, this childhood delight in helping my mother morphed into contempt at thirteen. One of the things I developed the greatest contempt for was the mah-jongg games. They struck me as the pinnacle of middle-class banality. One bam, three cracks, five dots, the women would call out all afternoon, then have coffee and cake and go home to fix dinner.

How pointless, compared to the Renaissance. Mah-jongg and the Renaissance came to represent for me polar modes of life, and I had no doubt which I was meant for, if only I could find it—as if it were tangible and resided in a place.

By the time I learned about the Renaissance I had stopped helping my mother set up for the games. If I came home from school to discover an afternoon game in progress, scorn rose in my throat like bile. It was all I could do to greet the women cordially, as my very civilized mother had instructed me. I would have preferred to roll my eyes but didn't dare. I grabbed a handful of salted peanuts from one of the bowls and clattered upstairs to my room, where I flung myself on my bed and mused about the Renaissance.

It would come. It had to come. Once I was allowed to ride the subway alone, the spell would be broken. Like the youngest son in a fairy tale, I would set out to find my true destiny.

David L. Ulin

A Tale of Two Cities

FROM THE DEPARTMENT of blurring boundaries: Last summer, in the neighborhood formerly known as Hell's Kitchen, I was brought face-to-face with the difference between my son Noah's New York and mine. Noah was sixteen, living with his grandparents in the city, and working at New World Stages, as a lighting intern on the off-Broadway revival of *Rent*. Brought up in Los Angeles, where my wife and I moved before he was born, he'd long considered himself a New Yorker in exile, counting down the minutes until he could escape the sprawl of Southern California for Manhattan's concrete corridors. Throughout his life, we've visited New York a few times each year—for my work, to see family, while passing through on our way to someplace else. He knows the city, in other words, or at least an aspect of the city—but it's an aspect circumscribed by having had to rely on me as a tour guide: a vision of New York through my eyes.

All that changed over the summer, with Noah working in Manhattan, commuting between my parents' apartment and the theater, running errands, going out. He told me about this when we talked or texted, but it wasn't until I came to town in mid-July that I realized the extent to which he had carved out a New York of his own. By then, Noah had been east for nearly a month, and *Rent* was in production, running eight previews a week. The night I arrived, a Saturday, he returned from the theater at 11:30: tired, a little frazzled, with the look of someone who'd been working too hard. We talked for a bit, but he soon slipped off to his room to iChat with his friends. *The more things change*, I thought with a measure of satisfaction, even relief. I want my kids to grow up, but I also want them to grow up slowly, and my only trepidation at having sent Noah to New York was the understanding that it would help to pull him out of our orbit, by offering a taste of independence, of experience, in a city twenty-four hundred miles from home.

And yet, of course, this is precisely what happened—how could it not?—as I recognized the following afternoon. Noah had gotten me a ticket to the Sunday matinee of *Rent*, and so around noon, we left my parents' place together, taking the subway from the Upper East Side. My first inkling that things had shifted came as Noah led me station-to-station, from the Lexington Avenue line to the E train, following the signs for transfer, deep below the streets. I knew where we were going, but I hung back, letting him direct me, until we were back above the ground. My second inkling came moments after we emerged from the subway and were standing at the corner of Forty-ninth and Eighth. "We should get some lunch," Noah said, but as I started for a Sabrett's stand, he lit out across the avenue for the Food Emporium, where, he assured me with the equanimity of a longtime resident, the sushi was both cheap and fresh. Wait, I almost said, leaning towards the vendor, so close I could smell the hot dogs boil. But Noah *wasn't* waiting; he was showing me his version of the city, the way he lived when I wasn't around.

After lunch, we went to the theater; Noah introduced me around and gave me a quick tour, before heading off to work. From my seat in the orchestra, I kept glancing at him, sitting behind the audience with the rest of the lighting team, going over the grid on a computer, making adjustments, taking notes. In the dim glow of the console, he appeared cocooned, encased in shadows, somehow a part of and yet outside the experience, as the techies often seem to be. This is Noah's territory—that of the theater and, more specifically, the light crew—and it's one I've had to learn to navigate as I try to understand what he's doing and who he is.

It's both strange and oddly moving to watch your child work, especially when he's doing something so distinct from your abilities, leaving you nothing else to offer but support. When it first seemed that Noah might get this internship, I tried to frame it through my point-of-reference; "It's as if," I explained to my father, "I had spent the summer after tenth grade working for Kurt Vonnegut." That, of course, is equally true and untrue, since one conundrum of the parent-child dynamic is how little each side predicts the other, how, despite my desire to draw comparisons, equivalencies, Noah's experience is unique to him. To watch him in that theater was to glimpse the adult he is trying to become, one with his own skills and affinities. That's part of the point here also, to let him see from the inside what it means to work on a professional production, even as this, too, can't help but draw him away from us, by immersing him in the contours of a broader world.

When the matinee was over, I went with Noah to pick up some replacement fixtures, then took him to a quick dinner at Joe Allen before dropping him back at New World Stages for the evening show. Afterwards, I wandered slowly up Eighth Avenue and into

Central Park, past the pond where Holden Caulfield, another sixteen-year-old in the city, had wondered where the ducks went for winter, up the Park Drive with its bicyclists and skaters, and across to the Upper East Side. This was my New York, the New York where I'd been raised, although tonight, as dusk thickened into bruised plum twilight, I felt as if I were seeing it through a different set of eyes. It's been twenty years since I lived in the city, a generation of intense change and turmoil—from the rise of Rudy Giuliani to the aftermath of the towers' fall. Yes, a generation, in which I've long since given up the notion that I have any purchase on the place, that this New York is the one I left behind. And yet, my afternoon with Noah had shown me something unexpected: that as much as the city might not be mine anymore, it was, in some important sense, becoming his. Living on your own in a place, even for a summer, will do that, but even more, it is a matter of blurring boundaries, of how our kids, as they grow up, can't help but grow away from us, even in a place we know.

Steven Harvey

Sputnik 2

IN MY IMAGINATION they both wake me, my mother nudging me quietly while shushing me so as not to disturb my brother, my father standing behind her holding my coat. I rub my eyes awake and see their faces glowing in the half-light of the room, my dad waving us toward the bedroom door. Outside it is cold—this is February, north of Chicago—but it must have been clear. The three of us walk into a grassy clearing away from trees and train our eyes on the evening sky.

Dad lights a cigarette for my mother and then for himself, the glow from the match illuminating their faces against the night sky for a moment like two crescent moons. He shakes out the match and takes a long draw letting the smoke out slowly. My mother fiddles with her cigarette before taking a quick puff, pulling her coat around her. We wait in the cold briefly, me standing between them, my mother holding me against her for warmth.

Suddenly, it appears. "Over there," my dad says, squinting from the smoke, and we turn facing east. The tree line forms a black horizon and above it the Milky Way shimmers in the chilly air.

Dad kneels down pointing up for me to see, the cigarette at the tips of his fingers tracing the arc against the sky. My mother sees it too and, putting an arm on my shoulder, leans forward to be sure that I have found it. I follow the glow of my dad's cigarette ash to the spot among the stars and locate it at last, not the satellite itself, which is too small, but the casing, a tiny oblong of light, tumbling silently across the constellations nailed into the night sky. It flip-flops in a regular rhythm, like a heartbeat, without glittering, and, despite its size, glows with a white-bright incandescence. In her letters my mother calls this satellite "Muttnik"—a phrase in the press at the time—because of the dog inside, but it is hard to think of a dog, or anything else, living in this slug of pure light.

I cannot imagine that night sky now without creating metaphors from the time three years later that I hid under the stairs and looked at the nails driven into the treads overhead, that coffin-lid of stars that still haunts me. Thinking of it now, other memories come flooding back as well. Of me at the top of the stairs watching my mother crying at the kitchen table while my dad stands off to the side. Of me stepping out of my bedroom to watch my mother with her back to me singing "Fever" all alone. No, those thoughts—those precious and horrible clues—don't go away, but they also don't erase that night, lost to memory but captured in a letter that I almost didn't read, when my parents and I, somewhere in Illinois, stood in a darkened field together and looked into the heavens.

Jennifer Finney Boylan

Why the Long Face?

DEVON, PENNSYLVANIA, the town where I grew up, is the place I loved with all my heart, and that I could not wait to leave. It was there, in a house on Waterloo Road, that I lost my virginity and saw my sons take their first steps, and there that my parents drew their last breaths.

I've been back to that house only once since we sold it in 2011. I drove past late one night, pulled into a neighbor's, and dissolved in tears. It was hard to remember how much I'd once hated the place, how all I'd wanted was to get away from Devon, and its oppressive preppy culture, a place where, when I was growing up, there really were Quakers who called you "thee."

But every year in late May, I still go back to my hometown, for one reason: to see the Devon Horse Show, an event that's like the Mardi Gras of the Main Line—the set of tony suburbs that stretches west from Philadelphia. The show raises money for the Bryn Mawr Hospital and goes on for eleven days; the climax is the Thursday night Grand Prix, in which jumpers race a course against a clock for $100,000 in prize money.

So there I'll be this week, up in the old grandstand in the box that bears my family's name, wearing a jacket colored "Devon blue." I'll be sipping something called a "Rum Swizzle," a concoction the people in the box next to us mix up, supposedly, in a washing machine. I'll probably also poke my nose in at the box-holders' reception, where Main Line aristocracy will be wearing plaid Bermuda shorts and orange sport jackets. There will be women in their seventies with names like Muffy, Portia, and Titania. People will speak with that spectacularly strange Main Line accent, most famously embodied by Katharine Hepburn, who graduated from Bryn Mawr in 1928.

I will be able to stand all of this for about forty-eight hours, before I'll want to go screaming back to my home in rural Maine, where you'll find me playing piano with my friends in a Down East rock-'n'-roll band called the Stragglers. Those boys have called me all sorts of things, but they have never called me "thee."

I used to walk past the horse show grounds every day on my way to the bus stop that took me to private school, a place where men in three-piece suits taught us the works of Thomas Mann in German. "You will never come to this place again," one of the masters told me, "unless you learn how to create it in your heart."

Creating Devon in my heart was the last thing I wanted to do in the fall of 1980, when I left, presumably forever, on a train bound for New York City. I remember looking out the window of the Paoli local at each of the little towns: Strafford, Wayne, St. Davids, Radnor, Villanova. I swore to myself, I am never coming back. I am off to some place less crushing, a place where it might feel safer to come out as transgender, a place where, at the very least, there was no one named Titania.

Back then I thought of myself as a fragile soul, as someone whose sense of self was so tenuous that an encounter with a pair of plaid shorts was enough to snuff me like a candle. But the passage of time has made me stronger, and more forgiving of the person that I was, of the place where I am from and the people who inhabited it.

The Devon Horse Show has changed, too. In 2012, a pony named Humble died after a regimen of drugs that included anti-inflammatories and muscle relaxants, in a case that drew national attention. Then, this spring, the president of the horse show, Wade McDevitt—whose grandfather was a founder—resigned after allegations of a conflict of interest in his pushing for the development of a retail center backed by Urban Outfitters adjacent to the fairgrounds. And yet, the event is as popular as ever, with a record-setting number of visitors last year.

The show goes on. The annual return I make there gives me the chance to re-connect with old friends, to take in the sights and sounds of childhood, and to walk around the Devon midway with a slaphappy expression.

When I was a child, I liked the Devon midway a lot more than the actual show. There were funnel cakes, a concoction called a lemon stick, which was a hollow peppermint stick stuck like a straw into a lemon, and the Ferris wheel. Many years later, I took my young son, Zach, on that Ferris wheel. As it rose, we could see the whole town—the run-down Victorian train station, the Mercedes-Benz dealers, even the house I had fled in anger, and to which I had finally returned. And above it all, a sky of Devon blue.

Meghan Daum

Home on the Prairie: Lincoln, Nebraska

THE THING you have to understand about Lincoln, Nebraska, is that it falls under the radar. Unless you're from Nebraska—or possibly South Dakota or Iowa—it's probably not a place you'd think of visiting, much less moving to. No matter how unafford-able life becomes in Brooklyn or Portland or Austin, Lincoln is unlikely to turn up on a list of "unexpected hipster destinations." But, being extremely unhip, I moved there anyway. In 1999, when I was twenty-nine, I traded New York City for it and stayed nearly four years. This was a strange thing to do, and it perplexed a lot of people, particularly because I did not, contrary to some assump-tions, go there for school or a guy or because I was in the witness protection program. As a result, there's a part of me that feels like an impostor whenever I write or even talk about Lincoln. I'm not from there, I don't live there now, and when I did live there, I occupied an often awkward middle ground between guest and resident. By this I mean that even though I lived in a house and had friends and a relationship and a book club and a dog, I was always regarded as "the person who moved here from New York for no particular reason." In Nebraska that translates loosely into "deeply weird person."

I could tell you the basics. That Lincoln is the state capital and the county seat and the site of the main campus of the University of Nebraska, and that the capitol building has a fifteen-story tower commonly referred to as "the penis of the plains." I could tell you that recent figures put the population at nearly 260,000 and the median household income at just under $45,000. I'd be obliged to mention, of course, that the biggest deal in town is, and always has been, Cornhusker football. The stadium has a capacity of more than 80,000, and on game days the normally wide-open sixty miles of interstate between Lincoln and Omaha goes bumper to bumper.

I could tell you the stuff that's slightly beyond the basics. That despite Husker pride—there's a disproportionate number of red cars and trucks on Lincoln's streets—and the beer-chugging, chest-painting, corn-hat-wearing (yes, as in a corncob on your head) all-American gestalt that comes with it, Lincoln's not as Wonder Bread as you might think. Since the 1980s, it's been a locus for refugee resettlement, and there are thriving communities of Iraqis and Vietnamese and Sudanese, to name a few. It's also got a visible LGBT (lesbian, gay, bisexual, transgender) population, a lot of aging hippies, and the kind of warmed-over, slightly self-congratulatory political correctness common to left-leaning university towns in red states. Unlike Omaha, which wants the rest of the country to know that it has tall buildings and Fortune 500 companies, Lincoln wants you to know that it's culturally sophisticated, that it's got a vegetarian sandwich shop and a public radio station and a wine bar. Like a restless kid from a small town, Lincoln wants to prove to you that it's not a hick. All the same, the country comforts of its steakhouses and honky-tonks make you want to put your arms around it as though it were a big, shaggy sheepdog.

But all that stuff always seems slightly beside the point. The Lincoln I love—the reason I stayed as long as I did and have returned nearly every year since—actually starts where the city limits end. Drive five minutes out of town and farmland unspools before you, replacing the car dealerships and big-box stores with oceans of prairie grass and corn growing in lockstep rows all the way to the horizon. This is where I spent the bulk of my Lincoln years; in a tiny farmhouse on the northwestern outskirts of town with an eccentric boyfriend and lots of animals (dogs, horses, a pig—the whole tableau). It would be a lie to say I didn't have some dark hours. My total income in 2001 was just over $12,000. My debit card was declined at the Hy-Vee supermarket more than once. I seriously wondered about whether I had it in me to seek work at the Goodyear plant. (I didn't.) As quiet as the days and nights were, there was chaos all around—animals that got sick, propane tanks that ran out of gas on frigid weekends. This wouldn't surprise a Nebraskan. It is not possible, after all, to live on a farm with a boyfriend, eccentric or otherwise, and animals five times your size without wondering if your life is piling up in snowdrifts around you. You can't live through a rural Nebraska winter without succumbing to at least a little of the "prairie madness" the early homesteaders battled when the wind blew mercilessly for weeks and months at a time.

Still, that landscape is the place my mind summons when I'm asked (usually in some yogic or meditative context, now that I live in Los Angeles) to close my eyes and "imagine a scene of total peace and serenity." In those moments, I picture the Rothko-like blocks of earth and sky, the psychedelic sunsets, the sublime loneliness of a single cottonwood punctuating acres of flat prairie. I remember the sound of golf-ball-size hail hitting the roof and denting the car. I remember sitting on the front porch and watching a lightning storm that was miles away but cracked the whole night open nonetheless. It was there, under that sky and at the mercy of all that weather, that I began to understand the concept of a wrathful God. In Nebraska, storms are a violence from which no amount of caution or privilege can protect you. Their warnings crawl across television screens in every season. They'll blow you or freeze you or blind you into submission. They'll force you into some kind of faith.

Lincoln gave me a faith in second chances. In third and fourth chances, too. I'd had a nervous upbringing in the tense, high-stakes suburbs of New York City, after which I lived hungrily and ecstatically, but no less nervously, in the clutches of the city itself. This was a life that appeared to have no margin for error. One mistake—the wrong college, the wrong job, embarking on marriage and family too soon or too late—seemed to bear the seeds of total ruination. Terrified of making a wrong move, of tying myself down or cutting off my options, I found myself paralyzed in the classic New York City way. I paid my rent, pursued my career, worked at temp jobs, and went on second (but not third) dates. I was waiting for the big score, of course (what is New York City if not a holding pen for people awaiting recognition of their greatness?), but in the meantime I was holding still, making no commitments or sudden moves, never venturing past the point of no return, honoring the nervous energy that paid my bills (barely) and delayed most of my gratification indefinitely.

Until one day I got on a plane and moved to Lincoln. Like I said, I don't expect people to get it. I didn't get it myself. Instead, I can offer this controlling metaphor. It concerns the final approach into the Lincoln airfield. It's a long runway surrounded by fields, with no built-up adjacent areas or bodies of water to negotiate. The runway is so long, in fact, that it was designated an emergency landing site for the space shuttle and, to this day, every time I fly in, even when the wind is tossing the little plane around like a rag doll, I always have the feeling that nothing can possibly go wrong. The space is so vast, the margin for error so wide, that getting thrown off course is just a minor hiccup, an eminently correctable misfire. Lincoln's air space, like its ground space, is inherently forgiving.

After those acid trip sunsets, that's the thing about Lincoln that rocked my world. That you can't really mess up too badly. You can marry too young, get a terrible tattoo, or earn $12,000 a year, and the sky will not necessarily fall. The housing is too cheap and the folks are too kind for it to be otherwise. Moreover, when you live underneath a sky that big, it's hard to take yourself too seriously. Its storms have a way of sweeping into town and jolting your life into perspective. That jolt was Lincoln's gift to me. It comes in handy every day.

Roxane Gay

There Are Distances Between Us

THE INTERSTATE HIGHWAY system in the United States is the largest and most sophisticated in the world. It is named for President Dwight D. Eisenhower. There are two points and between them, a distance between you and me. These two points are connected in ways we will never fully understand but they are connected. You are there and I am here. We are red stars on maps protected beneath hard plastic in highway rest areas tired travelers touch to make sense of where they are. I have counted the miles, yards, feet, and inches between us. There are too many. When I was young, my father had an atlas I liked to study, bound in leather, worn. I traced tiny lines with my fingers and said the names of cities like Waukesha and Cody and Easton and Amarillo. I once came home to a canopy bed. That summer was long, hot, terrible. Before I left, there had been an incident involving some boys who broke me right down the middle and, after, I couldn't pull myself back together. I simply stopped talking. My hair started graying. I stayed in my room. My parents fretted. A change of scenery, they decided, would be good. I went to Port au Prince, the city of their birth, stayed with an aunt and uncle

I hardly knew. Each time we needed to flush a toilet or take a bath or brush our teeth, we carried huge buckets to a well and carried those buckets back, warm water sloshing everywhere all to wash ourselves clean in some small way. It was never enough. I never felt clean. I only felt those boys. When I returned home, I walked into a perfect bedroom. The wallpaper was covered in little cornflowers. There was a canopy bed covered in gauzy material, draped perfectly. I loved to stare into the canopy and forget about all the ways I felt broken. Whenever we went on vacation, my father would study his atlas to find his way across America. My brothers and I sat in the back of our 1974 Grand Prix, bare legs sticking to the leather seat, hot and irritable, often bickering, forced to participate in my father's endless exploration of how far he could go. He often said the United States is a great country because with enough persistence, with enough patience, a man can travel from one end to the other. He said he never wanted to take for granted that he could not be kept from any place he wanted to be. Every morning, when I wake up, I think your name. I think, "Marry me," over and over and over. It shocks me, the clarity of those words, the intensity and depth, how the emotions behind those words defy logic, possibility. I do not say the words "I love you" often, not to anyone. Those words mean something. They shouldn't be used carelessly. In a photo album there is a faded Polaroid of my dad and my middle brother and me at the Grand Canyon before the third child came. We are painfully young, the four of us. I have no recollection of this trip. Behind us is our car and on the roof, the atlas. My father stands with one leg on a rock. My brother and I hug his other leg, hold hands. My father smiles. He is not a man who smiles easily. There is a gravity to him. When he speaks or acts, he does so with purpose and sincerity. I have spent the past several years trying to become like him so when I say, "I love you," you can know I mean it. My father is a civil engineer. He is always concerned with infrastructure, the strength of holding the world together. He has always filled my head with information about highways and tunnels and concrete. I've retained little. The ingratitude of children is staggering. I do know this, however: if nothing else were in the way, we would always be able to reach each other. We could close the distance between our two points. We could point to a place on a map and say, we are here.

Kim Barnes

Spokane Is a Coat: 1978

BECAUSE YOU'RE WEARY of the Idaho winter and country boys
in their barn jackets and think that what you must need is a real
city fix, you trade shifts at Lewiston's only disco, where you work
as a cocktail waitress, pack your curling iron and makeup in your
purse (you don't own a suitcase), pawn your deer rifle (you are the
daughter of a logger, raised on venison), and buy a round-trip bus
ticket to Spokane. No money left for food, but you still have two
Dexatrim and half a pack of Virginia Slims menthol, which will
quiet the hunger until you can reach a bar and fill a napkin with
celery sticks, sweet slices of orange—enough to get you through
the first hour of the night.

You know just where you're headed: The Ridpath—a real
hotel with room service, which you understand works like this:
you pick up the phone, utter a prayer for food, and it arrives like
a miracle at your door. The two-hour ride north provides time
to plan: you'll claim not to have a driver's license; you'll register
under your Oklahoma grandmother's maiden name; you'll provide a cousin's old address. You believe that the desk clerk won't
ask for more because you've curled your hair just like Farrah Faw-

cett. Purple eye shadow, a blouse that dips nearly to your navel—you're prepared. In fact, you're more than prepared because you're wearing a fur coat—real fur—which you were given in payment for some modeling you did for a clothing shop in town that couldn't pay but was willing to trade. The store once housed The Lewiston Fur Shop—all that 1940s inventory gone out of style. "Take your pick," the owner said, and let you loose to pet the racks of fox stoles, mink jackets. The coat you chose tufts up around your ears, brushes your knees. Its sleeves are weighty and largely cuffed. You feel like you might be able to pull yourself inside of it, hibernate for a while.

The Ridpath is a grand old dame, says the man at the door. Inside smells fusty, like hair oil, the back of your grandmother's couch. The lobby is dark and somehow heavy, like your coat, which you now let fall open. The middle-age clerk calls you by your grandmother's name, hands you the key, slides his fingers across your palm. You wince a smile, take the elevator to your room, which is bigger than some of the shacks you've lived in. You sit on the bed, stare at the phone. The dance club you've heard so much about—best bands, best booze, best boys—is too far to walk in your four-inch heels. You'll need to call a cab. No. You'll need to call the front desk. The front desk will do such things for you.

The coat waits with you in the lobby, bundles you into the back seat for the first taxi ride of your life. You watch the lights flick across your window, count the intersections, just in case. The disco's parking lot is full but the driver pulls right up to the door. You rummage through your purse, your coat pockets, while he watches in the rearview. You see by his eyes that he is smiling. You smile back. You can hear the music, feel the bass beating the air. He gets out, comes around, opens your door. "Next time," he says, and you think, yeah, next time.

But this time is real, and it goes like this: you order a double vodka tonic, start a tab that you will not pay. You find a table near the front, let the coat drape the chair. When you're asked, you dance. When the waitress says someone wants to buy you a drink, you say sure, ask for olives on the side. You smoke all of your Virginia Slims menthol. You consider. The man you choose is darkly handsome and looks like a French sailor boy—or what you think a French sailor boy might look like, since you have never been to Paris or even seen the sea. He wears a striped knit shirt, bell bottom pants, and has a way of staring at you that suggests arrogance. He helps you on with your coat, runs his hands down your shoulders. The fur lifts, settles. He pays his tab. He pays yours. He says, "Let's go get something to eat." You say, "I know where."

Spokane is a room at the Ridpath, a jacketed waiter who delivers your food on a rolling table covered in white linen. Spokane is lobster that you crack from its shell and pluck out with your fingers, steak that you take in large bites, bones that you suck and gnaw. Spokane is a silver bucket of ice, a bottle of champagne, and a boy whose skin is so smooth, you can only think of parachute silk. Spokane is a miniature envelope of fine cocaine—and, of course, you're hungry for that too. When he asks if it's your first time in the city, you say yes, because he may not be ready for the realities of your last time in this city, with a high school chum, now majoring in business at Gonzaga, who wanted to show you Spokane and took you for burgers at Dick's and then to a dank theater, where the double feature was violent porn and the floor was tacky and the men on both sides wore dark, ugly slickers and smelled like Valvoline. How you went back to your chum's apartment, back to his waterbed with its headboard full of mirrors and tricky little compartments full of illicit things. How he had another chum, already there, waiting for you, and that chum had a camera, and they didn't think they could take no for an answer.

If there is one thing you've learned about this city, it's that no is never the right answer.

But that was before, and this is now, and some part of you wants to feel more lighthearted than you are and make this boy with his smooth skin laugh. You think you might ask him, Do you know how hard it is to snort cocaine on a waterbed? Instead, you take the tiny straw he offers, keep your mouth shut, because this time, this time, this is your room, your rules, your reality. You're making it up as you go along, seizing this moment, because Spokane is never tomorrow, when you'll wake to find the boy has already set sail, when you'll curl your hair, pull on your elegant coat, take the elevator down, tell the clerk you plan to shop the day away, and walk out the door of the Ridpath into a world you have no idea how to live in.

Benjamin Anastas

O Pioneers!

WE MOVED to the suburbs with my lesbian moms in the summer of 1981. It was the end of Bohemian apartment living—the death knell of batik tapestries that doubled as bedspreads and room dividers and of the butterfly chair that scissored shut on anyone who sat in it.

We were pioneers in a land of backyard patios and lawn care, staking our claim on a neat white three-bedroom starter with an attached garage underneath the sunroom. The word "partners" wasn't used to invoke a partnership in bed, not yet. The phrase "same-sex couple," if anyone had coined it, would have drawn blank stares. The only word we had to describe the relationship between my lesbian moms—"lovers"—made it sound as if they met at an all-female bathhouse instead of in a gerontology semi-nar at Brandeis.

"You can't make me say 'lover'!" my older brother used to hol-ler when they fought.

"But that's what we are," our mother pleaded.

"That's right," Jan would join in. "Your mother and I are lovers!"

"I won't say it!"

"We're lovers!"

"Shut up!"

My lesbian moms knew what it meant to occupy the vanguard of sexual preference on our new block. I can still hear my mother's "Whoop!" on the day we moved in. It was a whoop of relief, tinged with the sadness of some bird calls.

"We did it, Jeane."

"I know. We did."

"It's ours. It's really ours."

"Whoop!"

I was twelve that summer. So was my twin sister. My brother, who got his own teenage sanctum in the attic, was sixteen. We were pioneers, too, but only by proxy. We were not prepared for the savages behind the hedges and the front gates, their radar for what was different about our house.

"Your mom's a lezzie?" asked a boy named Howard. It was the first week of school. I picked the wrong moment to practice the spirit of openness we were coached on. Howard hung out with the juvies at a place in the woods behind my school called the Shoe.

"Lezzies can be moms?" He chuckled.

"They can," I said. "Yeah." The blood was rushing to my face. "You're supposed to say 'lesbian.'"

"You're lucky I'm so stupid," Howard said. "I might forget your mom's a lezzie before I tell everyone."

I've read about a recent study suggesting that adolescents from lesbian homes turn out happier, better-adjusted and higher-achieving than teenagers from traditional families. I have an easy time believing it. Lesbian moms can now be as attractive and nonthreatening as Annette Bening and Julianne Moore in *The*

Kids Are All Right. If having two moms makes you special, then it stands to reason that children brought up in lesbian households would be off the charts.

Here's what I can tell you about having lesbian moms in the suburbs in 1981: It made me a liar. Afterschool was a time of evasion and dread, of postponing my friends' inevitable peek inside our house for as long as I could. But I always found myself, at some point in the trial period before the bond was sealed, standing in the doorway to our lesbian moms' bedroom, gazing at the lone queen bed, the pair of dressers with their matching jewelry boxes, rows of lotions and perfumes. "Where does Jan sleep?" my friends asked.

It was a natural question. That didn't make it any easier to answer. I used to claim, improbably, that Jan slept on a rollaway bed and folded it up every morning to store in the closet. I even felt a note of triumph whenever I opened the closet door and pointed out the bed frame. "See?" My sister had more dignity. She let their bedroom speak for itself and spent her afternoons doing homework with her other straight-A-student friends.

My older brother? He didn't last long in the suburbs. He shaved his head, joined a hard-core band and cut school to practice the bass and spend his days in record stores. Pioneering with our lesbian moms was not his choice. He still remembered what it was like to have a father in the house, and that was a hard imprint to give up. He was hardly ever home, but when he was, he fought with our moms so bitterly that I worried about the police showing up. I can still see my brother on the day he left for good, peeling down the driveway on his moped, bare head gleaming, the Tupperware breadbox that my mother's lover had just tossed at him sailing over his back and bouncing on the asphalt. We were down one pioneer.

Jill Talbot

Stranded

~ for Tracy

THIS NIGHT LIKE a photograph neither one of us can make out when I call you fifteen years later to ask if you remember the gun, the men, the comet. The two of us are on the side of Highway 82 outside of Brownfield, Texas. Forty miles from Lubbock. It's been a day-long drive, and my white Nissan is parked on the shoulder. No clouds and the moon is waning. A flash holds steady in the northern sky, the Hale-Bopp Comet. You are standing behind me, a gun in your hand. We're both wearing our long-sleeved flannel shirts, khaki shorts, flip-flops. The truck that pulled up behind us is dark, quiet, and we can't see the men who got out of it. The back right tire of my car is flat. Flat landscapes like this make it hard to hide, but standing out here in the dark, we understand how we might easily disappear. Two states away, I read aloud as you drove us through the red dust of the Tucson Mountains. "A postcard. Neat handwriting fills the rectangle: *Half my days I cannot bear not to touch you. The rest of the time I feel it doesn't matter if I ever see you again. It isn't the morality, it is how much you can bear.* No date, no name attached." And then I stopped, the lines too close to the things we were doing back in Lubbock. You with that one man. Me with that other. The two of us taking turns driving out of the state to change our state of mind. But every time, we'd turn your navy truck or my white car back toward Lubbock and give ourselves over to them, give ourselves away. But this night, the one right here, we're as still as the stars, trying to hear if the men are moving, if they're making a plan behind the slats of the truck bed to hurt us, or worse. Together we scratch down the postcard details of a close call, and I tell you what I remember most is the comet. Even now, I can still see it solitary in the clearing, the lights of a passing mystery suspended, and the two of us, not knowing how long we would be stranded by the miles of choices that defied measure or what we would, years later, be asked to bear.

Rebecca McClanahan

Things Gone the Way of Time

NOT THAT YOU CAN'T outbid perfect strangers in online wars
for your history—that vintage flour sifter, this Lionel train complete with smoke pellets and uncoupling track, the white cotton
gloves you've been dreaming for months. My mother had gloves
like those, with hand-sewn beads and scalloped edges, and as
I leaned against her on the hard church pew I'd close my eyes
and trace the route around each intricately bordered finger, the
only Sunday softness I can now conjure as I accelerate into the
past, Road Runner dust clouds roiling behind me, my father's
Route 66 coffee mug in my hand, a catalog gift I gave the year he
turned so sad that I schemed aloud, *One more time, Dad, we can
make the trip again, the whole family, the whole shebang.* I'd not
said *shebang* for so many decades, I had to say it again, *the whole
shebang.*

He shook his head as if to say, *Let it go,* this tenant farmer's
son whose life had been a series of letting things go—the rug
beater he'd wielded like a bat, the butter churn, the singletree
hitch, the corn husking glove with its dangerous hook. And
when I refused to take no for an answer (why should we have to

take no for an answer?) he wrapped his hands around the mug and leaned toward me. *You don't understand*, he said. *I want it to be then, NOW*, which sent me back to the whole shebang—him and Mom and all six kids in the blue station wagon, the red plaid thermos beside him, one of the boys in his lap, his small hands beneath Dad's pretending to steer us through electronic-free days of luxuriant boredom, past sage and cactus and tumbleweed, the dripping Desert Water Bag strapped to the hood ornament that pointed us home, where we fell into bunk beds and trundles and woke days later, or years, sprawled before the Motorola watching Laura Petrie or Lucy lumber across the screen in a maternity smock—whatever happened to maternity smocks? Mom sewed her own from Butterick patterns, or McCall's. Or Simplicity, the only dress line I could manage in my pimply, gangly years, the transparent tissue spread flat on the carpet, all pure and unsullied hope, until scissors rendered dismembered body parts splayed like a forensic puzzle beneath me, a pins-and-needles plot taking hours to solve. Hours of kneeling in submission until the carpet waffled its design onto my knees. No designs yet on my thighs, those would form in a year or two with my first nylon stockings and the garter belt with its tricky metal grips that dug into skin if you sat too long—beside a boy for instance, in the back seat of a car—and yes I know you can still buy snappy contraptions to coax vintage moments like that into motion, but that's just nostalgia, it costs us nothing and is beside the point.

Of memory, I mean, which takes us for all we're worth. Memory that hand-knotted string of pearls, that black locomotive spewing out smoke clouds, dragging its precious cargo in circles around the living room and over the uncoupling track with its power to disconnect everything we've snapped so carefully together, leaving the rest of our story stranded—the boxcar, the coal loader, the cartoon-red caboose signaling the end, the open platform asking to please be filled with something, oh please let it fill with something, we could name it the future, that all-thumbs, fumbling-in-the-dark set of hands whose touch we close our eyes to accept.

Jeff Oaks

4 for Easter

1

When I was a little boy, my mother used to construct elaborate Easter baskets and hide them, with a trail of jelly beans that she wove to help me find them throughout the house. I don't know what she did with our cats and dogs who would have eaten the trails before I woke up, but they never seemed to. It was one of her favorite things to do, she told me. Even years later, when I was living far away, she mailed me chocolate treats for Easter. All that pure love catches me in the throat now. What better candy to be given than to know that you were so loved?

2

Of the Easter Bunny itself, I was afraid. A rabbit the size of a man was wrong. I'd had rodents by then as pets and knew their sharp teeth and claws. I wanted no part of a giant one. I didn't understand the silliness of it, which is how adults, I think, think kids will see the Easter Bunny: a big, stupid, but kind-hearted creature. But kids, who often suffer the same sentimentalisms, know differently. A giant rabbit would be weaponized at that size. Anything giant is to be feared, is at the very least a cause for great alarm.

I was so glad the Easter Bunny never actually showed up in my house. I figured out early too He was really my mother, the first lie I recognized.

3

I have eaten rabbit. I ate a particularly good wild rabbit once, and was surprised by how tasty I thought it was, how it tasted like something that had enjoyed life and passed it on.

4

One of the earliest pictures is of me in a playpen with a lamb, which might have been an Easter lamb. It may not have been but in those days we weren't given to much sentimentality about the ways an edible creature might be used. We ate and we ate and we ate, as I've written elsewhere. You had to be strong because the Depression might return. It was after all only thirty some years before that picture of me was taken. You had to make your children love to eat so they had a chance. It was old magic. My grandfather could fix anything you handed him; he disappeared into his little workshop filled with drawers and tools and vises and a small stove over in one corner, and voilá, your watch was caught up in time again. My grandmother could make fantastic chocolate cakes out of pocket lint and old coffee grounds. The basement was full of jellies and preserves for the long winters. My father somehow made money out of sand and gravel, which made no sense to me at all. Maybe in that strange world I understood so little of, the lamb I briefly shared quarters with was in fact given a suit of clothing and twenty dollars and put on a bus. Who knows where he got off and how he started a new life? Who knows when we'll meet again and tell each other our stories of how we survived?

Bill Capossere

Chess Piece

You will be put in increasingly complex situations.
— from *Bobby Fischer Teaches Chess*, given to me by my father

- *Play takes place on a chessboard that contains 64 squares, alternately colored white and black. The board should be arranged in such a way that each player has a white square in the corner at his right.*

THE FIRST BOARD I remember was not particularly impressive—made of some kind of synthetic, vinyl maybe, certainly not wood or marble or onyx. But it was firmly rigid, didn't fold in the middle like most starter-set boards, and was smooth and slick. The pieces themselves were good quality plastic. Heavily weighted at the bottom, they moved almost silently on felted cushioning across the board, slow and steady. Stately even, one might say. If you lifted rather than slid them to move, when you dropped them down again onto an empty square or, if the space was occupied, when you marked your capture by striking whichever piece you had just taken, they landed with a muffled thud or thunk respectively, the perfect complement to the quieter slides or moments of thoughtful silence that preceded each move. Usually this low-key music was all the sound of the game, and as play entered into a rhythmic move and countermove—thud, thunk, slide, silence, thud, thunk, silence, slide—the hushed nature of it all lent the game a kind of gravitas, the pieces performing a muted dance of black and white, like a procession of nuns performing a sedate allemande in the chapel, their arms folded into their wide sleeves, the only sound the whisper of cloth and the occasional scuff of shoe on stone as they weave in and out, the disciplined stiffness of habit and face unable to hide the furtive pleasure, their fluid if serious grace.

- *The King can move one square in any direction. Castling allows you to place your King on a square that is reasonably safe from enemy attack. If you lose the king, you lose the game.*

I learned how to play from my father when I was in second or third grade, only two or three years before he left home. Unsurprising of a King, he chafed at the restrictions laid upon him, the growing sense of being hemmed in—wife with cancer, four small children. His moves to escape were:

1. King to nearby apartment.
2. King to Washington, D.C.
3. King quits the board entirely.

He was not far off in regarding Washington, D.C., as "*reasonably* safe," since none of us—my mother, us kids—ever visited him there. Nor would he have to witness the effect on my mother of her illness, her therapies, her raising a family on her own. It turned out however that Washington was not *entirely* safe, and when he died of a heart attack there, alone at his desk, a year after his move, I question if he regretted having fled so far to such an empty citadel, where nary a Pawn nor Queen could be seen.

- *The Pawn moves forward one square at a time. When a
  Pawn reaches the back rank it is promoted to a Queen,
  Rook, Bishop, or Knight.*

There were ten or twelve of us who showed up to Fourth Grade
Chess Club at West Ave. Elementary. The sets were cheap but
serviceable, most with missing pieces that had been replaced by
odds and ends someone had picked up around home—a metal
washer, a wooden spool, a mismatched piece from another set that
looked unnervingly out of proportion as it lumbered across the
board, twice the size of its surrounding brethren. Our skills varied
widely, with some games lasting mere minutes and others being
more evenly matched, but the highlight of the weekly club was
having the chance to match ourselves against our faculty advisor.
Unlike my father, Mr. C was a talker during games, keeping up
a running commentary on the sequence of moves, a patter that
would increase in jovial volume and intensity if he was ever in
danger of losing. Such games were always a good show, attract-
ing a crowd of spectators who, not allowed to offer tactical advice,
would root on their peer, groaning with each piece lost or cheering each time they thought Mr. C cornered. It might not have
been Spassky-Fischer, but I can still recall how the pressure built
while the game's possibilities winnowed as pieces disappeared one
by one, as a King was hectored ruthlessly across the board. Or as
sometimes happened, when a pair of opposing pawns, the smallest most powerless of pieces, raced each other one tense square at
a time toward their respective back rows and what lay there just
at the edge of our ten-year-old understanding: transcendence and
transformation, an exchange of shape and power, the yearned-for
guarantee of a future metamorphosis.

- *The Queen can move as far as it wants in any direction unless it is obstructed by a piece.*

My mother, during the three years of life she had left after my father died, knew nothing but "obstruction"—a traitorous spouse, four needy children, a body consuming itself from within while the cure did the same from without. Once, I remember the two of us driving home from somewhere, her asking, perhaps more to herself than to me sitting in the back, "Wouldn't it be nice if we could just keep going?" We didn't, of course, but for that moment, she must have, as beginner players are sometimes taught to do, visualized the board of her life as wholly empty, an open landscape of potentiality with unobstructed paths as far as the eye could see, allowing her, for a moment at least, to plan an infinitely variable universe of moves. No wonder we never played.

- *Since the Bishop can only move diagonally, it is confined to squares of the same color. Here, Black's Bishop interposes.*

When the neighbor who, with his wife and Old English sheepdog named Gandalf, moved in four doors down the street, he had, I'm sure, no idea of what they were letting themselves in for when they invited that twelve-year-old into their yard to play with the dog. No idea that soon that kid would be sitting at their kitchen table on a regular basis eating peanut butter sandwiches and swinging his feet back and forth above the linoleum floor, that he'd be learning algebra at that same table a year in advance of his peers, the Xerox engineer showing him shortcuts that would get him in trouble the next year in eighth grade math with Mr. Lily, no matter that the answers were correct. Or that he'd be playing game after game of chess, pushing back the moment he would have to return home, to that house. No idea how much it would mean to him, sitting at that table with the young couple, eating and talking about school and books and TV and then clearing the table and taking out the board with its familiar grid, then setting the pieces in all their right places, each ready to move just so, and always and ever only so, because those were the rules. Because that was how the game was supposed to be played.

- *The Rook can move horizontally or vertically. The Rook captures by removing the enemy and occupying its square.*

After my mother died, her parents moved in with us and became our guardians, as had always been, they said, "the plan." Years later, though, I learned that my oldest cousin Kathy and her husband Denny had wanted to take us instead, but my grandmother had fiercely overridden them, and so our lives became our lives.

It couldn't have helped but have been different. My grandparents were in their sixties, products of the Great Depression, World War, the Old Country. Denny and Kathy weren't even thirty, products of the Beatles and Camelot, Apollo and Vietnam, Martin Luther King.

They wore cool clothes, listened to hip music, drove cars without tops, and took us kids screaming up the hill near my aunt's house and over the one-lane bridge that crossed the canal so fast we couldn't tell if the thrumming in our body was from the steel crosshatch decking beneath the tires or simply from being so alive. They had big laughs, big sunglasses, big plans, big hearts.

And Denny played chess. When I approached him at family gatherings in my grandparents' basement with my usual blustering challenge—"Ready to lose Denny?"—despite so many better choices, he'd just smile, weave his fingers together, and stretch like he was warming up for the piano, then drawl out a scoffing, "Ahhhhlll right," that said, "Sure kid, give it your best shot," or "I see right through you, kid." Then he'd settle down on the floor and play a stream of games, keeping up a good-natured heckling throughout. "That's where you want to go, huh?" "Ho, didn't see that comin' did you?" "Uh uh uh. You took your fingers off. No take-backs in this game."

I loved those games. Calling them up in memory, sometimes I replay my life somewhat differently, sliding my grandparents back to their well-earned comfort in that last home of theirs with the screened-in garage, and slipping Denny and Kathy into their abdicated position. I let them rest there for a moment's space and speculation, a reconsideration of moves, of end games, and then restore them to their original places. Denny, after all, was right.

- *The Knight is the only piece that can jump over other pieces.*

My wife's father began teaching our son the basics of chess when Kaidan was five, on a beautiful stone set at their home, one we still use when we visit, though it is my mother-in-law's home alone now, ever since Kaidan's grandfather died seven years ago. And so already chess has some of the sad same associations for him as it does for me.

When he was seven, I began teaching him in earnest on a plastic set I'd picked up from a garage sale, my own having long ago vanished into the past. As had my copy of *Bobby Fischer Teaches Chess*. We picked up some newer books though, and as I had done with my father's gift, he often stayed up late doing chess problems in bed.

They must have paid off. Last week, for the first time ever, he beat me in a game I hadn't purposely thrown. A dumb mistake on my part, sure, losing my Queen to the Bishop I hadn't seen. But once I would have been able to recover from even such a blunder. Not this time. Try as I might, I couldn't escape his tightening, relentless web, and eventually there it was—checkmate. *Le roi est mort, vive le roi.*

We were playing on a set my mother-in-law had bought him, its carved pieces based on the terra-cotta warriors of China, an exhibit she'd traveled with us to see. It's a beautiful set, nicer than any I ever owned, and I imagine that when he pulls it out years from now it will call up warm memories of his grandmother, who just turned eighty-five. And through her of his grandfather as well, and that first stone set. And, of course, of his father who taught him to play. As he'd been taught by his own. One to another, memories like a sequence of moves in his mind.

*

And so here I am. Writing as ever about fathers and mothers, grief and loss. The pangs of my own mortality. The pieces come and go, I hop here and there, but always land on the same damn board. "How do you get over it?" friends used to ask. "You don't," I'd answer. "You move past, but you never get over." And sometimes, it turns out, you find yourself back where you started, and the moving has to begin all over.

Set them up again.

White opens.

Jericho Parms

Red

It is not the form that dictates the color, but the color that brings out the form.

—Hans Hofmann

"IT MIGHT HELP YOU better relax," my father told me as he tried to explain an exercise he learned in art school to focus the mind on a single color and every instance in which it occurs. "Try red," he said. And because often my father's ideas have a way of taking root in my mind as a steady preoccupation, I try his exercise. On my way to work I take inventory: traffic lights, stop signs, a fire engine. A tinsel holiday wreath tied and forgotten on a telephone pole. An array of lipsticks and nail polish, headscarves and jewels. The laces of a young boy's tennis shoes. The looped handle of a baby's rattle. And just when it seems the world is alive in red, the cat that sleeps on the floor of the neighborhood bodega slinks lazily from around a corner with a fresh bead of blood on its whiskers, as if to remind us coffee-and-cigarette "regulars" that something is always dying.

*

For centuries, red was the treasure of the Incas and Aztecs, and then the wealth of red belonged to Spain. When it is fresh, the pigment, carmine, made from the blood of a cochineal beetle, is one of the purest dyes produced in the natural world. But it is also the most fleeting.

JMW Turner painted with carmine even though he knew of its impermanence. And so his work, his bequest to the nation of England, was far more colorful than the signature grey storm-scapes we see today. Imagine an artist trying to capture the moment of a setting sun unleashing a brilliant slash of light through the clouds. As he reached to dip his brush, how could he not choose the best pigment, the perfect red, even though he knew it wouldn't last? What if words became illegible after they were written? Wouldn't we write them all the same? Unconcerned with posterity, Turner cared little of a painting's longevity but of the very moment it was created. Red, vanishing and imperma-nent, was his immediate—near fugitive—desire.

*

When I was eighteen and moved west to Colorado, I thought I would mourn the East Coast foliage. My mother sent care pack-ages filled with origami cranes and folded stars, nestled in a bed of pressed maple leaves. "Pieces of home," she called them, as if titling a shadow box or still life. But "home" has always been a variable. And some years ago, when I finally left Colorado and returned to the Northeast, it was the red rock canyons I craved.

I prefer red in its organic incarnations—rust-red creek beds, sea oats and sumac leaves, the blooms of algae that color the Red Sea. But the human hand that paints in red or the manufactured, commissioned varieties of red satisfy my belief in the duality of things. We have co-opted the natural shades of fruits and flowers and assigned them to passion, seduction, and—be it forbidden or sanctioned—to love. Pigments and paints are poised to accentu-ate and allure. And yet we color stop signs and fire engines red.

Emergency exits and security warnings all bear the color of fear and trepidation—of warning. Waves of taillights and sirens color tragic nights.

No wonder then that the reason stones appear red is the same reason our blood runs red: iron colors human and earthly temperament. Science teaches this. But what about the stories and myths we tell ourselves, the meaning we make, in order to endure? Native Americans believed that after the hunters killed the Great Bear, the animal's blood fell from the sky to color the leaves. And because I learned this in elementary school, in the portable planetarium our science teacher erected in the gymnasium, and because it still strikes me as hauntingly beautiful, it is the story I will tell my children if ever they are born: that death and demise can lead to beauty. Because what we hold most dear, what we claim to live for, is as much inherently necessary to life as it is dangerous and threatening to live. Red is the dying leaves just as dying stars exhibit a Mars-like tint before they go—evidence of their passing, yet just as much evidence of their life.

*

Before death, there will forever be the injuries of love. The first: my father, who against a table broke the bones in his hand as my parents negotiated their divorce. The second: my first love, who caught a ricocheting shard from the glass he threw against the wall on the eve of our inevitable split. His ring finger, nearly severed, glistened scarlet to the bone. And though *he* was the patient in the hospital emergency room, my whole body ached as if over and over I had fallen, pieces of me lost upon impact, calcified, dislodged. I would ache this way for years after, recoil at the thought of the raw vacancy, the bare tissue.

*

When I look up the word *red*, I find its origin in the Indo-European *ruedh*, and later the Greek *erythros*. In Sanskrit, *rakta* is the word used for *red* and for *blood*. In Comanche, the word *ekapi* is used for *red* and *color* and *circle*, too, which suggests something fundamental, something all-encompassing. Red is the color of beauty in Russia, of luck and good fortune in China. It is the color of Greek tragedies, epic battles of glory and salvation. Ancient Romans painted their gladiators and heroes in red; they washed the statues of gods and emperors with the same ruddy pigments that can be found in the murals of Pompeii. Here, we might gossip over red-carpet celebrities in the same breath we recall catching a red-handed thief. We might anticipate the pomp and circumstance of a red-letter day inasmuch as we curse the red herring of deceit. We hang flags of patriotism and revolution, landmark districts of prostitution and lust.

*

We say, *red-eye* and we mean flying overnight. But it is also what I call crying until morning. The kind of weeping—silent, full— that might be reserved for blue, except that it hoods our lids and circles the underside of the eye in red. This, the kind of weeping I learned from my mother, the kind you wake to the next morning and nurse like jet lag, like a hangover, face puffed, swollen, a little older around the eyes. The red of rage and grief and euphoric sadness; the red-eye of weightlessness, of rebirth.

*

Or maybe it's the dim-tint of an evening bar, which used to lure me, like a moth towards light. Nights after all my friends retired into taxicabs and slinked away to their Brooklyn apartments, I wandered the city looking for clues into unexplained grief, and found the inevitable cliché cocktailed in the pouty stranger at the end of the bar who, once we had stumbled back to his apartment, showed me his paintings—all brooding drips and globs that, in the dark, hinted at kindness. He went on and on about the New York School, until I threatened to leave. And when I did slip away, the air a little bit pink as it turned heavily to day, I remember the metal door to his walkup that shut forcefully behind—a door that still floats like a buoy in the shadowy sea of the Bowery—was solid and padlocked and red.

*

And while on the subject of doors, let this serve as an entryway into my memory of the red-door church in the old neighborhood—landmark of my greatest curiosities, my greatest shame—that I used to circle as a girl, trying to learn something, waiting for its sober advice. In many foreign cities houses of faith and worship are marked by similar doors signifying safe haven. Once, Hebrew slaves were instructed to brush lamb's blood on their doors to protect their first-born. Catholic churches paint their front doors red, the blood of Christ and martyrs, to mark the borders of holy ground, the threshold where physical or spiritual harm could not penetrate, where pursuers could pursue no further. The red of sanctuary and protection.

*

If I were to return to—if I were to safeguard or time capsule—one image of red, it would be the paper hearts, royal insignia of my girlhood make believe, of the simplicity of young desire. As my brother and I, parading as our heroes: Superman, Wonder Woman, Captain America—that patriotic threesome, that fantastical *ménage à trois*—three hearts to save the world. One Queen to issue the brutal destiny of beheaded hope. And if paper hearts seem too naïve, perhaps instead, a package of red doilies I bought in college at a thrift shop—the same shop with the stunning vintage Schwinn—that I strung into lacey curtains, still believing in paper-made pleasures. And they lasted, too, nearly as long as that first bout of love, before the wind took them. I think sometimes of their fate, wonder what bird may have swooped up their shreds to insulate its nest, what child discovered them littering the sidewalk during a game of catch, how the paper crimped and fell to the ground like fresh autumn leaves.

*

The next time I visit my father, I tell him I no longer see things the same. And to some extent, that's true. Color seems more evident now, more laden with testimony, with consequence. "Try red," my father had said. So simple. And now, I notice it everywhere: in the cranberries and rhubarb stalks at the farmers' market, the cider apples and bell peppers, and yes, the pomegranates, too. In the book-bindings that wall the library, the neon sign kept open at the diner, or the historic brick buildings that accentuate downtown.

Of course the painters knew how color is not only revealed in form, but how form—a synthesis of light and reflection—is just as much revealed in color. In the city, sirens sound through the streets delivering pain and sadness as cargo because a nineteen-year-old took one in the gut on Heath Avenue after holding the door for some thug's sister, and the red pool that must have swelled beneath him—the stain of chivalry's passing. But what if the sirens signify a heart being rushed for transplant, or an expectant mother about to birth her only child? The fire engines rush too, and a family may have lost their house, but what if a child is rescued from a fearful height or a battered home? Stalled traffic lights on Broadway mean frustrated commuters, waiting. But they also mean more time to breathe—stillness in a frenzied city.

*

"Color has taken possession of me," Paul Klee once said of his work. His canvases, like quilted patterns, reveal color and shapes—stick figures and fish, houses and hearts—in a childlike, sophisticated meditation.

Here we begin and end again with the heart, because what greater possession exists? Not just in color, not simply through this red (by which I mean rose-colored) lens, but as it adheres and tears, as it is pinned and stripped bare. It may be an impossible idea, to tell the story of a color, but perhaps we might glimpse a chapter that contains a single human experience, a retrospective of memory, the folded edges of paper and pleasure and pain, tucked into a chamber, a studio, a cabinet of curiosity. When oxygenated, when exposed, it pulses in crimson and scarlet, carmine, red—at once the longest wavelength of visible light, and the first color we lose sight of at twilight.

Nancy Geyer

Umbrellas

THEY'RE THE FIRST THING I see of the world beyond my bedroom window, bobbing along in the hands of children and their escorts on their way to the elementary school two blocks down the street. They form a colorful, if sporadic, procession. A navy blue umbrella followed by a smaller, red one. A giant rainbow umbrella trailed by pink, then purple. Umbrellas patterned after bumblebees and ladybugs. From above, I see little of the people beneath them.

Or, take the scene I love from a poem: "I stroll along with all the others, our umbrellas raised over our heads until the street becomes a garden of damp black flowers." Where was that dark garden? I wonder. All I can come up with are old paintings— Gustave Caillebotte's *Paris Street; Rainy Day*, say, in which fashionable men and women carry capacious wood-stemmed umbrellas with handles like shepherds' crooks.

Perhaps in 1870s Paris the only umbrellas to be had were black. Or maybe Caillebotte felt black umbrellas best suited a gray city whose orderly boulevards had only recently displaced medieval warrens. In the same spirit, Christo and Jeanne-Claude chose blue for all 1,340 umbrellas they planted in a lush Japanese valley, its waters mirroring the sky. And yellow for the 1,760 umbrellas installed among the parched hills of southern California, gladdened by shrubs with golden blooms.

Umbrellas-all-of-a-color make me think of Arles, from the vantage of the crumbling rim of the Roman amphitheater. Our backs to the arena—that deep bowl of lost voices—we looked out over townhouses all lidded in red clay. What is it like to live in one of those centuries-old stone homes, in that ancient city? As if you are borrowing it for only a moment?

Everything that individualized them—street numbers, the hues of shutters and doors and window box flowers—was largely hidden. Rooftops can haunt you with their evocation of our common vulnerability, of our need for protection from whatever blows through or comes down from the sky.

The beauty of the rooftops, compounded by the weight of history, was almost too much to absorb. The umbrellas passing below my bedroom window are a much lighter pleasure. They fix me in the present, with nothing behind me and with little thought for the day ahead, though that too is not for long.

Jane Brox

Star Light, Star Bright

I AM BEGINNING to forget things about the island where I once lived, and the remote house on a dirt road where I spent two winters more than twenty-five years ago. I'm not sure anymore how long the ferry ride from the mainland was, or when the scallop season started. I've lost the names of acquaintances. But the one thing I'll never forget is the night sky above my home those winter nights, which I anticipated as I drove out of town with its bright clusters of shop windows and then outdistanced the last of the streetlights.

Beyond their glare the road narrowed and the human lights grew more and more sparse until, when I turned down my rutted road, my own headlights were all I had to orient me in the dark. Once I arrived home and turned them off, I often couldn't see my hand in front of my face, certainly not when the moon was down. I always was aware of the phases of the moon then. There would be more stars than dark, just as Chekhov once wrote—so many stars one could not have put a finger in between them—and they seemed close enough to reach up and touch. Even so, I didn't have to look skyward to feel their presence. I sensed their weight—

that's the only way I can describe it—a kind of pressure bearing down on me.

As much as I tried, I found it almost impossible to stand and ponder them for long, for as beautiful as they were, they also made me apprehensive. Part of that may have been my own young solitary self in that remote corner. It may have been the cold and the wind. All I know is that I encountered those stars each time with mixed feelings of awe and loneliness, and often I hastened to feel for my keys and then the lock on the door. Once I moved inside, I saw to everything that would cut me off from the outer night— the lights, the fire, the radio, supper—the small tasks that people turn to so as to make themselves at home.

Still, the feeling I had beneath the stars lingered long into the evening. How must it have been for so much of human time when people had almost no way to take cover from the night—no more than a smoky fire or a lone candle that at its best also smoked, and stank, and lit only a meal, a face, a hand? Not much to do after a while but talk on in the dark, and then sleep.

Now I live in the heart of a modest town, so, like most people in this country, I don't see many stars anymore, and the sky between them isn't really dark. The streetlights outside my windows are so bright I can wander through my house without turning on a lamp. I see illuminated windows in every direction; the neighborhood forms its own constellation of far, near, bright, dim, upstairs, downstairs, which carries its own kind of beauty. When I walk through the streets at night I notice the moon above the windows and street lamps, and can sometimes spy a planet or a major constellation—Orion, Cassiopeia—more easily than I ever could before. The sparse stars feel familiar, part of the neighborhood, although they seem much farther away than they did on the island, and I never feel the pressure of them.

Sometimes I try to imagine the night sky I once knew shining above the town, as if starlight and human light could coexist with equal strength. But even if that were possible, I don't suppose the night sky would conjure the tumult of feeling that rose up within me all those years ago. Abundant artificial light creates a different kind of night for the human spirit, one in which it's a simple thing to travel through the dark, and which can be full of leisure or as full of direction as day. As the dusk draws down, I merely have to flick a switch to continue with my work, and I only have to look out the window to feel the company of others doing the same.

The star-struck sky belongs to a spare world, unbounded and without distraction, where it's never a simple thing to take cover from the night, where every attempt to do so is small and self-conscious. Perhaps it's age and experience that make it so, or the rarity of it, but when I chance to see such a sky now—atop a mountain, along a deserted stretch of coast—it feels like a privilege as I fall through the years toward ancient time.

Cheryl Merrill

Wild Life

IT BEGINS WITH the nonhuman other. Tooth, thorn, claw, tusk—sharp punctuation points, big and small, in lives other than ours. It begins with footprints in the sand, telling the twin stories of where we have been and where we are going. It begins with a puddle of rainwater, an ocean, a desert, a jungle. It begins with the soft despair of aloneness. Not loneliness, aloneness, staring at the wilderness within ourselves. It begins with the wild places hidden in the corners of our hearts.

IT ENDS WITH . . . it never ends. There is no map for this wilderness, no end to the exploration—for how else do we measure anything but against ourselves, over and over and over again?

*

I look into a face unlike mine, yet a face with a mouth, a nose, two ears, and two eyes, recognizable as a face.

Her eyes, like mine, are protected by bony sockets and eyelashes and eyelids and tears. Her eyes, like mine, sit high on her skull and light the darkness within.

Three-inch lashes cast shadows down her cheeks. She blinks and her lashes sweep against her skin like small brooms.

Each of the more than two hundred lashes of my eye is shed every three to six months. Has anyone ever done research on the shed rate of elephant eyelashes?

I could. I could stand here forever, peering into an iris that has sun flecks and shadows in it.·

The face that is not unlike mine looks back at me.

*

Off in the distance zebras nod as they plod past. *Yes*, this is the right way; *Yes*, this is the right way. Striped nature's bar codes, no two are alike.

In his book *Origin of Species*, Darwin speculated on whether a zebra was a white horse with black stripes or a black horse with white stripes. He compiled extensive examples of the occasional striping on all horses, arguing that a trait from a distant common ancestor, white on black, is brought to full fruition in the zebra. Occasionally zebras are born with white dots and blotches, incomplete stripes on a black background, Morse code instead of bar code, natural proof that a zebra is a black horse with white stripes. The white is lack of pigmentation.

So—here's the question that pops into my mind as I watch the zebras: do zebra foals imprint on the black stripes of their mothers or on the white stripes? The accepted belief puts money on the black pattern. But isn't that the human response, the bar code response? Not one of us knows what a zebra knows.

*

Just at the edge of darkness, where the light of our fire does not penetrate, an elephant thunders by, trumpeting the whole way, a classic illustration of the Doppler Effect, sound that condenses, rises in pitch, crescendos, blows by, drops pitch, recedes.

We lift our heads in surprise. Waves of sound undulate away from us, kin to ripples on a pond. We use sound waves, Doppler Radar, to see rain, to know when we should run for cover. There is no such radar for an incoming elephant.

Resonance fills the night air around us, yet we are deaf to the sounds he makes below our range of hearing, his messages warning other elephants.

Eventually his outrage is extinguished by the night.

HOW MUCH of the world are we missing, circle upon circle, ripples in the pond? Perhaps instead of placing ourselves at the center, we should move to the edges where our skills are low and our learning curve high. We should extinguish our fire and sit in the darkness listening, really listening.

Liz Stephens

American Animal

I AM RESISTING the urge to put the fox in my pocket. I am standing in the hallway of a wild animal rescue center, in the basement of a vet clinic, in the middle of a city in Ohio. I am holding a three-week-old red fox by the scruff of her neck, hanging her facing me in midair, and I am not supposed to pet her, talk to her, or hold her by anything more intimate than the back of her neck.

But what I can't help doing is return her stare. We are both amazed. Her littermates are in a crate across the hall from the hospital room, the crate set down between a desk full of paperwork and a folding table littered with take-out containers and magazines and donated towels. When I set her down into the crate, the littermates shift to make room in the hot pile of tiny foxes. There are five, I think. We think they are all going to live, the vet techs and I, after being fed every couple of hours by the head tech in the dark of her bedroom all night and day for a couple weeks.

She must have held them, I think. She must have sung them to sleep, lulled them with chatter, tucked them inside her shirt.

THE ORIENTATION at the rescue center did not prepare me for these things: Judy holds her hands around an opossum's mouth and lowering her head starts giving it mouth to mouth resuscitation. We all stand completely still listening to her breath, staring at the delicate feet of the animal, like a ballet dancer in a children's book, pointed towards us. The small pads of the opossum's feet, as he goes into shock and dies, fade from a lovely pink into a fleshy splotchy peach, and then, finally, into white. Judy sits back. "Shit," she sighs. "Will you get me a trash bag?"

And there is a green heron in the shower stall of the medical center staff bathroom that is the only place in our facility tall enough to hold him. I must wear safety goggles and leather gloves just to hand him dead fish; his snapping bill made the dream swords were made from, whip-thin and vicious. There's a loon with a flat feather coat of supple shiny spots like the emperor's imaginary cape, a bird that has a call so mournful I can hardly keep walking while she makes it. They hate me. I am soothed cleaning up their crap, making the slush of lettuce in a blender to put their fish in, but they beat the back of the containing cages with their wings at half-mast when I open the doors. I picture the burst of empty air left in hands when they are released, and that makes it marginally better, having to terrify them now.

Also, it was not mentioned at the orientation that though we use frozen secondhand lab mice to feed the hawks, we don't want the wild mice that appear in the kitchen, but will rescue mice brought in to us. A dead baby squirrel may lay tenderly wrapped in a dishtowel on the counter—"Don't put your hand there!"— but we will feed it to the owls. I will think a lot there about the surprise of meeting what's normally roadkill up close. I will begin to stare at roadkill. I will think about the time my husband shot a

162 | BRIEF ENCOUNTERS

bird because I'd just had a baby and the bird wouldn't stop throwing itself against the windowpane of my bedroom, where I finally slept after three days, because it took its reflection as an enemy. I cried for my husband to shoot it and then cried when he shot it. . I will think of that when I see the vet tech Lisa hold a bird on its back, talons up, and say to it, "Well, count to three, buddy," as she shoots a needle into its chest, full of antibiotics and hope.

We float further and further from a sympathetic instinctive relationship to animals. Backwoods doomsayers like to imagine the end of civilization as we know it, like to picture the way they'd survive on their wits out in the woods with the animals as both food and guides. They like to picture the way office workers won't make it through. They are probably right. Anyone who is surprised at a coyote eating their cat has a lot of learning to do before they would survive in the woods themselves even half as well as the smallest prey species.

But it sure doesn't look that way, as if animals might win, from here in the tiled hall of a rescue center, where ducks dodging cars and rabbits outrunning mowers is a best-case scenario. Ohio, where I felt so little wildness, was wild when Thoreau longed for it from the tended fields of Maine in the 1850s. Now, of course, that is reversed, the forests of Maine allowed to recoup, the twiggy and thorny native trees and bushes of Ohio painstakingly hand-chopped and pulled away generations ago, tossed into hedge-rows. Large fauna are just about gone here. Black bear is rumored somewhere nearby, but I'm not going to get so lucky, not off Rural Route 143.

Still, one morning at Bob Evans, a snake as long as my husband's body lay tight against the sunny edge of the faux barn siding of the restaurant. Adults shuddered and rushed inside. Children covered their eyes and then peeked through. Tall hands snatched short shoulders right and left. I crouched there with my daughter, as close as the panicked busboy would let us go. "If they'd just let me go get my rifle, I'd take care of this easy," he said. It's not poisonous, I said. And it'll eat your mice. Don't matter, he said.

I WAS SURPRISED, during the orientation, when I went out to lunch with a dozen other trainees, to hear them spend the time telling horror stories; botched attempts to save roadkill, abused pets. Work stories. They were all vet students and interning zoologists. I sat at the table with my increasingly unappetizing salad, my emotions, my book-reading on wildlife, my gut reactions.

They were dispassionate in many ways, twenty years old and inured to trauma. They knew, and perhaps it was a consequence of that, how to handle the animals. Adrenaline buzzing through my hands, I could fumble the meekest squirrel, and did: When I realized one rainy day that the vet tech had handed me a squirrel she'd just euthanized, in the moments before it died, I set it into a shoebox and I shook, mourning it, petting it, as it faded. Dog kennels full of damaged geese were shoved into my legs from behind me, the quotidian carnage stacking up while I stood in the way. The vet tech, the students, the lowest interns, could tell me how many squirrels were overrunning the yards of homeowners every spring. From twenty feet away, I don't even like squirrels. But in my own hands, I could feel its heart.

EVEN OUTSIDE THE CITY where I worked, every curve of those roads revealed a nest of trailers, disused trampolines, chickens penned in chicken-wired cattle feeders, scraping at the less than wild dust under their feet. It was rural outside town, but none of it was wild.

At least, I did not feel wildness there. Not in myself, not on the land. Not, surely, in the thin shade of ratty second-growth forests surrounding fallow, battered fields.

But my friend Mateo sees coyotes. He and David watch the baby coyotes jump hay bales in their back field, every cool morning. Mothers watch nearby, from the edge of the forest I call unimpressive. Handfuls of young coyotes leaping up the huge circles of hay, rolling off, going again. I wanted them in my backyard. I had dozens of deer, sweeping my hill in lapping waves, bedding in unmown tall grass where my daughter later played "being in a boat," but the does were as common as cats on the highway.

Coyotes at least seemed rogue to me. Inconvenient, bitey, elusive.

In the sweaty humid summer of 2008, a coyote walked through the downtown business district in Chicago and sat down in an open cooler in a sandwich shop. In newspaper photos, she doesn't look scared so much as relieved. Of course she looks wary; she is wary, that's the coyote's genetic make-up, and also their characteristic expression. Her chin points down and her eyes stare up. Her butt sits on cold glass bottles. After her photo op, local animal control officials took her away, and because the largest, most comprehensive urban coyote study in America is in Chicago, they relocated her as nearby as possible instead of euthanizing her in the truck.

Habituation surprises me, as a slow mover, a slow decision maker, myself. I habituate to newness so incrementally, interrupted by re-seeing even the old things again and again as newly changed. A new sweater is the New Sweater for nearly a year. The New Dog is new nearly all his life because he came after the Old Dog.

But it seems that dog species re-enact in every short generation the intelligent instinct that acclimates them to us, the great leap between never near us and always at hand. They figure out anew the conflicted instinct which keeps them skirting the edges of neighborhoods, which are after all only aggrandized campsites built around the pumping central heat of our camp fire. They smell the frazzled air of left-out snacks, the mice that hover in our insulation, the hothouse blood of delicate housecats. And then they rush into dens in the woods in a space so close and dark to us it seems like a Grimms Brothers fairy tale.

They get the best of both worlds. And us? We are the opposite. We sit royally out in exactly the spot we've earned in our brush-cleared well-mowed tightly-built homes. We are surprised every time those "rascally" coyotes eat a cat inside the perimeter of the moat of our perceived fiefdom. Indignant. We have an uneasy relationship with animals, most of us urban and suburban people. Large wild animals are usually entirely outside our experience; stories about encounters with them sound vaguely mythological.

But in truth we are surrounded by other animals, ones we often choose not to see as mysterious: inconvenient deer and mice, raccoons, snakes. And as our houses spread further into old farmers' fields, we alter the paths of these small animals. But we are all wandering the same world, our kids walking their deer paths, our lawn care chores kicking open their dens, as they slip away from under us, the animals as firmly as ourselves just trying not to make eye contact.

I like to imagine that at night in the city, or in the rushing energy of spring, behind our feet where our footsteps are dissipating like heat, the animals can creep back. Coursing through sewer tunnels, under bridges, the edges of parking lots. I imagine it like a film in reverse, a fairy tale of adaptability. The insects first, then the mice, then the squirrels, then the skunks, opossums, deer, coyotes, fox, wolf. Bear.

Pam Houston

What the Osprey Knows

IT'S A COOL WINDY EVENING on the Palomarin Trail at the southern tip of Point Reyes National Seashore. Vultures play in the cliffside updraft and a solitary osprey fishes just offshore. I am hiking with a man who has flown all the way to California from a city in the east on the off chance that I might find him irresistible. He's got the sad and honest features of a big dog you trust instinctively, a bloodhound maybe, or a St. Bernard. I've wanted to touch the unmatching lines that run under his eyes since five minutes after I've met him.

I, too, am a visitor to California. My real home is at nine thousand feet in the San Juan Mountains in southwestern Colorado where the light is gold and the air is clear and sharp and the Continental Divide rises up behind my ranch and cuts the sky in two. The Rocky Mountain landscape is chiseled like the cheek and collarbones of a working man, the mountain ridges as direct and unequivocal as the bones in the back of his hand.

California is a woman, soft and blue and given to shapeshifting. I spend two months a year here to remind myself of her gentleness, her cascades of wild roses, the part of me she calls to that in the bright Colorado sunlight I rarely let outside. I am opened by this landscape, softened, gentled, tenderized. My skin is drunk on the liquid air here, my mind is drunk on all this oxygen. As we climb out of the eucalyptus and calla lily forest onto the narrow and deserted coast trail I have the decidedly odd sensation of being one woman walking up another woman's backbone, combined with the sweet and terrifying anticipation of being a woman alone for the first time with a man.

We stop at a high point on the cliff and we can see all the way to San Francisco in one direction, all the way to Point Reyes Lighthouse in the other. Hundreds of feet below us the ocean smashes against the cliff we stand on, and tangles of kelp as big as wheat fields bob and sway together. Months from now gray whales will cruise this coastline like teenagers, and the great white sharks will return to these waters to breed, but today, only the osprey is here to convince us of our incurable loneliness, convince us that if we don't kiss each other, and fast, the earthquake of '99 might come and crack this massive promontory of rock and sand and manzanita wide open, convince us that there are such a very few things in life we really need to keep going, and passion, maybe, is at the top of that list.

In wild places like this one, passion is everywhere and unavoidable and feels so much bigger that any passion we humans can own. Maybe this is because wild things accept their passionate nature fully, submit to it easily, while our overdeveloped brains, in the face of overwhelming passion, send up billowing clouds of smoke and noise. In Point Reyes today, every time the ocean strikes the cliffs it says, *Take me in your arms*, every time the wind whips the branches of the giant eucalyptus it says, *Open your eyes and watch me while I touch you*, every time a pelican dives into the roiling ocean it says, *I surrender to you completely, I believe you will fill me up.*

The dog-eyed man is making conversation, and I am making conversation back. It is what we do, as humans, to keep our lives from happening too fast. He is talking about a place he goes hiking outside his eastern city, he is describing the power of the waterfalls in spring, the feeling, on a hot day, of plunging into the sunlit pool below. I am talking about the Continental Divide again, how it wraps itself three sides around my ranch, encircles me like a cradle, like a lover, how in the spring the snow melts into shapes that reappear in my dreams. The dog-eyed man is not saying he wants to bathe in me like an Appalachian plunge pool, I am not saying I want to trace the ridges of his spine, to memorize its silhouette as I have memorized the backbone of mountain that I call home. Inside our heads there are more conversations, ones where almost all the sentences begin with *This will never* . . . and *I'm afraid* . . . A pair of deer whisper through the manzanita above us, and the fog bank that's been sitting well offshore all day, soundlessly nudges in.

Now far above us, the osprey can see the whole boomerang shaped peninsula that makes up Point Reyes National Seashore. He can see the San Andreas fault, its stretch marks nowhere more obvious than here along the park's eastern border. The land mass that is Point Reyes sits on the Pacific tectonic plate, everything east of here sits on the North Atlantic plate, and what the osprey may not know is that Point Reyes walked itself all the way up here from Los Angeles over the last several hundred million years, and it has the soils and the record in the rock layers to prove it. Like everyone else from LA, it's headed for Seattle, grinding itself up the side of the continent leaving its long fingernail scratches in its path. It moved twenty feet closer in the 1906 earthquake and the misaligned fence posts are still visible at the Pierce Point ranch. For me this evening, even plate tectonics is about desire, the tenacity of the Pacific plate, its commitment to its journey, the painful brevity (geologically speaking) with which it gets to rest in any one given place.

The dog-eyed man and I met in person for the first time last night in a restaurant on the San Francisco Bay where the water gleamed midnight blue beyond the heat lamps and the waiters all wore Mexican wedding shirts and sang a song I'd never heard before which must have been Happy Birthday. We had first talked on the phone on business eight months ago, and had begun writing letters shortly after that, the kind you write when you feel a connection and are strangers and single and have nothing to lose. He wrote to me about tequila sunrise thunderclouds and twig flickers of far off lightning near Yuma, Colorado, of toothless men selling peanuts beside roads made out of red Georgia clay, of a photograph of a night blizzard in Central Park, Manhattan, of the precise combination of joy and loneliness one feels looking out at a brand-new landscape alone. I wrote to him when I saw my first green flash. I wrote to him after I spent New Year's Day alone with a monk seal on a deserted beach on Kauai and wondered if it was some kind of prophecy. I wrote to him one time because I knew I had to at least try to describe the shade of blue the sky above my ranch turns just before darkness falls for certain. I wrote to him from the west coast of Ireland where the surprise of unexpected sunlight on the rain-glistened field stones made me cry out with longing. The safety of two thousand miles of continent sat between us like permission and we traded landscapes as if they were kisses, again and again borrowing the passion of our favorite places to give us the language to describe our own.

The temperature has fallen, the chill in the air offering us another good reason to touch. We don't acknowledge the offer. We don't acknowledge the fact that even if we turned back now we'd never make it to the car before serious dark. Darkness intrigues us, and the crescent moon gaining purchase against what brightness remains in the western sky. The earth shine these last two nights has been overpowering. We think, each in our separate minds, that maybe the dark will teach us to be brave and helpless, we think, maybe the new moon will tell us the secret of how it holds the old moon in its arms. Maybe we will capitulate to the miracle of earth shine, to the miracle of earth itself. Our noisy brains shriek, *Love is improbable!* The earth says, calmly, *How improbable am I, then? How improbable is the moon? The spots on a young deer? How about the tide that's coming in and sending arcs of sea spray in perfect parabolas? How about this 400 square miles of mountain, marsh, and estuary that has traveled 310 miles from southern California at the breakneck speed of two inches per year?*

There is a quiet that comes with twilight, even though the wind still blows. The eucalyptus are still creaking, one minute sounding like bedsprings, the next like the cries of an hysterical woman locked away forever from the thing she loves. A black-crowned night heron cruises past just above tree line on his way to Tomales Bay and something big crashes around hard in the eucalyptus. I want the crashing to be a small herd of the shy Tule Elk. I want the black-crowned heron to be winging home to his life-mate but I don't even know if herons mate for life. I want them to. I want to know what the osprey knows. I want one gray whale who lost track of his internal calendar on his eight-thousand-mile journey to the south to raise all forty tons of himself out of the sea like the embodiment of all desire and then throw himself back in, sending out wave after wave of raw longing. I want to touch the lines on the face of the dog-eyed man and I want him to take my face in his hands and kiss me. I want to know how anyone can stand as we are, this close to the San Andreas Fault on this huge propelled plate that's moving some part of its yearly two inches even while we stand here, and want to do anything *but* kiss.

It is nearly true dark now, and the crescent moon oranges itself more and more deeply as it falls toward the sea. The dog-eyed man looks into me with hope and all its accompanying sadness and I look back. We are no longer making conversation. Our brains have grown tired of the smoke and the noise. No matter what happens next, he will board a plane tomorrow that will take him back to the other side of the continent. No matter what happens next, Point Reyes will move tomorrow, 1/182 of an inch closer to the north pole. No matter what happens next, no matter how good it feels, it won't mean a human can know what an osprey knows.

The first kiss is deep and long and suddenly everything smells like dew and eucalyptus. The wind stills momentarily and six vultures tumble languidly out of the sky. A cormorant spreads his wings to dry in the very lowest branch of an oak tree. Our kisses are the velvet on the antlers of a Tule Elk, they are the evening cry of the marshhawk. Our hands are the tumbling of Alamere Falls, our lips are the ripening of huckleberries. Three foxes pause before crossing the trail, all of them casting glances toward us over their shoulders, and our touching is the brush of their paws on the sand. The goldenrod, the fiddleneck, even the delicate orange poppies stop, for the first time today, their incessant swaying. Still kissing, always kissing, we fall to our knees. A barn owl asks maybe the only answerable question. On the ridgetop one bobcat bites hard into the shoulder of another. For the next several moments, there will be no passion greater than ours.

M. J. Iuppa

Clotheslines

STRUNG BETWEEN THE SHADE of two sugar maples, a double clothesline hangs taut, ready to hold our lavender-rinsed laundry, fresh from the spin cycle. Bundling damp clothes into the waiting wicker basket, I bend and hoist its heft up to my thick waist, wishing someone would waltz around the corner and offer a hand. Only our sleek gray cat appears, lacing his steps between my bare feet as I squeeze my way out the mudroom's screen door. Together, we go, down the worn porch steps to the privacy of the side yard.

*

Whenever I pin clothes to the white ropes, I hear my mother's instructions: give shirts, pants, socks, shorts, a good shake to snap out any creases; clip shirts from shoulders, pants by cuffs, and suspend socks in pairs, toe end up. My hands work quickly in the sway of wind & sound of cicadas buzzing in the sun's full heat. One by one, the clothesline fills with air. The summer dance begins . . .

*

Long ago, that is, not so long ago but unimaginable now, there was a time when everyone had a clothesline. Only in the early sixties, plastic-coated wire lines were strung between two metal cross pipes set in cement, acting as a division between yards; but, in actuality, were a meeting place where mothers would air their thoughts & the neighborhood boys would race their Scwhinns between the flap of Saturday's sheets. The mothers, with cups of coffee and cigarettes dangling from red lips, would say Stop—stop it between sips of gossip, until stop became a head-on collision with a set of brothers crumpled on clean sheets.

*

Bloomers—I won't forget *Ooh-la-la*, bicycling past the flat roof in Vichy, with its clothesline stretched out in plain sight. The billow of those full moons nodding in the breeze as the church bell began its solitary peal made me wonder if they belonged to the parish housekeeper or cook?

*

Driving in the country, on roads to nowhere, we spot clotheslines parading their colorful displays. There, among the farm's ruin, next to the blooming lilacs and rusted tractors, the delicates and denims flutter dizzy beneath the steady spin of the lone windmill. The family's life is the same as the generation of cat sitting on the porch railing, watching.

*

I sing, "The dame is in the garden hanging up the sheets"— Egyptian cotton, luxurious 800-thread, made to last and last, days into years of loving, of sleeping upon a pillow mattress that holds our shapes. Sheets, that do not take sides but let us fall together into the scent of sun, woo us all night long.

Greg Glazner

Foul Ball

WE CLIMBED into Pam's car on a cloudless May afternoon, headed to a Sacramento River Cats baseball game, and I was thinking about the word "community." I have no idea why. Pam's new novel was out, and she'd just gotten back to our part-time home in California from an Oregon reading. This was our first outing together in a while.

So of course I buckled up and said to her, "What *is* my community?" She just put it in reverse, not even shaking her head. She's used to me.

I said, "I mean, I belong to what, the pasty older poet guy community? Well, a) we're not a community, and b) it's pathetic, even as a metaphor. Who'd want to belong to that?"

She smiled, adjusted her baseball cap, and said, "It has been way too long since I've seen a hot dog cannon."

This is the way we talk anymore. Only our text messages stay on point.

I said, "I know there aren't any literal communities anymore, but couldn't I at least belong to some better *language*? Is that so wrong?" I arched my massive eyebrows to try to get a laugh out of her.

She glanced over, squinting at my shirt, and said, "Is that bird crap?" I looked down. It was. I looked at the sky. "What are the odds?" I said, feeling sort of unique.

She accelerated toward Sacramento and said, "I bet we see a couple of famous rehabbing big leaguers today."

*

The weather at Raley Field was ideal, our seats only a few rows from the short AAA backstop, and friends, John and Lisa, were sitting nearby. We spent the first inning catching up. Then I set out to scout for bratwurst for Pam, wandering the park happily, thinking a lot about food and baseball and almost none about what community I might or might not belong to.

I got to the Jack Daniel's Balcony over right field just in time to hear, "Now batting for Salt Lake City, Brad Hawpe." *Our* Brad Hawpe? We live half the year in Colorado and are Rockies fans. At Coors Field, I'd seen Hawpe bat quite a few times, bouncy and pigeon-toed, not to mention watching him nearly homer on TV in the 2009 All-Star game. In a couple of pitches, there was an unmistakable bat crack, and the ball sailed over the left center fence. I texted "Brad Hawpe!" in case Pam had been talking to John and Lisa. "*Our* Brad Hawpe?" she texted back, right on point. I couldn't imagine what Hawpe was doing playing for the Bees. Neither could the LA Angels, it turned out, who called him up a few weeks later.

The Jack Daniel's Balcony was devoid of bratwurst, but down on the concourse I found a stand and got Pam's the way she likes, peppers and onions, mustard, sauerkraut, got my own minus the sauerkraut, and with a plate in each hand, started down the steps, pausing to pick her out of the crowd near the backstop. There was a sudden white smear, a searing, unfathomable pain in my privates, one of the brats upside down on the concrete, the other right-side up in its plate, and I was down on all fours, meditating on the solar agony radiating from my groin. A baseball was rolling under the nearby seats. How had I gone so quickly from thoughtful bratwurst-bearing guy to butt of the oldest joke in the book? What are the odds? I concentrated on ruling out fainting or regurgitating.

Down by the backstop, Pam's world, I'd later learn, had been very different from mine. She'd said, "Did that hit somebody?" Lisa said, "Some guy just got it in the crotch," and John said, "Luckily it was an older guy," and everybody laughed, and in a few minutes there was some talk about what could be taking me so long with the brats.

Back in my world, an EMT was looking down at me, a kindly guy around sixty-five, curly hair, round face, glasses. And a stocky guy from nearby had stationed himself behind me as if I might fall off my step, even on all fours.

"Where'd it hit you? the EMT said. "Right in the?" I nodded. "Can you get up?" I shook my head no and stayed put.

A younger, female EMT joined the crowd I'd drawn. "Where'd it hit you?" she said.

"Right in the," I said. I longed to spend some quiet time looking at my concrete step, but I held my head up to talk. Alarmingly, she was pulling on some latex gloves.

"Can you get up?" she asked, and if all this echoing talk was funny, it was lost on me.

I wasn't about to get up, not with solar flares blazing out of my inheritance and no blood getting to my brain and her wearing those gloves and me as overdue as I was for that exam. So I permitted myself to study a whole stretch of concrete. The good bratwurst was upright near the wrecked one, and some younger EMT was on all fours at my level, cleaning up.

"Hey that one brat is still good," I said in an alien-sounding groan voice.

A kind but queasy look on his face, he said, "Who's it for?"

I couldn't remember how to answer that kind of question. I said "Pam" and pointed toward the backstop.

"Pam?" he said, glancing down there. "What does she look like?"

Language was being siphoned out of my head and used as fuel for the nova going off in my heritage area.

"OK, do you have your ticket?" he asked.

Meanwhile, down in Pam's world, everyone was still craning around backward. A woman who'd been on her phone asked, "What happened up there?"

"Some guy got hit," John said.

"Oh no, where?" she asked, and three answers came in simultaneously.

"In the nuts," Pam said.

"In the groin," John said.

"Where it counts," said Lisa.

And right about then, a guy in an EMT uniform, a bratwurst in one hand and a ticket in the other, leaned over from the aisle and said, "If you're Pam, this is for you."

After a brief wheelchair ride, my world was centered in some kind of cinderblock first aid room. The grandfatherly EMT took my blood pressure, 160/80. He was clearly impressed. The woman EMT, scarily thin, it seemed to me, all business, was pulling her gloves up, letting the latex snap. She asked, "How old are you?"

I said, "Fifty-five," and a sinister scenario started spinning out of control in my mind.

But then Pam was opening the door, wearing that ultra-calm neutral look she gets when things are dicey. She asked, "How ya doing?" willing herself, I believed, to keep her eyes from dropping to my pants. With Pam there, I knew I was in the clear with the glove-wearing EMT, who asked me if I wanted something to eat. I said "Bratwurst," and Pam filled her in on how I like them. Really thirsty, I added, "Could I get sparkling water, Perrier or something?" She laid a gloved hand on my shoulder and said, in her gravelly voice, "Honey you're at a ball park." And before long, I had a Sprite, a brat, a blood pressure reading of 120/80, and the offending baseball.

When Pam and I ambled slowly, arm-in-arm, back down to our seats, there was stadium-wide sympathy applause. Embarrassed, I still knew I had capital to spend. I asked Pam who had fouled the pitch, and true to sports-savvy form, she worked through the at-bats and pointed to #10 on her program, Trent Oeltjen.

I described my plan and headed over to the security guy assigned to the Bees' dugout. From his kind, wincing look under that riverboat gambler's hat they'd outfitted him in, I knew I was in business. When I'd told him what I wanted, he leaned over for a word with Bees' coach Keith Johnson, who waved the tall, dark-haired Oeltjen over. I handed the ball down to him.

"Sorry about that, mate," he said, signing. Was he Australian—maybe the only Australian in AAA? But before I could process this information, I spotted Brad Hawpe.

"Hey, could Hawpe sign too?"

Oeltjen shrugged and took him the ball, said something. A laughing Brad Hawpe signed it and walked over, taller than I'd expected, curly-haired with his cap off.

"How old are you?" he asked, handing the ball up.

Was I wearing some kind of older poet dude ID badge today? "Fifty-five," I said.

He half-grinned and said, "So it's mostly for show now anyway, right?" and walked back in to get his glove.

Sitting by Pam with my autographs, after inquiries from

friends and strangers alike about my, well, health, I swallowed the
embarrassment, studying the backstop's caution diagrams: a man
getting hit in the head with a baseball, a woman getting hit in the
head with a bat. I was grateful there wasn't a third diagram with
my name and situation on it. And I was grateful for other things,
grateful it had happened at Raley Park and not Coors Field, where
it would have been on TV, grateful it couldn't go viral on You-
Tube, spawning a new injury term, as in, "Oh, man, that dude
just got *Glaznered*."

We stayed to the end, trying to root for the River Cats, but
things kept seeming a little off. Pam texted our acupuncturist
friend Denise for treatment advice. I said, "Tell her not to even
think about needles." Pam's text ended, "Luckily he's a burly poet,"
and Denise replied, "Yes siree Bob." When Pam told me Denise
was suggesting a Chinese healing paste mixed into yogurt, I said,
"Tell her we're in row five for crying out loud." Denise asked if
we had ice and Pam texted, "No but we can get ice cream." She
replied, "Oh don't say that."

In fact, I wanted ice cream. To eat, OK?

Back on the concourse, people asked how I was. I could feel
them welding their eyes to mine to keep from looking lower.
What did they want me to say? "I think I'll still be able to? Nothing's leaking? Nothing fell off?" One woman said, "Did you get
hit in the stomach?" I said, "Oh it was a little worse than that."

Heading back with a scoop of chocolate, I met a succession of
older guys. One clapped my shoulder and said, "You OK?" One
smiled, told me a story of his own that involved a toddler with a
croquet mallet. A stocky guy who looked familiar said, "I was the
guy behind you. I made sure you didn't fall off your step."

"Thanks," I said, not sure how to come to terms with all this
solidarity.

"I was a catcher in college," he said, giving me a knowing look that only the deeply bonded could ever share.

*

On the drive home, I said, "This isn't going on your Facebook page, is it?"

She said, "We better get you some ice."

I said, "Couldn't you post something about your reading in Portland?"

She said, "And yogurt. We better get some yogurt too," and patted my knee.

That night, her Facebook page was flooded with sympathetic comments. Jeannie from Seattle said, "Tell him it was because the target was so huge. Guys love that." Sam from Arizona said, "I can't wait for the haiku that memorializes this." But it wasn't until morning that a post by Frank from Sacramento helped me see the bonding I'd be part of for life: "Let him know that guys are wincing with him throughout the nation."

And the haiku came flooding forth:

Spring's full blossom in
Older foul-ball poet dude!
Proud swell, belonging!

Jonathan Wilson

Post-Game

THE FIRST GOAL I ever scored that truly elated me was a header in the playground at Gladstone Park Primary School. The cross came in from the right and I rose, instinctively rather than intentionally, to meet the worn tennis ball with my forehead. The ball sped past the outstretched hands of the goalkeeper, between the green netball stand and an invisible post a few feet away, and smacked into the chain link fence that served as a net. I was seven. The fence shimmered in the October sun. A teacher came out and rang a hand-bell; break was over.

The sparkle and glisten of the goal stayed with me for the rest of the day, and clearly it has never entirely left me. Via soccer I know the world differently: people I would never have met, places I would never have gone, conversations that would never have begun, otherwise occluded or lost domains all open for exploration. It is the associative patterns and passions of soccer that hold me the most: ink-blot skies over delirious crowds, quirky moments, drama, beauty, sublime incongruity. I think of the Chinese blogger in Beijing who wrote from a soccer supporters bar, Paddy O'Shea's, on Dongzhimen Outer Street, happily innocent of North London historical memory, "Here we can sing and cheer like the Yid Army at the Lane." Or, the agile boys I saw last May playing in a Venice campo near the Rialto using the thick marble ornamented pillars of a church as goalposts, the ball slammed up a step, over mosaic paving and into the church's massive wooden door as if with the profane goal of demanding entrance.

Deep in my heart, where it all began, are Sabbath Saturdays in the 1950s and early 1960s, when, towards the end of the morning service at Dollis Hill Synagogue, the congregation would begin to get impatient if Rabbi Rabinowitz appeared to dawdle through prayers. The rabbi, aware of the emergent restlessness, sometimes took a moment to scold us. "I know that some of you have your cars parked nearby" (orthodox congregants all were supposed, like my father, to walk to temple), "I know you want to be on your way to Arsenal or Tottenham." He would glare and tug his prayer shawl tighter around him. "But do you have time for the Mourner's Kaddish?" Silence, murmurs, a glint of heavenly approval in the form of sunlight through stained glass. As I left the synagogue I could already hear the feverish cough and spurt of engines turning. Suburban houses in the distance seemed suspended on the horizon like a faraway big city against the smoky background of a red sunset. My father held my hand and we walked down a narrow path bordered by nettles and dock leaves. I turned my head like Lot's wife; there was the convoy of cars, bull-nosed, all moving up the hill toward the great diversion of soccer.

Eduardo Galeano

The Fan

ONCE A WEEK, the fan flees his house for the stadium.

Banners wave and the air resounds with noisemakers, fire-crackers, and drums; it rains streamers and confetti. The city disappears, its routine forgotten. All that exists is the temple. In this sacred place, the only religion without atheists puts its divinities on display. Although the fan can contemplate the miracle more comfortably on TV, he prefers to make the pilgrimage to this spot where he can see his angels in the flesh doing battle with the demons of the day.

Here the fan shakes his handkerchief, gulps his saliva, swallows his bile, eats his cap, whispers prayers and curses, and suddenly lets loose a full-throated scream, leaping like a flea to hug the stranger at his side cheering the goal. While the pagan mass lasts, the fan is many. Along with thousands of other devotees he shares the certainty that we are the best, that all referees are crooked, that all our adversaries cheat.

Rarely does the fan say, "My club plays today." He says, "We play today." He knows it is "player number twelve" who stirs up the winds of fervor that propel the ball when she falls asleep, just as the other eleven players know that playing without their fans is like dancing without music.

When the match is over, the fan, who has not moved from the stands, celebrates his victory: "What a goal we scored!" "What a beating we gave them!" Or he cries over his defeat: "They swindled us again." "Thief of a referee." And then the sun goes down and so does the fan. Shadows fall over the emptying stadium. On the concrete terracing, a few fleeting bonfires burn, while the lights and voices fade. The stadium is left alone and the fan too returns to his solitude: to the I who had been we. The fan goes off, the crowd breaks up and melts away, and Sunday becomes as melancholy as Ash Wednesday after the death of Carnival.

Tod Goldberg

Joltin' Joe Has Left and Gone Away

I CAN'T SAY for certain how much of my father's life was a lie. I know a few things are fact: he worked as newsman for a variety of television stations in the San Francisco Bay Area and the Pacific Northwest. He once won a local Emmy for a documentary he did on stewardesses. He tried—and failed—to produce his own talk show in the 1960s called *International Airport*, an experience my mother says led to a nervous breakdown and their eventual divorce in 1973, but that may not be true. I know that my father adopted his own stepdaughter's son and never told him that his sister was his mother, and then abandoned the boy as he had his own children some twenty years earlier. And I know that my father loved baseball. I know that for the five years I tried to get to know him, before finally deciding on my own that he wasn't a good person, baseball was often the only thing we shared, a kind of filament to a life neither of us had lived.

"Did I ever tell you about the time I played catch with Joe DiMaggio?" he asked. We were sitting in his condo in Rancho Mirage, the last strings of another long fight balled up between us.

"No," I said, "you never did."

"He'd just gotten a job with the A's," he said, "so this was 1968 or 1969, so you'd already been born . . ."

"No," I said, "I was born in 1971."

"You were? I always thought you were born in '69."

"That's Linda," I said. Linda, at the time, was suing my father to recover hundreds of thousands of dollars in back child support.

"Your sister is an angry person," he said. "You know, I suffered, too. You kids weren't the only victims here."

"I have to go," I said. I'd heard it all before. I'd heard the lies and the truth and I didn't much care to dig out from the divots they both left inside me.

"Don't you want to hear about DiMaggio?"

Though you're always a child to your parents, the truth as it relates to my own father is that he never knew me as a child. Between 1976 and 1995, I'd see my father a handful of times— funerals, weddings, a chance meeting or two—and in those times we'd talk about nothing in particular, a gulf of anger and sadness filled with ellipses of conversation. When those silences became too much, when it became clear that genetics alone could not fill in for words, he'd turn to baseball.

"You still a fan of the A's?" he asked me during a lull in his mother's funeral. I was thirteen and hadn't seen him in nearly five years.

"Yes," I said. We were sitting beside each other and I could smell his aftershave, a sweet perfumed cologne that seemed wrong for the day. His tie had been cut in half by the rabbi and I remember wondering if it had been expensive, if he'd spent child support money on it, if he was sad to lose the tie. His face was covered in small bumps of razor burn and I remembered the last time I'd seen him: he'd come to our house in Walnut Creek and my mother, who raged at the very mention of his name, had kissed him on the cheek, touched his face with her palm, and told him he needed to shave. This is the only memory I have of tenderness between them, a yellowed snapshot in my head, though today I'm not sure if that's how it happened at all.

"They're not looking too good this year," he said. "Did I ever tell you I met DiMaggio when he worked for the A's? Played catch with him."

*

I'm not a very athletic person. My legs are short, my torso is thick, my arms are skinny. The only sport I ever played competitively was soccer and for a time I was good at it, if only by virtue of the fact that I wanted to hurt my opponent. When I stepped onto the field, something in me switched and I became the kind of aggressive person I wasn't in real life—during father/son games, where I was frequently the only son without a father, the coaches had to pull me aside and tell me to dial it down a notch, that I couldn't slide tackle Jeremy Joseph's father. I played for over a dozen years and only scored a handful of goals, but that never mattered. I wanted to drop people. I wanted the players on the other team to be afraid of me; I wanted to be as intimidating as Goose Gossage was on the pitcher's mound, a fat, burly mass of anger who simply did not care about the score, only the one he had to settle.

My father loved Gossage. Or, maybe he didn't, because when you have so few memories of someone, you cast importance on the smallest things, like a visit to a television station in Portland, Oregon, where people called your father "boss" and where you two watched a bank of TVs filled with Seattle Mariners highlights, Gossage rearing back and striking out one Mariner after another and your father saying, "Gossage does it the right way." But that's not your father. It's not even mine. You hang on to things when you're young. You control what you can. And maybe, when you play soccer, you imagine you're a baseball player your father admired the last time you can remember seeing him.

*

"I'd like you to come to my wedding," my father said. This was in the mid 1990s, my senior year in college, the beginning of a stretch where I would attempt to get to know him from an adult perspective. My grandfather, my father's own father, had implored me to decide on my own whether the man I'd vilified in my childhood mind for his abandonment and failure to take responsibility for . . . anything, simply, anything, was indeed the monster I imagined. Separate from the silences I and my siblings had endured. Separate from the court judgments. Separate from the stories of how he was going to really take care of his adopted son, only to excise him like so much garbage.

"Why?"

"It's time we started acting like father and son," he said. "Your brother is coming."

"That's because you were a father to him," I said. I said it to hurt him, to get a reaction, to drop him. But what made my father incredible, what made the difference between his lies and his truth murky and disturbing, is that he didn't react, never reacted.

"It'll be fun," he said. "We'll even have a little bachelor party." When I didn't respond, because I was somewhere between crying and vomiting, the two poles I typically battled in his presence, he changed the subject. "Your A's aren't doing so well, I see."

"Why do you do that?" I said. "Why do you never address what I'm saying?"

"Because it's the past," he said. "Let's move forward."

The night before his wedding, in a hotel bar in Longview,

Washington, while my father's friends tell me what a great man my dad is, how they don't understand why they've never met me or any of my siblings, I watch the reflection of a baseball game in a smoked glass mirror. It's such a simple game. The rules concise. The human contact limited. The chance for redemption as near as the next pitch.

"A toast," my father says, "to my sons," but my brother has long since gone to our room, where, I'll find, he's just as sick as I am.

*

I can't remember the last time I saw my father alive. It might have been the time I drove to his house and asked him not to sue my sister, not to force her into bankruptcy after her attempt to retrieve the child support was thwarted by the courts. It might have been when I drove to his house and asked him not to sue my mother for the same reasons. It might have been another time altogether. Scar tissue has formed over many of my memories and when I peel it back, everything rushes together and I'm nine years old, memorizing the statistics of every major league player, filling my head with numbers and names and all-time records and minutiae, anything to stop me from concentrating on what is empty about the rest of my life. By age twelve, I know more about Rickey Henderson than I will ever know about my father.

"Your father is a great man," his most recent wife said to me during one of those last visits. "Why you and your brother and sisters can sit around and say such terrible things about him is a wonder to me."

"He never paid child support," I said. "I didn't see or hear from him for decades at a time. He was legally not allowed into California because he was such a deadbeat."

"You could have picked up a phone," she said.

"I was ten," I said. I tell her he's doing the same thing to his adopted son.

"Well," she said, "he's adopted. And half black. That was all a big mistake if you ask me."

Later, when his wife had stepped away, my dad would tell me how much her son reminded him of me. Her son was a petty criminal, the kind of guy who got drunk, ran from the cops, and crashed a Camaro into a bank. "You're a lot alike," said my father. "But I can't talk to him about baseball like I can talk to you. Did I ever tell you about the time I played catch with Joe DiMaggio?"

*

The day after my father died, I called my mother and asked if she remembered the time Dad played catch with Joe DiMaggio. "What? No, that's crazy," she said. "He never did that."

"He said it was about 1968 or 1969," I said.

"I'd certainly remember that," she said.

We talk for a while about my father, about what he was like long before I was born, about their life together. She tells me I would have liked him then. She tells me he was a good person but that something drove him crazy. She tells me she is sad for the man she married, but not for the man he became. That night, I leaf through old scrapbooks my mother keeps high on a shelf in her house. In these books my father is young and handsome and happy. There are pictures of him with my brother Lee, my sister Karen, my sister Linda, me as a newborn, my mother (who in these pictures is his wife, a notion I cannot imagine), his own long-dead parents, and in each of them I am struck by the sense that I've never known any of these people, at least not in the context of these photos. The more I stare, the more I feel like I'm invading someone else's memories.

And yet, in one of the last pictures, I see a baby sitting in a high chair wearing an Oakland A's baby-shirt, while a man, who looks so much like me that it snatches my breath, stands in the background, smiling.

Bernard Cooper

The Insomniac Manifesto

SLEEP IS THE OPIATE OF THE MASSES, a retreat from the teeth-grinding and ceaseless thinking that is our true calling as humans! What use is a body sprawled on cotton, as still as a statue? We who toss and turn each night, we sentries fretting in the moonlight say: Deep-breathers everywhere, awake! Rise from your beds, free yourself from the stranglehold of blankets, shed your flimsy bed-clothes and don a scratchy woolen suit, chafing shoes and belts and watchbands, the glorious clothes of consciousness!

Dreams are nothing more than deception: You hold the winning lottery ticket, the dead one returns to your arms at last, the exam is passed with flying colors, the speech delivered even though you are nude. Oh, dozers and catnappers and denizens of Nod, you must turn your backs on the illusory satisfactions of the dreamlife! Surrender yourself to churning worry, to indecision, to doubts as bright and numberless as stars!

Warm milk, bounding sheep, amber bottles of Halcyon—where have they gotten you? Half your life squandered, time that would have been better spent regretting the past and dreading the future. Think of it (if you're not too groggy): You might have constructed, grain by monotonous, painstaking grain, a mountain out of a molehill.

You say you need your forty winks, to knit up the raveled sleeve of care? Go ahead and make excuses, each as thin as a well-worn sheet. A life where pale dawns are lost is no life at all! We the bleary-eyed, the perpetually restless, the not-for-a-moment-seduced-by-sleep, we tell you there's light in pots of black coffee, high adventure while pacing the floor. While others slumber, insensible, we urge you to make yourself irate by recalling old slights, to see the unstoppable progress of time by studying your face in the bathroom mirror, to embrace the terrors of kidnap, plane crash, and coronary by watching late-night TV.

You must make your pallets from brittle straw! You must fling your limbs at uncomfortable angles, each less conducive to sleep than the next! You must picture the mites, mandibles and all, who inhabit your mattress!

Listen! Rousing new tunes have replaced the quaint music of crickets, the mumbling of doves on a window ledge, the rain's drowsy, insistent whisper. Gunshots, sirens, car alarms. Raging dogs, squalling babies, couples fucking like wildebeests. Why ignore this wealth of noise for a meager lease on oblivion? What you hear is an anthem throbbing through the walls. Stand up, comrades. Look alive!

We must reconsider the meaning of sleep! We must think again. And again and again.

Amy Gerstler

Viennese Pathology Museum

WITH THEIR VAST LAWNS and lordly trees wielding floral authority, the grounds make one feel small. At least they did me. Housed in a squat, rotund tower of dun-colored brick built in 1784, the museum had once been a jail for the insane, chains still attached to the walls in small dark cells with barred doors. Exhibits are shelved along corridors, and in the old cells. The word "dungeon" fits well, though the building's politely described in guidebooks as "fortress-like." From outside, the tower looks like a giant bran muffin. This resemblance led to a German word for "cake" becoming slang for "mental asylum." Five stories high, the ex-nuthouse/museum could be mistaken for an ancient observatory. The building's ringed by rows of vertical slits, which, since windows read as eyes, give it a sinister look. Visitors climb stone stairs between floors. That summer I was twenty, all I thought about was the great river of suffering, meaning my own.

Large specimen jars are what I recall, contents suspended like plums in heavy syrup. And how cold and dark the building felt, earlier centuries' air sifting into one's lungs, tainting one's brain. Only the jars seemed lit, by murky brown beams, like sun through muddy water. Light-headed with dread, I wanted to flee as soon as I'd entered. Yet the museum seemed a test I had to pass by remaining, despite growing faint, to stare at a room of jarred infants, each representing some birth defect. Was this what came of procreation? Why was their fate not mine and vice versa? Did the specimens in glass canisters cry out, however illegibly, from their formaldehyde naps? How long had these babies been sleeping? Was theirs a heavenly rest—bloated, alone (Siamese twins the sole exception)—each afloat in his own final solution, unable to say if something itched or hurt? A greenish fetus, junior mermaid, embraced her tail. Suffering seemed to drip from the stone enclosure as molasses trickles down walls of old sugar refineries.

A tourist, nursing twenty words of German, afraid everyone could tell I was a Jew, I also felt tugs of connection to Vienna. My grandparents on my father's side had come from Austria. People eating pastry in cafés and walking avenues of linden trees looked like me, so much so that I was often asked directions, by other tourists, or even natives in their rapid-fire German. No help at all, I was happy to lend my laminated map, which I flapped at askers like some kind of stiff flag. I was able only to order *kaffee mit milch* and say *entshuldigung* when I bumped into locals, which I frequently did, forgetting I had arms and legs to keep track of, alive only in the furious hive of my head, wondering if the bees in there would ever learn to get along or make honey. Was the pathology museum an endurance test? A shove towards *schadenfreude*, towards embracing the fate of this mortal coil, always in mind, though never yet faced?

I wouldn't mind getting back the complexion or energy I had in those days. But you couldn't pay me to reinhabit that younger, seething, bottled up self. *You're a freak! Decay and chaos await you* something with bat guano breath kept telling me, and I would drink, smoke, or kiss anything to reduce the volume of that constant hissing. Getting older has helped, I guess. At twenty, I ran down the stone stairs of the Viennese pathology museum and burst into the park. For an hour or so, I lay on my back in manicured grass, waiting for the tour to end and my friends to exit. Breathing carefully, like I had just learned how, I opened my eyes every few minutes on blinding brightness to watch butterflies flit. It's hardly ever like that now. But in the pathology museum I was ashamed and afraid of being found out, afraid of waking up floating and ravenous in some dusty jar.

Jennifer Culkin

Ichthyosis

I KNOW I will not remember her name.

I remember instead the labels attached to her. Ichthyosis. Hydrocephalus. Looking back, I realize there was probably some error in her very fabric. There's a text, *Smith's Recognizable Patterns of Human Malformation*, that I think of as the "syndrome" bible: nearly a thousand pages on what happens when the most basic stuff of a body goes wrong. There are pictures of malformed babies and children, hundreds of them, all with black marks, like a blindfold, over their eyes. Protection for their privacy, their identities. But there is also the prurient eye of the camera, recording the places where the coding of a human being stumbles. Where cells, multiplying one by one in the darkness of a womb, branch away from the well-lighted, well-provisioned road of normality.

I loved the language of medicine from the first, and I still love it—the precision of it, the way it gives shape to chaos. If I look up ichthyosis and hydrocephalus in *Recognizable Patterns*, I may find some imperfect understanding of where her cells failed her. I may find a photo of a baby with an immense head, a wasted body, and the skin of a fish, along with a bloodless description of how such a baby might come to be in the world. I would take comfort in it. The language of medicine names the unspeakable, and moves on.

Yet her name is all she had to announce herself, and I've forgotten it. That feels like failure.

I can see her, though. The fine scattering of reddish hair that covered her huge, fluid-filled head, the dilated blue of her veins, mapping out her scalp. I see how the bones of her skull were like islands, separated by wide straits of soft tissue. And I see the scales that covered every inch of her, except for the palms of her hands and the soles of her feet. Scales that flicked off, left raw and bleeding places, if I rushed with the washcloth when I changed her diaper. Dead scales that sloughed off in her incubator. She was a sacrifice for a primitive god, pinned on her slab by the sheer mass of her head. Entranced and alone behind the translucent leavings of her skin, a halo made of insect wings.

And I have muscle memory of her: the medicine-ball weight of her head in the crook of my left arm, the sweet hint of her body lying across me as I rocked her. Half of her irises were sunk below the rim of her lower lids, forced down by the pressure in her head. There was no way to tell for sure what lay behind the gray half-moons of her eyes, what thought or absence of thought. She cried in infrequent, weird bursts that trailed off, like the clatter from a windup toy. I know now, from scores of babies that came after her, that it was a neurogenic cry, an emblem of brain malformation or damage. When I hear something like it now, twenty-seven years later, I know right away how much is wrong that no one can fix.

But she was able to take comfort, my little pea. Her eyelashes were red and sparse, like her hair, and she blinked faster, more ostentatiously it seemed, when she was happy. When I held her, she settled in, turned toward my warmth with hers. Her own heat was so slight, like her hold on the earth.

By CT scan, her brain was grossly abnormal. I remember that

her family stopped visiting after her first few days of life, expecting her to die, and that there were plans for institutionalization as the weeks went on. And institutions conjured the image of some Dickensian orphanage, even as late as 1979.

I remember wishing, in my unformed, twenty-one-year-old way, that I could adopt her. Someone, I thought, should be able to save a brand-new baby from becoming a forgotten cog in an institutional wheel. Wasn't that a given? I was fresh from the nursing homes I had worked in during my undergraduate days, where spirits in an unknown state of grace or damnation were frozen in hellish, twisted bodies. That setting seemed all wrong for someone with the clean slate of a newborn, someone who so recently arrived in this life.

I remember the day I came to work and her incubator was empty, like a lung that has just exhaled.

BUT that isn't the whole story.

I know that the more experienced nurses on the unit didn't share my soft spot for her. They cared for her with economical movements, the casual grace of expertise, but they turned their inner gaze from her, females of a herd refusing to feed an orphaned runt.

"Why do you hold her all the time?" Karen asked me one evening as I sat with the baby in our accustomed place, the scarred wooden rocker in front of the isolette. Karen was smiling, teasing me. The little pea and I traced a section of institutional flooring over and over, slow and measured, back and forth. Karen was about fifteen years older than I, and she had spent at least ten of those years in that place, the neurology/neurosurgery unit of a large children's hospital. A few nurses there had desiccated into wasps, penetrating but venomous. Karen wasn't one of those. It was just that she was hundreds of brain-damaged babies, thousands of tragic stories, ahead of me.

"You've seen that baby's CT scan. You know she has about as much brain power as an earthworm," she said, chuckling.

I could feel the little pea's pale fire against me, right over my heart, but at the same time, rising on my inner screen like a vision, was the earthworm I had dissected in tenth grade: one nerve running up the length of its body, bifurcating at its head into a simple Y. The Y is its "brain." Nothing is much more basic than the brain of an earthworm.

I snorted back a laugh. I'm still not sure if that laugh was salvation or damnation. But I do know that when you take a scalpel to the nervous system of an earthworm, the trick, then as now, is to expose that tender bifurcation without destroying it.

Emily Rapp

Los Angelitos

AT THE MUSEUM in the birthplace of the artist Diego Rivera in the city of Guanajuato, Mexico, there is a gallery of portraits called "Los Angelitos." The museum itself is like a stop-time photograph from a different age. Various rooms of the house are staged although some are off-limits, and visitors move through the available spaces as if moving through an imagined day in the life of a family whose furniture remains intact though its members are dead: the bedroom with thick wooden furniture and canopied crib for a tiny Diego surrounded by a braided cloth rope to ward off those who might be tempted to touch; the impressive entrance halls lined with art in gold frames; once-used dishes now stacked behind spotless glass. The only sounds are the shuffling of curious feet and muted voices in English, Spanish, and German.

On the top floor of the house, in the upper rooms full of light, are the little angels, two white-walled galleries of carefully curated photographs of babies being held by parents, siblings, sole mothers, and single fathers, all dressed in fancy clothes that are neatly pressed and seldom worn. In some of these family portraits, older children with dark wings of hair over their eyes lean on one elbow over the baby, who is usually on a table or in the arms of a solemn-looking parent. Solemnity was usual in the nineteenth century photograph, so this does not surprise me. I look at the dark-haired families; I stare into the faces of the children, the parents, the babies.

Because my son Ronan was blind for a year before he died when he too was still a baby, it takes me a full twenty minutes of looking at the photographs to realize that the babies are dead and not just afflicted by the unique vulnerability of being a baby and having no choice but to rely on the goodness of others, of the world. I am used to the sight of the sightless after so many long hours singing into the face of a baby who would never see me fully, never know me apart from the animal instinct he was born with that told him I was his mother. I assumed they were baptismal photos. My partner has been walking silently behind me, and only when I turn around and see his beloved face do I realize my mistake.

"Are they dead?" I ask him, as if they have just died and I am asking for confirmation. He nods. His eyes are dark and glittering. He can see me.

"I thought they were being baptized." The babies in the portraits mounted on the walls where Diego Rivera was born are wearing burial gowns that are frilly and white and as elaborate and delicate as baptismal gowns. Looking more closely I can see that the way the living person interacts with the camera is different from the stillness of the babies. In death, even their bodies are mute, although it is those silent bodies that tell the whole story of every other person in the photograph. I feel dizzy with the weird meaning of time in this lit upper room: everyone in these photographs is long dead, but in this isolated, unrepeatable, documented, mummified moment only the babies have marched forward out of measured time. Their blank eyes offer only a reflection of where they have gone, which is a place from which there is no return, no going back, an unknown we are all headed for and about which there are no believable reports. Why can't these babies tell us what we need to know?

The room is suddenly loud with Ronan's voice, the way it faded and quickened in the minutes before he died and then stopped. The way it was always a collection of sounds that never shaped into words because there was a neuron path that had been burned to the ground of his brain and, smoldering and useless, became part of a decimated forest it would take a figure from a fairy tale to heal or resurrect. A forest of personality and personhood that nobody—not even he, the inhabitor of it—would ever visit or know or recognize. I feel a surge through my body of something that is not grief or anger, but a necessary numbness that acts as a net through which I view the rest of the gallery. I am light-bodied and cold. I do not want to run out; I want to see these babies the way I did not want to see my son's face in the hours after he died but did so anyway, lifting the embroidered shroud again and again, not wanting to see, wanting to see. His eyes would not stay closed although his body was heavy so I closed them again and again, trailing the bitten edges of my nails through his long eyelashes. I was not weeping then, but choking and dreaming with disbelief, relief, release, alienation, attention. *This is woe* I thought then, a brief, single syllable that seemed to sum up the simple, crushing fact that he was gone. I would be left to tell his story and not the other way around. A fairy tale grinding backward, a gruesome reverse.

I descend from the top staircase of the museum, through the rooms of modern art and sculpture, and out into the street where it has been raining for hours, slowly and lightly. Our clothes smell like the strong detergent used at the *lavanderia* where we have had them washed by a young mother whose three-month-old baby coos and kicks in the cot next to a long line of washing machines. He was fussy when we went to collect our clothes. I put my finger on his forehead and he looked at me with his dark, seeing eyes and then fussed a bit less. "Look how well you can calm him," my love observed. This compliment flattened me, for what good is a mother whose child has died?

The week before we arrived in Mexico I discovered in a dresser drawer I was cleaning out after a year of stuffing into it receipts, underwear, and stray gym socks, a single red mitten that was Ronan's, and the shirt that I cut from his body after his death, printed with rockets and planets arranged in a whimsical pattern, a little boy's dream of space, of the beyond. I had been moving both items around in various drawers for months, always wondering what happened to the pants that went with the shirt I cut off. Where were the matching space pants? But I never bothered to actually look for them. "Ronan's not an angel," I say all the time, to anyone who will listen. "God doesn't have him." Who does?

It is Christmas in Mexico, and all around this city with its winding, cobbled streets and ringing bells we have watched people marching purposefully to cathedrals, holding their baby Jesus figures decked out in festive costume and plucked from the home crèche to be blessed by the priest. It is men who do this ritual shuttling of the doll, their precious, inanimate bundles wrapped in brightly colored blankets printed with the image of wide-eyed animated bears and Hello Kitty.

Dry leaves cross the Zócalo, the plazas, the polished holiday shoes of the living children headed to Mass or headed home.

Angels. Perhaps they exist in some other world, but it is not enough. Rebecca Solnit, in her book *The Faraway Nearby*, quotes Mary Shelley, author of *Frankenstein*, writing in her journal in March 1815 about the death of a child: "Dreamt that my little baby came to life again—that it had only been cold and we rubbed it before the fire and it lived. Awoke and found no baby. I think about the little thing all day." The parents of the dead babies in the photographs in the Diego Rivera museum hold them as if they are alive, as if they are looking for a fire before which to rub them awake, their faces drawn with resignation and an unspoken ambition to solve the unsolvable. Sometimes I hold the plaster cast a friend made of Ronan's hand and pretend it is warm and real. I trace the creases in the palms and examine the white material of his fingernails for imagined dirt.

My love and I hold hands in the street and kiss on the corners like other couples. In the bakeries we select hot loaves of bread and glistening pastries with silver tongs and arrange them on a tray. Guanajuato is known as the haunted city because of its museum of mummies. We do not visit the mummies, a deliberate and necessary avoidance. We've heard some of them are actually not so old, which is somehow more horrible, and that their families don't have money to bury them. A newer mummy is scarier than one that has long been dead.

At night, when the otherwise non-stop dance party on the roof next door to our rented house takes a brief hiatus and we are able to sleep, I have dreams in which Ronan is helpless in some foreign land. Someone is putting him on a plane but they don't know how to care for him, how to support his head, how to feed him, and he will die. People want to hurt him, but I don't understand why and this makes me murderous. People are trying to blind him with acid although he is already blind. They want to hurt him, cross every boundary of cruelty, and in my dreams I try to kill them with my hands, bombs, knives, rockets, words, anything that can be fashioned or shaped into a weapon. I wake up frightened: by my rage, by a feeling of impotence that is the loss of love. I thrash around, slobber and pant, and cannot be coaxed back to sleep. I listen to the music next door. I think, suddenly, *I should get up and dance* but I lie still and think of the portraits of dead babies, *los angelitos*.

The sounds of the techno music and shouts of the living mix with the imagined voices of the unnamed dead babies, who leap from their portraits and form a circle on the floor of the well-lit upper gallery in the home of the dead artist, in a country where skeletons walk with the living in artwork and lie half-buried in the ground, and inside the circle sits my son, telling a story of what we need to know, although nobody can stay awake or asleep long enough to hear what he's saying. Only the babies cheer him on with their language of coos and kicks and hiccups; beholden to no one, they say only what they want to hear. Ronan keeps turning the pages of a book that nobody else can read, his own story, the story of ordinary babies and ordinary time, and the people who are left behind to mourn both.

Tracy Daugherty

The Summer After

"THERE'S AN ALPHABET in every child's hair," she said, scratching the river with her oars. "A's and E's in the curls. I's in the thin, straight bangs."

She was speaking, I knew, of her son, who had died on an icy road in Oklahoma the winter before, far from home, miles from these hushed piney woods in Oregon where we fished together now.

He had left to learn electrical engineering, or maybe astrophysics, though—his mother always grinned at this—he couldn't spell worth a damn.

As she spoke and cast her line she was calm, having spun her grief toward the bottom of her mind months ago. We drifted on the Siletz, trying to read the water, the weather, the dizzying script of insects in the air. Our conversation drifted too, to meaningless things, the pleasantries of our safely dull domestic lives.

Then the trout took her fly and the physics of motion took over; the fish shattered the surface, silver as a wedge of ice, and her face stilled in wonder, in shock, as it had the day she'd heard the news about her son. Startled, unguarded, she lost her hard-won control. I helped her struggle—the reason I was there, after all—until she said, "Let it go, please just let it go."

That was three months ago. I see her in town now, self-possessed once more, laughing and shopping with her friends. We say hello, promise to cast another line or two sometime, and say goodbye.

I spell trouble for her, as an embarrassing witness to her last public display of sorrow. She maneuvers past me on the street, a skillful engineer, so she won't encounter sadness again.

Lately, I've read that Oklahoma's another Dust Bowl. No rain, no ice predicted for the winter—maybe not for years. The conditions that killed her son are nowhere, now, to be seen . . . though surely they're hovering like history, ready to burst unexpectedly into the light. Family comes and goes, friendships start and stop, and in this gasping struggle we'll always strain to read what lies beneath the calm: need, silent grief, drifting us slowly, steadily apart, mornings we pull winter from the river.

Abigail Thomas

How to Banish Melancholy

YOU WILL NEED three dogs, one of whom has caught the scent of something interesting wafting through the second-floor window. She is a hound. They are all hounds and the four of you sleep together on a double bed. When you open your eyes (her warm doggy breath on your face) she will be staring at you with such intensity that you burst out laughing. You will throw on yesterday's clothes (which are lying conveniently on the floor) and head downstairs without tripping over Rosie, Harry, or Carolina, all of whom are underfoot. When you open the kitchen door they will fly into the yard and immediately commence hunting, noses to the ground, some small creature whose zigzagging trail resembles an electrocardiogram. You follow them onto the wet green lawn. So now you're outdoors and it's five a.m.

For the last month you've been inside while it rained. Perhaps you are a fan of rain, but this may have gone on too long. You have stopped answering your phone. You don't gather the mail. You have noticed that bad as it was when two dogs followed you from room to room, it's even worse with three. Every time you get up, they get up. *Please don't, it's not worth it*, you want to say as you rise from your soft red chair to wander into the kitchen on an errand you forget before arriving. You look out the window while the dogs settle down on a rug by the stove. They are so good-natured. Moments later you drift into the living room and again the dogs trail along behind, and if you do this often enough, the aimlessness of your day is driven home. From here it is but a hop, skip, and a jump to the pointlessness of your existence, which is why it is so excellent to be outdoors with your clothes on at five this morning.

Next, you will need a bed of nettles five feet high. Perhaps you already have a garden like this, having neglected it for the two years you have lived in the country. You have told yourself that you don't want to put anything into the ground so you will not have to hate the deer who will certainly eat it, but the fact is you are bone lazy and prefer drinking coffee and sitting on the stoop to weeding or raking or digging a hole. But nettles have closed over the heads of three pink peony bushes you could swear you saw two summers ago, and you are experiencing an unfamiliar surge of energy. You dash inside and good, there they are, the gardening gloves given to you as a housewarming present two years ago still stapled together. You rip them apart, don them, and charge back into the yard.

Your first nettle comes up with the perfect amount of resistance—none—you can yank it out by the roots and you do so, flinging it with joy behind you. You yank another and another, and pretty soon you are a madwoman, pulling nettles three at a time, caring nothing for the stinging on your arms and ankles, and the mound grows on the grass behind you. Sometimes you get a stubborn old grandfather and pulling as hard as you can you reach the big root snaking just under the surface and you get that too, dirt flying as you tear it out, and now you are *the old woman and the nettle*, destroyer and giver of life, and you understand the ferocity of the gardener.

After five or six minutes you will tire and stand back from

your work. A tiny patch has been thinned. Perhaps you will now make coffee and bring the cup outside. If all goes well, a perfect pink peony bush will be revealed by lunchtime. There will be slim yellow irises too, and the big throaty purple ones that remind you, alas, of an old man's scrotum, but you will weed there too. By early afternoon the sun may burn through what has been a heavy mist, and should you not be ready to be dazzled, do not fret. It is time for a nap anyway. Inside you may notice that what you thought was dust is instead a layer of golden pollen blowing through the open windows. *If only life were more like this*, you will think, as you and the dogs traipse up to bed, and then you realize with a start that this *is* life.

Michael Martone

Brooding

SEVENTEEN YEARS AGO. The house in Syracuse, on Fellows Avenue. A sunporch on the second floor, windows all around, she had painted a pencil yellow, a school bus yellow. The squat computer, a putty color, sat on the sterilizer table, dialed up, squawked for the first time. Tone and twinkle, hiss and static sigh, ripping zip, twist and ratchet. O. O. O. "Hello."

In the cloud of trees, canticles of cicada barked, waxed and waned, tinkered with their tuning.

> *still*
> *the hush peals the rock*
> *sound of cicada*
> —Bashō

May. Now. Seventeen years later, Brood II emerges in the east.

> *Magicicada Septendecim*
> *Magicicada Septendecula*
> *Magicicada Cassini.*

Cicada, cicada, cicada. The name (though it is not ono-matopoeic but Latin for tree cricket) mimics the song. The long sibilant. The cawing caw. The dada da of the of the of the denoue-ment, a trill falling off, entropic, unable to escape the gravity of, of, of a marble, dribbling on, each rebound lessening, dribbling on a concrete floor.

Just now, just now (another window is open on this machine, a program running) the chirrup of an alert. As I type this this, a comment has emerged in my timeline. The comment palimpsest-ing into place on the Facebook. Two tones, two tones like like the clicking cricket the nuns (I remember) used to use to time our genuflections.

> a cicada saws
> there and there and there and then
> star and star and stars
>   —Issa

One billion buried grubs per square mile. Buried for seven-teen years but not asleep, no, no suspended animation, no dream-ing dreams of waking, of falling upward. A lot of rooting around down there. Rooting for roots. The earth crawling with them, coiled like the watch springs they are.

All one needs to do is type into a field and enter. In seconds, millions of returns return in seconds, scores and scores of hits, hints from hither and yon, hinterlands come out of hiding. The lists and lists come back in instants and after years one wonders no longer about an other, another one. Another other emerges. Emerges.

Now that I think about it, the @, the "at" symbol, the amper-sat, that balled-up bug, has the look of a burrowing bulging-eyed nymph. Or the @ is a map of absence. A sink of seeking. A sink of sought. All that time circling down the drain. Screwed. Worm-holed. Bored and bored.

Then, the elm trees were still living, and they were scaled with the spent shells, the papered and papery leavings the bugs bugged out of. I had to pry them from the trunks they were stuck to. Pointing up the brick siding of my grandparents' red brick house as well, grappled in the grout, a kind of fossil ivy. I kept them in a glass jar, a mess of little brittle blisters, those bugged-out eyeless eyes, blown glass, goo goo googly, bulging orbits. Shifting shifts. Slit open sleeves. A thousand thousand-yard stares. What were they thinking? Thought balloons configuring their own empty empty-headedness. And all around me, invisible, was the busy full-bodied buzz buzz babbling of the brooding.

> *cicada shell*
> *Singing sang itself*
> *absolutely away*
> —Bashō

I wonder what happened to her or her or her. Carol Clay Clay Clay. The scuffed anthills on the walks home from school. Nancy Carrollllllll. The lightning bugs made into ashy jewelry. Maripat Golf, an estuary of silence after that graduation party in some-body's backyard where seeing her through the screen of the lilac bush, obscenely in bloom, touch David Esinbarger's hand (I've looked him up—he's dead, he died after that but before this writ-ing now) I ran back home through the alleyways of North Highlands and the tunnels of screaming sirens, cicadas sawing, seeing what I saw again and again. Where are you now? You and you and you. Why after all these years can this song or that one or this one here not be unsung?

> *Over the course of an emergence, male periodical cicadas congregate in huge choruses or singing aggregations, usually located high in trees. Females visit these aggregations and mate there. Males of all species have typical calling songs as well as special courtship songs, the latter being given only in the presence of females. In* Magicicada septendecim, *the calling song is a prolonged buzz that drops in pitch at the end: weeeeeee-ah. This song is very low pitched around 1.3 kHz . . . When a male approaches a female, she responds by clicking her wings after each song, and he slurs his songs together.*
>
> —*The Songs of Insects* by Lang Elliott and Wil Hershberger

I stare at my screens. Images of zombies back from the dead staring back at me. I believe I am to identify with the living in these dramas, but secretly I have much empathy for the re-animated dead. Their staring reminds me of my staring. Their predation of brains is done too literally, I think, for the sake of an audience's visceral response. I like to think of that hunger more metaphorically, a desire not for the biological nutrient but the virtual one. There is a mad curiosity I see. "What'd I miss?" Suspended underground, out of time, as you were, poor zombie. It is a hunger for the synaptic recording of time, the looping tapeworm of memory. The past needs to be tapped. Stare at me now, staring at this screen as I scroll through the searches, searching for what?

What? What? My shuffling, stuttered scroll. My clicking. My stalling. My missing. My finding.

> *even with cicada*
> *some sing*
> *some sing not*
> —Issa

Hilton Als

Fats

FATS WALLER. Even when he couldn't get his feet off the ground, he walked on clouds. He was irrepressible in his joy when it came to music, voices, the sweet and sour smells of backstage life; his clergyman father's disapproval of his son's chosen style of music only brought more joy to Waller's enterprise. This didn't mean he denied the truth—listen to "Black and Blue"—but Waller didn't wallow. Why do that when there were other options, such as good looking women and good music and rent parties and stories to be told and his big face? One loves him as one does a relative—the uncle who slips you a five against your mother's wishes. You bury your child face in his big suit that smells, equally, of sweat and violet candy and hair tonic, and that is the smell you look for forever. Waller's songspiel—his patter—is as significant as Brecht and Weill's, and just as joyful in its made-up-ness. When Fats died, his family carried out his wishes, which were to be cremated, and have his once solid body spread over Harlem, which changes and does not change, like home.

Marjorie Sandor

Hoffmanniana

HE'S THE KIND OF WRITER you don't think you know, but you do. You meet him first in childhood, when your innocent parents give you *The Royal Book of Ballet*, and you fall in love with the enormous and delicate illustrations of the Mouse-King and Clara in her party dress, Herr Drosselmeyer's gleaming shoe-buckles, which make his boots look unnaturally long and black. The sinister eye-patch worries you slightly, as does the voluminous black coat. But his magic is nice, and Clara returns from the enchanted realm safe and sound. Then there's the one about the student who falls in love with a dancing doll. Hectic passion, poet-shirt undone, the automaton's pale perfect limbs graceful and akimbo all at once. And again a creepy avuncular type appears, offering, from the lining of his voluminous black coat, thousands of gleaming eyeglasses, telescopes by the dozen. But it's all right: the hero is saved from madness and a violent end by his smart real-life girlfriend.

So why can't you sleep? Why do all the wrong images rise up? Not Clara in her party dress but Herr Drosselmeyer's long black shoes and eye-patch. Not the happy wedding-couple in *Coppelia*, but the student-hero alone on the clock-tower, peering through a spyglass, overcome by madness, by a vision of an evil ocularist nobody else can see.

*

Then you're nineteen, studying literature at a British university, and your intolerably handsome Scottish professor for "The Dostoyevsky Seminar" calls for a volunteer to present on the German romantic writer E. T. A. Hoffmann. He seems to be looking only at you, speaking only to you. "You don't know you know him, but you do," the professor says. And you raise your hand.

And suddenly the delicious wrongness is back in your life, along with the insomnia. You are granted a brief nostalgic interlude, in which you discover that Hoffmann wrote the original stories on which *The Nutcracker* and *Coppelia* are based. From there you melt into the student-thrill of discovering that Hoffmann not only wrote stories, but also painted and composed, and wrote music criticism so good that Beethoven wrote him a thank-you note. Oh, and in his other life he was a judicial councillor. As for his literary influence, Dostoyevsky is only the beginning: Gogol and Turgenev worshipped him, as did Hawthorne, Poe, George Sand, and Baudelaire. And clearly, clearly, Kafka.

There are no *doppelgängers* without Hoffmann.

And modern psychology? It turns out that Freud's seminal 1919 essay *The Uncanny* contains at its core an analysis of Hoffmann's tale "The Sandman." Without Hoffmann, no Freud.

His life-story alone curdles the blood. Born in 1776, his parents divorce when he's three; his father disappears for good when he's six. Later comes an unhappy marriage, and the loss of his only child, a daughter, to cholera. By age thirty-six, a reputation as "the best drinker in town." And through all of it, he works like

222 | BRIEF ENCOUNTERS

a demon, half-starved and penniless, sometimes at the mercy of Napoleon's victories in Prussia, and later, at the mercy of his own self-destructive habit of satirizing Officialdom in print—and getting caught. He dies at the age of forty-six, a literary lion paralyzed in his legs and hands, dictating his last story and cracking jokes with his friends.

And somehow, in that time, he manages to write several of the first truly modern short stories and novellas: works in which an artist-hero travels back and forth across the threshold between the hallucinatory realm of dreams, and the world of petty officials, café habitués, and impoverished students.

Come to find out that *Coppelia* has a different ending than "The Sandman." In Hoffmann's tale, the hero winds up on the top of the town clock-tower, crying, "Whirl round, Circle of Fire, Whirl round," as he tries to fling his flesh-and-blood fiancée over the balcony-rail.

Never mind how it ends. Let's just say it's no wedding.

"The Sandman," "Councillor Krespel," "A New Year's Eve Adventure": these are the tales Offenbach directly honors in *Les Contes d'Hoffmann*. But there are more. Discover, as did Robert Schumann, "The Golden Flower Pot," "The Mines of Falun," and "Mademoiselle de Scudéri." Schumann, himself susceptible to the music from the other side of the mirror, so identified with Hoffmann that he named one of his great piano pieces, *Kreisleriana*, after Hoffmann's fictional alter-ego, the half-mad musician Johannes Kreisler.

"Reading Hoffman uninterruptedly," Schumann wrote in his diary when he was twenty. "New Worlds."

Ernst Theodor Amadeus Hoffmann. You don't think you know him, but you do. But not enough to resist rereading him late at night, when everyone's asleep, for the insomniac thrill, the glimpse of the perilous edge of sanity. Not enough to resist introducing him to your own literature students, and giving them insomnia too. And this of course leads you deeper in, back to all the writers and composers Hoffmann inspired, not only in his time, but in years to come, those artists who read him obsessively, hoping to get closer to the fire without falling in.

Joe Mackall

When You Write About Murder

WHEN YOU WRITE about murder it's best to start with a few facts. The first one is this: The man killed was somebody's father and husband and friend and uncle. Fact number two: So too was the guy who killed him.

When you write about murder, begin with police reports. Police reports, while not artfully written, can tell you all kinds of revealing things. They can tell you that your uncle's body was found seventy-five feet away from a police call box. They can tell you that the killer used a .38 blue-steel revolver, an Arminius Titan Tiger, serial number 023805. From police reports you can learn what the victim was wearing and what he had in his pockets.

When you write about murder, even if the murder happened over thirty-five years ago, be sure to accompany your dad, an ex–homicide detective, when he goes to inspect your uncle's car, a 1971 maroon Lincoln Continental. Pay attention when your dad's explaining to his then-sixteen-year old-son—just by looking at the car—how it must have happened. "One guy in the passenger seat, another in back. The guy in the passenger seat fired the gun." Pay attention when he explains glass and blood splatter. If you can, turn your head away from the car every minute or so. Breathe in the cold outside air. Try as hard as you can to ignore the hair splattered on the driver's side and stuck on the headrest. Don't worry about the stench. No matter how many times you try, you'll never be able to describe it to anybody.

When you write about murder, regardless of how many scenes you visit or police reports you read or cops or witnesses you interview, you'll never be able to fathom why good friends of your aunt and uncle—friends who lived directly across the street from them— bought the Lincoln, forcing your uncle's then-ten-year-old daughter to have to see it every morning she left for school, each day she went out to play. When you write about murder, understand that why the guy killed your uncle is the easier question to answer. Why his friends bought the car he was murdered in will remain forever inexplicable.

When you write about murder—say the murder of a family member—always be sure to justify yourself within the text. Never pretend you're justifying it to yourself, because you don't have to, but not everybody will understand your willingness to betray your family. Say something like this: "Somehow I always knew much of what happened to my uncle had become a family fiction. Maybe it was the way the story never changed, as if one detail out of place would cause the entire narrative edifice to come tumbling down, resembling a collapsed cathedral, its glory betrayed by the sudden clutter of its bricks. For whatever reason I have remained selfishly, seriously curious for over thirty-five years. I know I loved him, and I'm hoping this love is enough to attempt to tell his story." When you write about murder, ask yourself if love ever has a thing to do with any of it.

When you write about murder, don't be too excited when your reporting reveals what you had suspected. It's unseemly. It's beneath you. As you ride down the elevator in the Justice Center in Cleveland, try hard to hide your glee—yes, your fucking glee—upon learning that at the time your uncle was murdered other men also claiming not to be gay were robbed and beaten at Edgewater Park. It seems some kids were preying on closeted gay men, luring them down to the lake's edge with the promise of sex, and then robbing them. It was a good scam, until the kids went too far and killed somebody who put up a fight.

When you write about murder ignore your uncle's marriage to your aunt, how it must have been for her after the separation; what it must have been like for him before.

When you write about murder, pay heed to the woman at the coroner's office who warns you about one of the autopsy pictures. She says you don't have to pay for the one if you don't want to. You thank her but insist on seeing all seven. She says okay and hands them to you, back first, so the photographs face her. "What relation was he to you?" she asks. It should be a simpler question but has gotten considerably more complicated. Story to storyteller? Subject to writer? Nephew to . . . ? "He was my uncle," you tell her. "Three and a half years ago my daughter came through here," she tells you. "That was hard." "I'm sorry," you say. "You do what you have to do, huh?" When she says this you almost think you hear her ask, "Why are you doing this?"

When you write about murder, for Christ's sake, stop what you're doing long enough to ask a helpful woman about her murdered daughter. The story will wait. Your soul is in peril.

When you write about murder work hard to get the details right and the right details. Drive a 1971 Lincoln Continental. Hold a .38 blue-steel revolver, an Arminius Titan Tiger. Visit Edgewater Park at six p.m. on Friday the thirteenth, December, the exact date thirty-five years after the murder. Be sure to remember how much has changed. A tree grows a lot in that time. So don't assume anything. Get pictures of the time and place and study them for clues of the way things were, whether the murder was last month or long ago. Check with the weather bureau so you have the right weather on the right day.

When you write about murder, never forget you're writing about human beings, and never forget you must transform them into characters. People who had one precious life, just like you, and then that life was gone. Remember that the whole life was not defined by a murder—only ended by one. Do months of reporting and researching and soul-searching and rationalizing and then give it your best shot. When you write about murder, do not make up a single thing. Remember: this is somebody's father or husband or uncle Don.

"On the night of the murder, Don maneuvers his 1971 Lincoln into the entrance to Edgewater Park and moves slowly up the drive to Perkins Beach, where, unbeknownst to him, a guy named Barnes waits, finishing take-out chicken, and sipping a can of RC Cola.

"Perhaps Don checks himself out in the rearview mirror, slips his glasses into their black case, nods in a knowing way that he likes what he sees. Although he's still wearing his work clothes, light gray pants and matching work shirt with Houghton Elevator sewn over the right shirt pocket and his name stitched over the left, he looks fine, dapper even. His brown dress shoes ease up on the accelerator as he nears the portal to Perkins. The temperature this close to the lake is only a couple degrees above freezing; Don's lucky he wore his blue nylon work jacket.

"He backs into a spot along the cul-de-sac, turns off his headlights, and then the engine. To his left and across a more inland section of the shoreline, the lights of Cleveland shine through the oncoming darkness. He sees the Terminal Tower. Behind him sit leafless trees, and beyond the trees a black drop-off to Lake Erie, the shallowest of the five Great Lakes. On the other side of the cul-de-sac stands a sixty-three-year-old statue of German composer Richard Wagner. Wagner's beret-topped head angles away from Perkins Beach; his coat looks as though it has been blown open, and he holds a sheaf of music in his left hand. Don gazes around casually, noncommittally, perhaps clicking the ballpoint pen in his shirt pocket or fingering the yellow-handled pocketknife in his pants.

"When he sees the young man approaching his car, does Don's heart pick up speed? Does he quickly rehearse his lines or does he know the drill? Does he check his hair one more time, frustrated by the tinges of gray growing above his ears? Does he lower his power windows a bit to convey a welcome? Is this the first time, the first time he's fantasized about, the time he's forbidden himself to fantasize about? Does his conscience tingle with the electric knowledge you get when you know something's wrong and you do it anyway, as if you're moving through everything you are and know to enter another place, whose passage you'll only worry about once you're safely back on the other side? Is this why, when the killer destroys the fantasy by pulling out his gun and demanding money, Don can't possibly give it to him? Can't possibly give in to him?"

When you write about murder, it is here you'll write about four bullets entering a body and killing a man, somebody's father, husband, or uncle.

When you write about murder and then wonder why you did, find an old photograph from Christmastime, 1960-something. Stare at Uncle Don and Aunt Dee standing in front of their wooden mantel. Two Christmas stockings—still a few years away from being three—hang behind them. In the background, in front of a window covered with soft, white, cotton curtains, a saint with a crown of gold and a gown of white stands atop a corner cupboard with glass doors.

Uncle Don's arms are wrapped around his wife's waist. Her right hand holds his left wrist. Your aunt's smile at his holding makes her beautiful. Uncle Don's smile rules and lines his face. Their smiles appear to be evidence of something, true evidence. Of something good. Of a story worth telling. They seem, at this captured moment in time, two people possessed of all the love that can possibly exist in a world where people are murdered, and where other people presume to write about it.

Jim Krusoe

Traffic

I CAN'T REMEMBER exactly how old I was—I'm guessing eight or nine—when I first learned that my father had killed a child. The actual event, if I can call it that, took place before I was born, I think, but I can't be absolutely sure. In any case, it wasn't until I was in primary school that my mother mentioned it, almost in passing. After that, when it came up now and again, it was never as a shameful thing or a crime, but always as an example of the unfairness of the world: a parable about traffic safety and greedy parents. The boy, the story went, had been lurking behind a parked automobile and, just as my father was driving home from work, dashed out in pursuit of a rubber ball with such little regard for his own life that my poor father never had a chance to stop. This would have been before, or maybe during the Second World War, and somehow that came into it as well.

The child died, though I was never told the details, only that afterward his parents had the temerity to take my father to court—criminal or civil, I'm not sure which. In the end, my father was found not guilty because of his car's skid marks that, I was told, showed he could not possibly have stopped in time. Or maybe they showed he had not been traveling that fast in the first place. In any case, it was the skid marks, along with a good lawyer, that kept him out of jail, and clearly, this child's parents had been monsters for thinking that a man as nice and as good as my father was would somehow strike their child on purpose.

And so it happened—although I certainly never connected these two things—that shortly after I first heard this story I started running out into traffic. Not traffic, exactly, but in front of single cars, like a bullfighter dodging a bull, on a narrow highway near my house. I would hide behind a bush, and then, when it was too late for the driver to hit the brakes, jump out and run straight across the road, as close to the car as I possibly could.

Sometimes I did it alone, but usually with a friend who could watch and describe the expressions on the panicked drivers' faces, because I was too busy trying not to be hit. If I were hit, though, the knowledge that it would be their fault was a powerful attraction. And so, over the space of about a month, one summer I got into the habit of doing this two or three times a week, until one driver, after an especially close call, turned his car around, pulled up, and yelled at us, at me. He was red-faced and trembling and furious, his eyes nearly popping out of his head, and I was scared to see anyone so angry; I quit then and there.

But there is one more piece of information to this story, one other fact I'm not quite certain about, but which I almost completely believe is true, one that nobody ever spoke of. Namely, back when I was a child, there were a lot of places people called "neighborhood bars," where men would stop after work to have a couple of shots, down a few beers, and talk. The places were—to use a curiously modern word—spots for them to network: to hear of jobs, of cars for sale, of houses for rent, or just to talk about current events and share complaints. By those standards, my father was a good networker. I don't think I can ever remember him coming straight home from work without the smell of whiskey on his breath, and there were countless nights I remember my mother complaining as the supper she'd prepared was left out cold, waiting for his return until nine or ten o'clock.

In other words, my father was an alcoholic, although in those days the only way I ever heard the word applied was to men like my Uncle Louie, who, my father said, "couldn't handle the booze." Which was probably true enough, because after Louie joined Alcoholics Anonymous he used the meetings to build a network of his own. Louie networked himself into such a career as to leave the rest of our family standing openmouthed in awe. Louie had a racing stable, a country house, and his kids went to private schools—all unheard-of in my world. At least until the day they found that my uncle was a criminal and had used his position of trust, the one he had established through countless AA meetings, to steal the company blind.

But my father could handle the booze; he kept his job even though many was the night or morning I would hear him in the bathroom vomiting, something I took to be the price of being an adult male. Those were the days, and maybe still are in some quarters, when, at least for a certain class of people, the first thing you did when a guest walked through the door was to offer them a drink. Then people would reply, "I thought you'd never ask." Those were the days that drunk-films—W. C. Fields and *The Thin Man*—were considered charming. So I'm as certain as I can be that my father had been drinking the day he killed that child. That would explain, for one thing, why the boy's parents felt they had a right to make their case; some witness or another had undoubtedly smelled the liquor on my father's breath. That would explain how the whole thing got as far as an actual trial, and maybe it would also explain why my mother, a legal secretary, kept slaving at her job in the firm that had defended him, even as my father complained about her bosses being pigs.

And it would also provide the answer as to why my father kept on drinking for years after his family and his doctors told him he had to give it up. To quit would have been for him to admit there was something wrong with alcohol, and therefore when he'd struck the child that he'd been wrong. That would have been more, I think, than he could have borne. So instead of quitting, when I got a little older, he would encourage me to take a sip of a ginger-ale-and-rye highball, or beer, or wine—though he wasn't much for wine—to keep him company. We were co-conspirators, in a way, and then afterward, for many years, for nearly twenty of them, it was the alcohol that kept me company.

I've noticed that in America no one admits to being old, and I can't blame them. The old are just repositories for loss, or worse— endless and self-congratulatory memories. When it comes to my choice of reading material, or even watching, I much prefer stories of the young caught up in their first flashes of excitement, or about the middle-aged in the first dawn of disillusion. Still, I find plenty in old guys like myself to listen to, mostly in the locker room of the local Young Men's Christian Association (three out of those four names untrue). In that context, I'm happy to report my fellow oldsters seem to have learned little, or if we have, we sure don't speak of it. So at the Y, the guys in the locker room talk about sports or food or nothing much at all, but certainly not how they have lived their lives in blindness, and not how the person they thought they were and the person they turned out to be is different. I don't blame them; it's not a subject for mixed company. And as for my part, I ask myself: do any of them need to know that while I lived much of my life thinking it was one kind of book—

an adventure story, I suppose—it was already a sad history, one with whole pages torn and missing, with sentences, some mercifully and others not, illegible?

My father, my own son, and I have this in common: we are all dog lovers. My son was raised with dogs his entire life, and I've kept dogs for at least fifty years. But what strikes me as strange about my father and his dogs is that right until the end of his life, his animals would often get away. Sometimes a gate would be left open, sometimes there would be a hole in a fence that should have been mended but wasn't, or, walking out of the house to check his mail, my father, who should have known better, would leave the front door wide open. And then his dog would be running down the street, into traffic, with my father shouting after it, sometimes catching up to it, and sometimes not. Sometimes, arriving too late, he would watch it killed.

Or such is my conjecture.

J. Malcolm Garcia

Securing District Four

WE PREPARE to go out on a night patrol.

The captain however must pick up an Afghan policeman first. On paper, the American and European soldiers of the international security forces provide a "supportive role" only to the central Afghan government. Therefore, protocols require an Afghan police officer to lead patrols, the captain explains to me, an embedded reporter. He calls me by my last name as he does his soldiers, and tells me to ride with him.

We leave Camp Julien in south Kabul for the District Four police station in a convoy of four Humvees, six soldiers in each vehicle. The dawn light rinses the sky with an umbrella of pink light, and then the light fades almost instantly and the sky darkens to an impenetrable depth without stars. Kids wave to us from the shadows as they always do when we go out on a night patrol, but it seems to me they also have one hand behind their back, and sometimes I'm right because I'll hear the rocks they throw ding against our doors.

"Last week on our way out, this kid was throwing rocks at me," a soldier tells me. "In Iraq, parents'd beat the shit out of their kids for doing that. This kid didn't look slow. It's not like he's a retard. If that's how a kid thinks about us what about his dad?"

"It's a game, dude," another soldier says. "How many rocks do they have to throw to make a gunner duck." "They need to start a baseball league here then. He was whizzing them."

The dirt road we follow climbs a hill. A stone castle swarmed by birds circling its broken towers overlooks our progress.

"In Bosnia, we had Kurds, Muslims," a soldier seated behind me says. "Here it's everybody. In Bosnia, we tried to study the enemy. Here, we try to figure out who the enemy is. We're all scared. This is not our country, not our culture. Going out at night in town with all these people with weapons; it's very different for us. My gun is nothing compared to their cache of rocket-propelled grenades. The minute we stop being scared is the time something will happen."

We continue driving until we reach the ruins of a square cinder block building. An oil lamp lights one small window. We stop and get out, stones crunching beneath our boots. We hear someone approaching and then a man in a green uniform materializes before us like a mirage come whole, illuminated by our headlights.

"Who are you?" he asks our translator.

The captain shows him a paper.

"What do you need?" he asks glancing at the paper.

"We need a police officer on our patrol," our captain says through the translator.

"Which spot is your patrol?"

"District Four. Your station is part of District Four. We're here because we are mandated to bring a policeman along with us."

"We'll get you a guy."

He turns around and disappears into the dark. He returns a short time later—first the sound of his boots and then the sight of him again materializing in the headlights—with a short thin man in a green jacket much too large for his narrow body. His pants form pools of cloth around his ankles, and mud clings to his sandals. Patchy stubble mars his face like a burn. He introduces himself; Saif Ali.

Without another word, he gets in the front seat of my vehicle and sits next to the captain beside the passenger door. He turns around to shake hands. He does not distinguish me, the American reporter in the backseat wearing a helmet and Kevlar, from the other soldiers in the Humvee.

We start up again and follow a narrow stone road that takes us behind the police station and into some woods. The opaque shapes of leafless trees loom above us. Dogs bark in a disjointed chorus. Mud huts stand stark and mute in the sweep of our headlights. We cross a bridge, listen to water rushing invisibly beneath us until we reach a checkpoint. A man on a cot outside a shack kicks out from some blankets and waves us through.

The captain tells me we have entered a bad area. Lots of robberies. But we should be fine because we won't be stopping to do foot patrols. Don't need to. We're on a "presence" patrol only. We're not to do anything. People just need to see us drive through and know we're here, nothing more.

The captain turns on the cab light to illuminate Saif so the locals can see him. Saif stares out the windshield and raises a hand and smiles as if to reassure anyone watching us. Veiled women appear fleetingly on the side of the road revealed by the sweep of our headlights. Stooped old men hold the hands of boys and watch us without expression turning their heads slowly as if pressured by a heavy wind. Ribbed dogs snap at things in the rushing gutters.

The crackling of the radio pulls our attention away from the road. A static-filled voice shouts that an unexploded ordnance has been found outside the Canadian Embassy in downtown Kabul. We're needed to assist in cordoning off streets around the embassy while engineers from a Canadian security detail detonate the ordnance.

The captain orders the driver to stop. We slow to a halt. Dust swirls enveloping us as if we had been consumed by a gray cloud. The radio makes sporadic hissing sounds and then the hissing stops altogether. The captain looks at Saif. No unauthorized national is allowed to enter an international staffed security cordon. Saif's police station is in the opposite direction of the embassy. We don't have time to drop him off, the captain says.

"Where's the translator?"

"In the vic behind us, sir," a soldier says.

The captain shrugs. "Thank you," he says reaching over Saif and opening his door. "Thank you."

Saif doesn't move. He looks at the captain, head cocked to one side, "What?" written all over his face.

"Thank you," the captain says again and shoves him. Saif shifts away, moves one leg out the door, and looks at the captain and says something that sounds like a question but none of us can understand him.

"Thank you!" the captain snaps pushing Saif the rest of the way out the door. Saif waves his arms to keep balance but collapses in the dirt. A soldier beside me gets out, steps over Saif and sits in his seat, and slams the door shut.

Twenty minutes later, we arrive at the Canadian Embassy and take positions at two intersections. An electrical storm quakes the sky and the ground appears to shudder beneath our feet. We wait for the engineers from the security detail to disarm and remove the ordnance.

To break the monotony, we shout, "Thank you," back and forth to each other because really there was something hilarious about the captain dumping Saif off like that.

After a while, we stop shouting, "Thank you," having wrung the joke of all its humor, ground into the tedium of waiting. We get quiet and become irritable, and we shrug off the children clutching at our pants begging. In the silence, I think of Saif, the look on his face.

We were out of there so fast. Did Saif make it back to the police station? I don't know. I do know we left him in our dust, and he scrambled backward crab-like as our Humvees spewed stones and raced past him. I turned around and watched Saif staring after us, staring through me, the what look on his face changed to fury. Then he was swallowed whole into the night as in a movie when the camera pulls back and the image left behind shrinks in an ever tightening circle of dimming light.

I mill around the perimeter of the Canadian Embassy in what feels to be an endless night. A dirty moon holds the sky. The silence fills spaces. That look of Saif's. It bores into me still more than an hour later, a presence demanding to be addressed. The captain decided to toss you out, Saif, not me. What could I have done? I am not a soldier.

Saif's expression does not change. When the captain dumped him in the middle of nowhere, the captain became any one of us.

I close my eyes but Saif stays with me. He bides his time. But the captain cannot wait. He has his duty. He will need Saif tomorrow, and the day after that and the day after that and the day after that.

Paul Auster

Winter Journal: *The First Three Pages*

YOU THINK it will never happen to you, that it cannot happen to you, that you are the only person in the world to whom none of these things will ever happen, and then, one by one, they all begin to happen to you, in the same way they happen to everyone else.

Your bare feet on the cold floor as you climb out of bed and walk to the window. You are six years old. Outside, snow is falling, and the branches of the trees in the backyard are turning white.

Speak now before it is too late, and then hope to go on speaking until there is nothing more to be said. Time is running out, after all. Perhaps it is just as well to put aside your stories for now and try to examine what it has felt like to live inside this body from the first day you can remember being alive until this one. A catalogue of sensory data. What one might call a *phenomenology of breathing.*

You are ten years old, and the midsummer air is warm, oppressively warm, so humid and uncomfortable that even as you sit in the shade of the trees in the backyard, sweat is gathering on your forehead.

It is an incontestable fact that you are no longer young. One month from today, you will be turning sixty-four, and although that is not excessively old, not what anyone would consider to be an advanced old age, you cannot stop yourself from thinking about all the others who never managed to get as far as you have. This is one example of the various things that could never happen, but which, in fact, have happened.

The wind in your face during last week's blizzard. The awful sting of the cold, and you out there in the empty streets wondering what possessed you to leave the house in such a pounding storm, and yet, even as you struggled to keep your balance, there was the exhilaration of that wind, the joy of seeing the familiar streets turned into a blur of white, whirling snow.

Physical pleasures and physical pains. Sexual pleasures first and foremost, but also the pleasures of food and drink, of lying naked in a hot bath, of scratching an itch, of sneezing and farting, of spending an extra hour in bed, of turning your face toward the sun on a mild afternoon in late spring or early summer and feeling the warmth settle upon your skin. Innumerable instances, not a day gone by without some moment or moments of physical pleasure, and yet pains are no doubt more persistent and intractable, and at one time or another nearly every part of your body has been subjected to assault. Eyes and ears, head and neck, shoulders and back, arms and legs, throat and stomach, ankles and feet, not to mention the enormous boil that once sprouted on the left cheek of your ass, referred to by the doctor as a *wen*, which to your ears sounded like some medieval affliction and prevented you from sitting in chairs for a week.

The proximity of your small body to the ground, the body that belonged to you when you were three and four years old, that is to say, the shortness of the distance between your feet and head, and how the things you no longer notice were once a constant presence and preoccupation for you; the little world of crawling ants and lost coins, of fallen twigs and dented bottle caps, of dandelions and clover. But especially the ants. They are what you remember best. Armies of ants traveling in and out of their powdery hills.

You are five years old, crouched over an anthill in the backyard attentively studying the comings and goings of your tiny six-legged friends. Unseen and unheard, your three-year-old neighbor creeps up behind you and strikes you on the head with a toy rake. The prongs pierce your scalp, blood flows into your hair and down the back of your neck, and you run screaming into the house, where your grandmother tends to your wounds.

Your grandmother's words to your mother: "Your father would be such a wonderful man—if only he were different."

Dinty W. Moore

If Mr. Clean Had Been My Father

SISTER ANN, my fifth-grade teacher, raised one eyebrow and pointed to the door after my name crackled across the school's public address system. I was ordered immediately to the principal's office. What I expected was to be handed Saturday detention for some unremembered act of rebellion, but instead, when I turned the corner in the dark hallway, there was my mother, dressed in a shabby gray sweatshirt and blue jeans—an outfit she only wore when doing heavy cleaning.

"I've left your father," she told me. "We're moving to a new house."

Sister Mary Ellen, the principal, had apparently been briefed. The elderly nun touched the large rosary at her waist, made some odd sympathetic noises, then stood aside.

"The movers," my mother continued, digging in her purse for something, avoiding my eyes, "are loading the furniture right now."

There have been few moments in my life where thought simply stopped. Nothing spun, nothing sifted, no words fought to reach the foreground screen of my mind. Not a whisper. Just momentary blankness. This moment was one of them.

In the five short hours since I had slouched at the kitchen table that morning to wolf down cornflakes and milk, my mother, my sisters, and I somehow acquired a new home, new lives, and utterly altered circumstances. Mom knew what was coming, of course, had planned it for months, but I had absolutely no forewarning. Neither, it turned out, did my father.

Mom led me to the car, and I sat mutely as we drove four miles uptown to an unfamiliar, unappealing neighborhood. I shuffled up the broken sidewalk and opened the front door, where my older sister Sally was busy scrubbing the wooden floors with Murphy Oil Soap.

I registered the unfamiliar, unpleasant smell, ran to the kitchen sink, and promptly vomited.

THE COINCIDENCES begin here.

Murphy Soap was first brought to market by Jeremiah T. Murphy, an Irishman who settled near the shores of Lake Erie in the late 1800s. Murphy based his product on an easy-to-make vegetable-oil soap, and at first, made the soap as a paste, packed it into barrels, so that consumers in the Cleveland area could just scoop out whatever quantity they needed.

Like the Murphy clan, my own Irish ancestors also settled along Lake Erie, and at about the same time. These ancestors— the Moores and O'Briens—were entrepreneurs as well, though they favored illegal rum and real estate.

In addition to the soap, the J. T. Murphy Company eventually expanded into other oil-based products, including an item used in service stations and automobile garages—Murphy's Tire Mounting Lubricant.

It is entirely possible, then, that at the moment *his* life was unalterably changing, the moment his fearful wife and puzzled children were disappearing with no warning, my father—a mechanic for the local Chevy dealer—was, through an odd quirk of fate, using a J. T. Murphy product as well. Mounting a tire.

Perhaps he too was sickened by the odor.

HAD I BEEN given a choice, I would have preferred not to move away—from our home on Ninth Street, or from my dad. But if we had to move, and if the new wooden floors had to be scrubbed, I would have much preferred that my mother buy Mr. Clean, not the Murphy stuff.

Mr. Clean cleaned "stronger than dirt," which seemed to me to be the perfect attribute. And Mr. Clean was a man I easily admired. He had biceps, fortitude, dependability. He was always smiling, his eyes wide and friendly, his bushy white eyebrows arched constantly in pleasant surprise.

My father's hands were dirty, scarred, forever covered in deep gashes coated in oil and grease. Fixing cars was physical work in those days. You didn't read a computer print-out; you got in there with a wrench, loosened nuts, maneuvered hunks of metal.

He was not a particularly happy man. Nor was he often around.

My guess—at age ten—was that Mr. Clean would have been an entirely different father. He would have been steadfast, reliable. Everything at home would have been spotless and grand.

I could never know, of course, for many reasons, including the obvious—Mr. Clean wasn't real.

BUT BY PURE chance, I've lately met and become friends with the daughter of the man who invented Mr. Clean.

This man—the advertising artist who first drew the jolly character to life—was Mr. Clean's human counterpart, or as close as we will ever get. He moved away from his family when my friend Tracy was five. She tells me that her father was a distant man, hard to know. His marriage utterly failed.

So perhaps I was wrong about that too.

Perhaps Mr. Clean himself would have been a disappointment.

FOUR YEARS BACK, my wife and I bought a house. My father had been buried for fifteen years by this time, and I had become a father myself. The house had wooden floors, top to bottom.

I walked in from work one afternoon and Renita, by pure coincidence, was scrubbing with Murphy Soap. In an instant I was nauseous, not enough to vomit, thankfully, but enough that I had to stagger backwards out of the room. I was suddenly looking for air.

Smell has such absolute potency that my mind, for a brief moment, registered blank.

When I told my wife why, and related bits of my childhood story, Renita was horrified, far too apologetic. She threw away the near-full bottle.

These days, our floors are not so clean.

But at least the marriage is working.

Peggy Shumaker

The Nun

THE YEAR I IMPERSONATED A NUN, my marriage was falling apart. Pages torn loose from the binding, we weren't sure which verse we were on. Fresh out of my MFA in 1980, I went to work for North American Liturgy Resources, a publishing house that produced sheet music, hymnals, and record albums for post–Vatican II congregations.

Such upheavals! People were used to worship services unchanged for centuries, services offered in a language unspoken except in Catholic churches all over the planet. And now they could improvise. They could put things into their own words. The freedom was explosive, heady, vertiginous. Some churches resisted, threatened to break away. Some worshippers missed the prayers they'd chanted in Latin all their lives. Others felt cool breezes, fresh water, renewal. The vernacular. Miles of felt banners. Liturgical drama and dance. Guitars and drums in church. Women reading scripture.

People on the phone would assume. "Thank you, Sister," they'd say, deferential to my vocation. "You're welcome," I'd reply. I was a mongrel Protestant not even guilty that I was taking bread out of the mouths of somebody's Catholic child. I needed the work.

Everything with words on it came across my desk. I wrote catalog copy for religious supplies and knickknacks, ramped up desire for polished wooden offering plates. I wrote articles for in-house publications aimed at music ministers and choir directors. I proofed lyrics, learning in great detail how words meant to be sung should be divided.

The irreverent in-house composer who received stacks and stacks of heartfelt drivel showed me one scrawled letter. "God gave me these songs." The handwriting, in pencil, was childlike. "Give them back," the composer wrote. He had the hunched posture, the brooding disposition, the prodigious beak of a night heron. We produced one "compilation" Christmas songbook with contributions from fourteen composers. Really, our in-house heron wrote all the songs. Even he cracked a smile as we made up his pseudonyms.

I turned into plain English articles submitted by people whose primary strengths didn't involve crafting graceful sentences. I had great conversations with those who could write, especially a gay Jesuit priest many years my senior, a man who was always reading something interesting. He spoke in parables. He asked me one day what my husband read. "He doesn't read much," I said. To be fair, my husband read *The Hobbit* and *Lord of the Rings* over and over. And he did like motorcycle magazines. I heard the pang in my voice. So did the good father. "It's not your fault you're married to the wrong man," he said gently. Ironic, those words of a man who could never marry.

I hadn't until that moment put words to what had been building inside me, hadn't realized quite the sources of the pressure. "No," I thought. "My husband's doing everything he promised to do. He's just married to the wrong woman."

IN HIGH SCHOOL, my nickname was "The Nun." Not for religious reasons, but because I didn't smoke or drink. (We didn't know that nuns smoke and drink. No clergy we knew would have dared, at least in public.) I dragged home my siblings after binge parties in the desert, but never found anything fun happening there. Out in the boonies, I was trying to figure out how to make a life that involved reading and writing, a life that didn't involve the screaming and fighting of childhood. I was trying to write a script for a life I wasn't sure was possible.

At work, I wrote liner notes for record albums that hadn't been produced yet. I'd get somebody to cover my phone, and head down to the recording studio where rehearsals (and fierce arguments) were eating up very expensive time. No matter how organized the project seemed ahead of time, players got flaky in the studio. Too much caffeine, too little sleep. The composer got stubborn, and wanted to get things right—meaning just the way he imagined them. He insisted on another take. He demanded a more intricate arrangement, more instruments, more background singers. The producer mentioned that they wanted lay ministers and choirs to be able to sing the songs. The pressure of the budget, always too low, hung over the sessions, mingling with cigarette smoke and the haze of cheap booze.

The liner notes had to be printed before the record was pressed. The notes had to work into the cover design. The artwork had to be done and the cover printed and assembled ahead of time so the finished record could slide right in. I'd listen, make my best guesses about what might still exist at the end of the process, then wing it. Laudatory, always. Not too specific. Notes to appeal to the folks who bought this person's work the last time. Notes to appeal to the people who held each church's music purse strings.

We met these folks at trade shows. Our boss, the patriarch of a family business that had grown a little faster than he could handle, had his flunky order what he considered "cute" little outfits for the women to wear in the booth. They were little all right. "Where's the outfit for the guys?" I asked. Oh, they'd be wearing business clothes. "Then so will I." The patriarch arched his eyebrows. I wore business clothes.

Once I was sent to San Luis Obispo to help with the release of a new album. Coming from bare-walled churches full of somber Lutherans predestined to depression, and later from Methodist halls full of entrepreneurs who made good business contacts on Sunday, I found the Catholic rituals foreign. The regalia and the old artwork were seductive, bringing me in touch with ancient stories. How would it feel to be born part of something so vast?

There beside the ocean, I breathed. Wave after wave, the same motions, changing. In the fine old church building, the singers warmed up, eager to try new songs. A vibrant young priest had revitalized the whole parish. Just before afternoon mass, before a packed crowd, he placed a wooden cross around my neck.

"BUT," I protested.

He grinned. "We're proud to allow women to take part in serving Communion."

"BUT . . ."

"You'll do fine," he reassured. He turned, hurried away. I was trying to tell him I wasn't Catholic. I didn't have a clue what I was supposed to do. The person next to me whispered in my ear. The woman lining up the shining vessels handed me a chalice of wine. As the communicants came forward, I tipped the grail, murmuring, "The Blood of Christ, the Blood of Christ."

I felt light in my body, floating. Strangely moved. I didn't believe what they believed. But I can testify to a powerful calm, a peace that surely passeth my dim understanding. Afterwards, with the day's last sunlight slanting through stained glass, I told a musician friend that I hoped I hadn't sent all those people to Hell.

"No, of course not," he said, his hand on my shoulder. "You're the one going to Hell."

In some ways I was already there. I couldn't find words for my restlessness, couldn't manage to negotiate my pain.

My husband's mother, studying to be a minister in the Unity Church, had all the answers, prepackaged, ready-made. When Jehovah's Witnesses knocked on her door, they had no idea what they were inviting. They figured they'd nudge someone Awake, they'd offer the view from their Watchtower. Phyllis invited them in, sat them at her Formica table, poured tall glasses of sweetened iced tea. Then she started talking. Unity, her religion, believed in seeing the good in everyone. (Her son would say, "Yeah, when little Billy sets your pant leg on fire, you say, My, you sure know how to handle matches.") She'd tell them about her dream to visit Unity Village, about all her projects to enter the ministry, all her studies—"Those nomads never stayed in one place very long!" They'd try to ease a word in edgewise, but she never came up for breath. After three glasses of tea, they asked, politely, to use the bathroom. After a couple more, stunned by caffeine and laughter, not really understanding how it happened, the Witnesses agreed to come to her church. They couldn't see any other way to get out the front door.

I couldn't find words.

Sometimes I wished I were Catholic. Not for the dogma, not for the hierarchy. No. I coveted the chance at absolution. All you had to do was find the words, then give voice to your shame. If you confessed and repented, you could wipe the slate clean. But the lapsed Protestant in me couldn't really get behind this. How could another person, even an intercessor, offer this? Wouldn't it take a god I didn't believe in? (Brief aside: When my sister was engaged to a Catholic man, they'd enjoy the sweaty and gymnastic sex of the very young. Then he'd go to Confession. She was outraged. "If you think it's wrong, we should stop doing it." No, no, he didn't want that. But his conscience wouldn't let him revel in their bodies' exuberance without acknowledging what he knew HAD to be a sin.)

I couldn't find my way.

So I did unforgivable things, things that even if my husband forgave, I couldn't forgive. In this way, bewildered and broken, I broke out. I rewrote the whole album. It's been more than thirty years. I'm still looking for words. I wish I could have been kinder.

Brenda Miller

Swerve

I'M SORRY about that time I ran over a piece of wood in the road. A pound of marijuana in the trunk and a faulty brake light—any minute the cops might have pulled us over, so you were edgy already, and then I ran over that piece of stray lumber without even slowing down. *Thunk, thunk,* and then the wood spun behind us on the road. Your dark face dimmed even darker, and you didn't yell at first, only turned to look out the window, and I made the second mistake: *What's wrong?* That's when you exploded. *You're so careless, you don't even think, what if there had been a nail in that fucking thing?* you yelled, your face so twisted now, and ugly. *And I'm always the one that has to clean it up whenever something breaks.*   I'm sorry, I said, and I said it again, and we continued on our way through the desert, in the dark of night, with the contraband you had put in our trunk, with the brake light you hadn't fixed blinking on and off, me driving because you were too drunk, or too tired, or too depressed, and we traveled for miles into our future, where eventually I would apologize for the eggs being overcooked, and for the price of lightbulbs, and for the way the sun blared through our dirty windows and made everything too bright, and I would apologize when I had the music on and when I had it off, I'd say sorry for being in the bathroom, and sorry for crying, and sorry for laughing, I would apologize, finally, for simply being alive, and even now I'm sorry I didn't swerve, I didn't get out of the way.

Stuart Dybek

Between

guilt and desire, thought and act, *déjà* and *vu*, between ampersand and cross, wing and air, all she made possible and all she made impossible, between river and eel, loving and leaving—a life like the exhalation that separates wine and whine—between mute and mime, between the rhyme of night and light, dream and waking from a nap in the afternoon darkness of what could have been a total eclipse but actually was an April thunderstorm, I thought the sound of men lifting long lengths of rain gutter from a pickup truck was a meteor shower rattling the metal awning over Sun's Oriental Food Store.

Lance Larsen

A Brief History of Water

LAST SUNDAY a displaced water snake interrupted our nightly walk. My beloved and I watched it roil under the streetlight, metallic in its shimmers. Overhead, a companionable moon, which can move seven-tenths of the earth's surface without lifting a finger. Also overhead but not so far away, the firmament, which possesses a simple job description: divide waters above from waters below. What are we but walking bags of the stuff, over 60 percent liquid. Sow a rill, reap a tsunami. My cat turns up her nose after I've freshened her dish, but will risk life and limb to lap from the toilet. Pick up a water snake, it will musk you every time, a stink worse than pee. Unlike desert snakes, it can afford to lose the liquid. I picked it up anyway. My first computer password was Chacmool, Mayan rain god. Drowning is easy. Drunks can pull it off with a puddle. The wives of sailors lost at sea require no more than a thimble of stars. I first attempted drowning at age three by falling in a river. My father fished me out so damned quick his wallet stayed dry. Thanks to surface tension, certain insects stay dry all the time, striding the water like the Son of Man. What is a cloud but an overhead lake that likes to cross-dress? Now a race car, now a refrigerator, wait make that a goose, make that a gnome. "Making water"—a euphemism that manages to sound generative, resourceful, and Native American all at once but is only pissing. In August, snow fields in the Sawtooths grow a pinkish mold that tastes of watermelon. The night we found the water snake I must have looked like an idiot walking home: one hand holding the snake at a stinky distance, the other holding my wife's hand. Or not so much an idiot as a crippled plane searching for a runway. Water, one of those rare gods you can drink from a tap. During my first trip to London, I stayed in a Bayswater flat where Ernest Shackleton, the explorer, lived with his brother. Even the warmest days in that flat nipped like Antarctica. Noah: first mortal to heed a sketchy weather report. Icicles, artesian springs, vapors rising off a lake: before all three I've bowed my head and said amen. I love snakes but feel sorry for them because they don't have hands, one of many errors in misplaced sympathy. I once left a love note to my beloved in an abandoned ice house in Red Wing, Minnesota. She found it twenty-eight days later. Certain skeptics have seen the face of Jesus in a seepy wall. In noir films, I like it when rain dripping down windows melts skin or causes tears to ooze from every pore. I've always wanted a water snake to guard my backyard fountain, so I let my captive go beside a daylily called Primal Scream. Capillary action: a wet uprising sneakier than gravity. My best stroke during swimming lessons was dead man's float. Haunted houses cry in blood. A friend of mine fantasizes the perfect suicide: drown herself in the city water supply so that friends will drink her demise for weeks. Does it count as skinny-dipping if it's just you and the one you love in a pool too small to swim laps in? Certain peat bogs in Ireland will pickle a body better than any funeral home. Every mirror comes with its private lake. Face off two lakes and they will leap each other into eternity.

When it rained at Ground Zero, a terrible mist of the lost wafted through the air. To breathe was to mourn. When I swam Walden Pond, I met a man in a kayak in the middle of the lake: bearded, shirtless, hair in a ponytail. When it began to sprinkle, he looked up: "No worries," he said, palms cupped, as if channeling a conversation from on high. Each morning I pinch off spent daylilies in my garden and look for my snake. The water cycle is the first lesson in reincarnation. What are narwhals but unicorns in an oversized pond? Even bones drink water. Here is my fountain, my man-made spring. Come sip, Gentle One, come sip.

Leila Philip

Water Rising

BEAVERS ARE the Shiva of the animal world. Who knows how a beaver chooses where to make her pond? But once she does, trees fall like spears of light then overnight disappear, dragged to underwater lairs, or left to float eerie carcasses, every branch and shred of bark stripped clean.

Last week I saw the beaver who's been cutting down the woods near my house. It was evening, the weary light thinning through the trees by the time I reached the bridge. Sound came first, a crack so loud I flinched, thinking my neighbor had shot his gun. But across the newly flooded swamp, I saw a brown head cutting a silver vee. Beaver, the first I'd seen.

One black eye visible, staring, back and forth she swam, a crease in flat silver, then she dove like some huge furious fish and her dark tail flicked up and slammed the surface. Another crack echoed through the trees, her warning.

Now my beaver swam faster and faster, back and forth before me on the bridge, fierce, her whole being focused on this one resolve, to make me go away. Again she slammed the water, sound booming through the trees.

This swamp was hers, her trickling dam, her fallen trees, her growing pond. Each day water rising. When I didn't move she began to track me, that dark eye locked on my standing figure.

This time, when she dove, she took me with her, my svelte younger self moving through the hot water ladled with silt, down to the bottom of the pond where she had carved her underwater trails, clawing roads through the deep muck.

When I surfaced I was middle-aged, messy in my ways as if I had grown four sets of yellow teeth, two layers of fur, claws, and dark scales cascading down the thick paddle tail. Half fish, but no mermaid.

Barrie Jean Borich

Crease

AS A GIRL I walked waterlines, sometimes on sand along oceans, sometimes on the paved paths downtown, between Lakeshore Drive and the waves, always parallel to the groove where destination folds into the present tense.

When I walked the Gulf Coast beach for the first time, age fifteen, I was that girl from the cold city, tanning too quickly in her stringy striped bikini, bare feet marking sand, sun-blond and uneasy in her long swimmer's body, no tattoos yet, or surgeries, or histories of love.

The crease is what the gaze inhabits but the body cannot. I walked out of time, stepping forward and forward again, for longer than I thought I could keep on, knowing I'd have to walk back again, past the same greased-up college kids, screeching mothers chasing toddlers into the surf, future architects building shell cities and burrowing limbs into the sand. The gauzy line, amber interrupting blue, hovered over first my right shoulder, later my left, the crack of waves standing in for the end of things.

I see her now, that blond girl, walking, pretending not to notice men watching her, the way men gaze after blond girls in bikinis, or after the figments they make of blond girls. She will not remember if she longed for any part of those bare-chested linebackers, collarbones glinting with Italian gold, their bodies taut as they dove into the breakers. She will only be sure of what she did not want: their babies, their houses, their hovering mothers, their jealous breath in her ear.

Though she may have wanted their wanting. As I do sometimes still, hoping to be seen as much as anyone walking the crease of future's plainness, even knowing too well the difference between fascination and erudition, that interruptible blue.

Kate Carroll de Gutes

The Wardrobe Series

YOU LOOK DECENT

I can't remember if the lapels of the tuxedo jacket were crushed velvet or shiny satin, some of the details are simply lost to the degrading dendrites and failing synapses of time. It was a black jacket, however, even though it was 1982 and it could have easily been powder blue. The shirt was a classic tuxedo shirt, the buttons and bow tie permanently attached. You actually slid into the shirt back to front and secured it behind with a bit of Velcro, the quicker to get the high school seniors in and out of the photo studio.

Still. Tuxedo.

This is how it felt to change from the black velvet drape to the tuxedo: it was like diving into a cool, mineral-laden river, the way water slides all silky over skin turned pink from too much July sun, the way a body moves with the current—slipping along seemingly languidly only to find itself much further downstream than expected.

Or it felt like this: like a sigh made at the end of a long day when at last you can crawl into your big, king-sized bed just made with clean, purple 600-thread count Egyptian cotton sheets—like a whisper across your tired body—the memory foam mattress a reminder of what soft is supposed to feel like.

It did not feel like sitting exposed on top of a white rock mesa in New Mexico's Chaco Canyon, the wind kicking up the fine grit of desert topsoil, the pulverized sandstone exfoliating the fair Irish skin on my cheeks and neck, searing my eyes, worrying my chattering mind about melanomas and carcinomas and survival in this too-bright landscape. No, that's what the velvet drape—off the shoulder, no push-up bra or pearls—felt like.

The way I remember it is that it didn't occur to me NOT to wear a tuxedo for my senior portrait. I felt handsome not beautiful, dapper not sexy. Of course tuxedo rather than drape. Of course bow tie rather than pearls.

Then the proofs arrived in the mail.

JEYDON LOREDO is on the cover of *Equality*, the magazine published by HRC, a civil rights organization working for gay, lesbian, bisexual, and transgendered rights. The transgendered teen smiles wide with teeth too big for his head, looking—maybe—slightly self-conscious about being on the cover of a national magazine. HRC has just successfully forced Jeydon's Texas school district to include his senior portrait in the high school yearbook. Jeydon with the impossibly smooth skin of a face not touched by the hormonal surge of teenage testosterone. Jeydon who did not receive his senior portrait proofs in a yellow five-by-seven padded envelope labeled "Do Not Bend." Jeydon who wants to have his yearbook photo reflect who—how—he feels. Jeydon in a tuxedo.

The superintendent in La Feria, Texas, ten miles from the Mexican border, claimed the photos violated the standards of community decency and refused to allow them in the yearbook. Or to even release them to Jeydon's mother.

> Etymological aside:
> *Decent*: polite, moral, honest.
> *Decent*: good enough but not the best.
> *Decent* (archaic): well-formed; handsome.

Please use the word *decent* in a sentence. "Dude, that tux makes you look decent." Or, "Dude, that tux looks pretty decent on you." Also, "Dude, you look decent in that tux."

MY MOTHER didn't use these words. Although I can't remember whether the lapels of the jacket were soft or silky under my fingertips, I remember what she said when she got to the last three photos in the stack of proofs, after all the various poses with the drape—looking left, looking right, looking back over my shoulder—when she got to the last three photos her voice rose half an octave, grew loud, and she said, "What in the world were you thinking?"

Good question, that.

For someone who was forbidden to wear her favored 501s and plaid flannel to school presumably because they accentuated the butch in her, someone who only allowed herself the most cursory of thoughts about what these clothes signified, someone who stood mute, scuffing a toe nervously back and forth across the sidewalk anytime Alison Green stood too close in all her Love's Baby Soft glory, what was I thinking? How did that kid find the courage to ask the photographer if he—and the photographer was a he—to ask if he would take her picture in a tuxedo? Did she find it easier to make the request while the photographer's head was tucked under the black fabric that hung off the box camera? Like the safety of the confessional her father entered on Saturdays, was it somehow easier to say to a face she could not see, *Forgive me Father for I have sinned. It has been six weeks since I last wanted to wear a tuxedo. And Lord, I want to wear one today, too, and be memorialized in color.*

I managed to kiss Alison Green. Once. Awkwardly. As if there is any other way when you are seventeen. Once—again, only once—we spent the night in my double bed, holding hands. Not sleeping and breathing much too quickly. It made sense to show the pictures to her.

"Give me them," she said. "You're getting these, right?"

The instructions that came with the proofs were clear. If you took a photo without paying for it, the company billed you for an entire package. And my mother had already purchased an eight-by-ten, two five-by-sevens, and forty-eight wallet photos twelve-up on a page—all of me in the drape, looking straight on at the camera, chin slightly dipped.

I like to imagine that Alison saw my true self—that my photo must have looked like what I now see in Jeydon's. Unlike Jeydon, though, I am flushed pink from shame and the excitement of transgression, my hair in a short, Farrah Fawcett wave, lips together, mouth turned up in a slight enigmatic smile. An image lost to fear and the chemical decomposition of a stack of photos from the San Marin High School class of 1983.

WHAT I WON'T WEAR

Mac or Bobbi Brown. Maybelline and Cover Girl are out, too. Although, Estée Lauder and L'Oréal make excellent moisturizers and everyone needs well-hydrated skin. And sometimes, I'll wear a little Aveda brand lipstick just to freak out my girlfriend and because, in a strange way, it's almost gender bending.

Mini-, midi-, or maxi-skirts. A-line, drop-waisted, jumper, or sun-dresses. A shirtwaist, a sheath, or a shift. A cocktail dress or a ball gown. A Kitty Foyle or a St. John's Knit. A tunic. A crinoline. A bustle. That said, I don't mind wrapping a sarong around my waist (and over my shorts) to visit Catholic cathedrals in Latin countries. It's sort of my butch version of a skort. Although, it's not exactly flattering.

A twinset, cap-sleeved T-shirts, or anything called a blouse. A chemise, a spaghetti-strap tank top, or a tube top. A smock or a turtleneck (because I'm not a painter and my neck's too short). A shirt with a Peter Pan collar. A choli or anything where my midriff hangs out.

Nylons, thigh-high or otherwise. Of course, Spanx are a miracle of modern technology for which our forbears fought—a twenty-first century alternative to the merry widow—and which I believe have their place in the well-dressed butch's wardrobe.

Court shoes or elevator shoes. Platforms, stilettos, or kitten heels. No to mules and pumps, too. No to Manolo Blahnik, Jimmy Choo, Charles Jourdan, Christian Louboutin, and Bruno Magli. Unless you're talking about his two-tone oxford or the big-buckled chunky-heeled loafer. But you're not, are you? You mean his wedges and his spectator pumps, don't you? In which case, no means no.

WHAT I WILL WEAR

It's fraught for all sorts of reasons.

Because when I came out it was not politically correct to be butch or femme—buying into the dominant paradigm of gender expectations and all that. Because I have been socialized as a woman even as I have railed against the Maybelline, and MAC and all those ridiculous outfits that require you to sit with your thighs demurely pressed together. Because—and it pains me most to admit this one—I care what you think. I want you to like me and not judge me simply because I favor patterned ties in a double Windsor knot.

It's easy to dress for everyday. There's no issue with slim-fit, colored chinos—especially if they have a button fly. Burnt umber, cobalt, sage green, fire truck red, and aubergine, all hang in my closet. A hard finish so the pants wear well is preferable, but brushed twill is all right, too. Everyone is wearing these now. Even Costco sells Gloria Vanderbilt colored jeans for women. And if I wear mine rolled at the hem like a J.Crew male model or a Kennedy summering at Hyannis Port you likely won't even notice.

Special events are more, shall we say, challenging. Do I wear the black, summer-weight wool, pin-striped pants, custom-made for my five-foot-four frame? Blue or black twill pants, the de rigueur look of business casual? Plain front or pleated? I'm starting to cross that gender line—now you're going to notice.

Crew neck T-shirts, I favor these. Long sleeve is, more often than not, better than short. (Somehow it's more formal and completes my favored highbrow/lowbrow look—jeans, a T-shirt, and an expensive vest or blazer.) Of course, I also like hip shirts cut from Italian cotton, and made by Bugatchi Uomo, Duchamp, or Robert Graham. Something with subtle checks, reversed-out cuffs and collars, and square buttons, something that when paired with my perpetually flushed Irish cheeks and soft face gives me a gender-bending look. I'm afraid you'll notice my transgression, but I also love to transgress. See, I told you it's fraught.

But now the tie, bow and otherwise. Patterned more often than not. This is the big one. A tie is like a big fucking billboard that says, "Ask me about my gender identification!" Here's the rationalization that I make each time I'm standing in the mirror, collar up, tying under, over, behind, and through: A patterned tie is ornamental, and loose at the neck, charming, less chance of people thinking you're just an angry dyke trying to make a point. And please don't call me that unless you are. A dyke, I mean. Straight people—even liberal ones—don't get to use that word.

The shoes. Ropers and cowboy boots can work. Frye boots if it's a hipster event—same thing with biker toe black oxfords. For meeting clients or dinners out, suede wingtips or saddle shoes with outrageously garish laces are stylish and whimsical. Wingtips made with shiny Cordovan leather dyed tobacco brown or midnight black are too much. Too much what, I'm not entirely sure. Too butch, yes. Too gender non-conforming when paired with the rest of my ensemble, sure. Too much of an in-your-face statement, maybe. Even though these shoes feel right on me, I don't think I have the ego-strength to carry off wearing them.

Finally, the foundation. Boxers or briefs? Sports or push-up bra? Wouldn't you like to know.

Joan Wickersham

Mom x 3

I. THE WAR

Neither of you ever called it a war, but that's what it was. It went on for more than thirty years. It was fierce, grim, and unevenly paced. There would be a series of bloody battles and then an exhausted silence. There were moments of truce. The most violent assaults were followed by periods of confusion: the two of you wandering through an unrecognizable bombed landscape not knowing where you were, how you'd gotten there, what the war was about, who wanted what. Had your mother actually thrown a box of Ring Dings at your head? Had you—not then, but three decades later, in the parking lot of a Publix supermarket in Florida—really told her to go fuck herself?

Nobody won, nobody lost. Nobody learned anything. Nobody added up the cost and realized it wasn't worth it. The two of you just kept blundering into skirmish after skirmish, because that was all you knew how to do.

There was a time before the war. A golden summer idyll when you were a skinny, tanned, quick little kid, when you didn't much like food and regarded meals as annoying time-wasters. There must have been a beginning; one of you fired the first shot—you ate something, she said something, which must have felt, to the other person, like an act of aggression.

Or maybe the first volley was exchanged because she saw your body growing, rounding, chunking up—she'd been patrolling the border, on the lookout for this sort of unrest. She saw movement in the bushes and shouted, "Halt!" When the movement continued, what could she do but squeeze the trigger?

She said, "Do you want to roll down the street? Do you? Do you?" She said, "I'm going to send you to fat-girl camp! Is that what you want?" If you just glowered at her, she kept on asking. "Is it? *Is that what you want?*" If you slammed out of the room she followed you. "You think this is *funny*? You think I'm kidding? I'm picking up the phone and calling one of the fat-girl camps in the *New York Times*, and then we'll see how funny you think this is." You and she both knew she would never pick up the phone.

Why did it matter? Why were the two of you so ferocious, so tenacious, so angry? You were both lucky compared to most people. The world was full of problems, things to be troubled by. So what if you got fat? The stakes were small and personal: it was a territory dispute, about your body and who owned it. Was it yours? Hers? Something shared—a colony inhabited by you, but that she felt she had the right to govern?

No matter how mad you got, you never pointed out that she was fat. No one in your family ever mentioned it. This piece of ground was a minefield. You never walked on it, and pretended not to know that anything was buried there.

2. THE DRESSING ROOM

All that flesh in the dressing room. She pulled and twisted her way out of her own clothes and into the ones she was trying on, red-faced, messy-haired, and panting. "Polyester," she hissed at the mirror, glaring at herself, and at the reflection of you, sitting on a little stool in the corner, pressed against the wall. "Do you see this? This is all they make in my size. Do you see?"

You saw her shape and her skin, her belly with its violent red horizontal line—the bite-mark of her slip's waistband—and its rutted purple scars, appendix, gallbladder (*I almost died. You were too young to remember, but I was so sick, I had to have a nurse. My mother came to help, but then she expected me to wait on her, I said, Mama I can hardly walk, and she said, What do you mean, you're young. At your age I was taking care of five children and my mother*). Her brassiere, another hiss the way she said it, brah-*zeeeeer*; and it looked violent too, a siege fortress girded with hooks and straps and seams. Sometimes she took it off, to try on new ones, and then you didn't know where to look: the dressing room and the mirror both full of spilling enormous pink-tipped flesh, of bending and cupping and adjusting. "Jesus Christ," she said. "Look at that. Just look. Why do I even bother."

Sometimes you tried to tell her she looked nice. You didn't know if this was the truth or a lie, you just wanted so badly to make her feel better. "Really? You really think so?" she said. But also, "You don't know. You don't know." Sometimes she moaned, "How did this happen? I used to be so beautiful. Do you believe that?" And, "This is why I can't look for a job. Who would hire me, with clothes like this?" And always, "Polyester. *Polyester*"— you were terrified and wanted to laugh, but you knew not to. You were eight, ten, fourteen; this went on for years.

She sat in dressing rooms with you, too, when you were trying on clothes. "Oh," she said during the bathing suits. And, "Lose it while you're young. Please. It gets so much harder when you're older." What she said didn't touch you. Her body was solid and permanent and hers; yours was yours and still changing, still fluid.

You would never let it harden. Someday you would shed this, your chunky young self, and move lightly into your own sleek permanence.

Meanwhile she kept taking you with her into dressing rooms. She needed a companion, a witness. She needed to warn and save you. "Is this what you want?" she kept asking, looking in the mirror. "Is it?" She expected you to answer. It felt artificial, like a play. Her part was to ask you over and over again if this was what you wanted, and your part was to say no, no, no.

3. WHAT DIDN'T COUNT

According to your mother: Chocolate after the dentist. Chocolate after the doctor. Chocolate on Christmas and Easter. Cake on your birthday or someone else's birthday. Ice cream to go with the cake. Ice cream when you were sick. Apple crisp in October, toasted marshmallows in July. Anything people served you when you were visiting them and anything, homemade or store-bought, they brought to your house. None of this was arbitrary. If you had asked about anything on this list, she would have had a reason. Reward. Reward. Of course, of course, of course. Medicine. Seasonal. Good manners.

Calories counted. She had some little books, their pages dense with columns, calorie counts of everything. She kept buying them, as if hoping to find a book with happier numbers, better news. But the news was always the same. Baked potato with butter, 362 calories. Baked potato with sour cream and chives, 393. Baked potato plain, 290. She had another book called *Calories Don't Count*, and some Weight Watchers cookbooks, which said nothing about calories but tallied everything up in points.

You were allowed to have one cupcake. Two cookies. If you asked for more, she got angry. If you sneaked them out of the box while she wasn't home, she knew—she had counted them, before she left.

None of this counted on winter mornings when she melted brown sugar on oatmeal laced with dates, or melted butter in Wheatena, or melted Hershey's kisses in Cream of Wheat. Her mother had done these things: this was how these things were done.

The one day your mother hadn't called her mother, a long time ago, her mother had died. "It's like all the other times didn't count," she told you—she told you this story for years, for the rest of her life. She was almost pleading, she wanted something.

"Of course they did," you said.

"You'll understand when I'm dead. When it's too late."

"Oh, shut up."

"You're a terrible daughter, you say such terrible things to me."

"What about all the nice things I say?"

"Shut up," she said.

Years later when you first met your husband, he couldn't believe the way you and your mother yelled at each other. He'd grown up in a house where yelling meant divorce, where nobody ever said "I hate you" but they did. The first time he heard you and your mother fighting, he didn't say anything, but you could tell afterward how spooked he was. You told him not to worry. His eyes were wide, he was shifting from foot to foot like a frightened horse. "It's okay," you said. "It's just how we talk to each other. It doesn't really count." You were sure, pretty sure, that this was true. She was downstairs, not crying anymore, making pot roast and baking gingerbread in honor of his visit; the house smelled rich and spicy and full of her mercies and grievances, her rules and rulings and dispensations, her way, her life, her multitudes.

Suzanne Berne

Gifts

DURING MOST OF THE YEAR my mother cannot give me any-thing, except by mail, and so our relationship remains decorous, though she does offer advice over the phone, about vitamin sup-plements she thinks I should take, for instance; but this sort of offering I can accept with grace, and at the end of these phone conversations I thank her and tell her I love her. When I hang up I feel well behaved and even grateful, having left her with the impression that she's given me something of value, which I don't then have to throw away. My mother is an unusually sweet and generous person. That her generosity creates tension between us confuses and causes both of us some grief.

My mother owns a summerhouse on Cape Cod, a gray-shingled saltbox surrounded by hydrangeas and English ivy tum-bling down the retaining wall, the sort of charming old house that hints at civilized leisure—croquet and badminton on the back lawn, handsome long-limbed people in rumpled linen clothing reading Tolstoy in hammocks, lobster dinners served on scrubbed oilcloth lit by antique glass hurricane lamps. Open the front door, however, and one confronts a musty wilderness, a dense thicket of mildewed throw pillows, inflatable beer coolers, scarified plastic place mats, dingy stuffed animals, sandy carpet squares, musical fly swatters, chipped china vases. Gifts. Treasures my mother has found in thrift stores and yard sales and flea markets and has given my sisters and me over the years, things that we have left behind or outright rejected. So these offerings collect here, in what has become a shrine of sorts, presided over by the cheerful, affectionate, capacious spirit of my mother, goddess-like both in the intensity of her generosity and her disregard for whether anyone benefits from it.

Already this morning, even before I had coffee, my mother offered me a set of china salt-and-pepper shakers shaped like spotted mushrooms. Also a black Orlon sweater appliquéd with sequined butterflies. Summer after summer, the front door bangs open and a moment later she sings out, "I've found something I think you'll like!" and then, with her lovely, sweet smile, she pulls from a plastic bag something I do not like, have never liked, never will like.

Each offering is followed by discouragement: "Mom, I don't need a teapot decorated with yellow smiley faces." Or: "I am not a size sixteen, Mom." Or: "I don't wear Argyll knee socks." Her lovely mouth turns down at the corners. "Really? But it seemed like something you would like." Sometimes I try evasive tactics. "Why don't you offer it to . . . ?" I name one of my sisters, or my husband, even one of my children. "It's very nice, Mom," I just said of the Orlon butterfly sweater, "but I just don't think I'll wear it." Her face fell. "Really? But it seems—" Before she could finish, I suggested she give it to our neighbor, who is eighty-six and has failing eyesight.

I am perfectly aware of how churlish I sound. My mother has provided us with a summerhouse on Cape Cod, for Pete's sake. What's a few musical flyswatters? One has only to think of immigrant parents and their first-generation American children to acknowledge that many parents and children can have different sensibilities. My mother is from Largesse; her children are from Ingratitude, a narrow country where it's customary to walk around with one's nose in the air.

Because clearly the problem of my mother's generosity lies with me, and my aspirations to join the patrician croquet-playing phantoms rising from the English ivy, the blue hydrangeas, the old sugar maple shading the semicircular driveway. I do sometimes read Tolstoy in the hammock and would not be averse to owning a pair of antique glass hurricane lamps.

But could the problem also be that my mother's gifts conjure an utterly different daughter than the one she has, even setting aside those genteel ambitions? A sturdy, sunny daughter, who joyfully accepts an extra-large fuchsia T-shirt commemorating a software convention in Philadelphia and three pairs of mix-and-match rainbow-colored shell earrings. An upbeat gal who hails from Scranton or Duluth and works as a sales representative or in the hospitality business and who, like my mother, never misses a good parade or a band concert and thinks bus tours to the Grand Canyon are a hoot—this is her daughter, this easy-going populist. Until I have to disappoint her again and reveal the snobbish changeling in the hammock, sulking behind *The Death of Ivan Ilyich*, the refuser of day-old doughnuts and thrift-store bathing suits and a ceramic cookie jar shaped like a cow in a milkmaid's outfit.

"I grew up during the Depression," my mother often comments at these junctures, with sad complacency. "I know the value of things."

And she does. More is more, especially if you can get it for nothing, or next to it, which is why most of our kitchen appliances are from the swap shop. As for gifts, my mother knows it's the thought that counts, and that more is always more when it comes to thinking of her children, even if those children bear only passing resemblance to the ones with whom she is eating dinner.

When it comes to love, more is always more.

And all happy families are alike in each being unhappy in its own way.

Here, of course, is where this essay should end, in a plangent celebration of love, no matter what form it takes, because there's never enough of it. That I believe this to be true doesn't soothe the cranky frustrations of being loved for who you are not. As Tolstoy observed in *Anna Karenina*, an observation probably directed to his mother, "When you love someone, you love the person as they are, and not as you'd like them to be." Although perhaps such an accommodating regard is possible only by the light of an antique hurricane lamp.

We all live with shades of ourselves, projected by other people. We also live with the ghosts of our own hopes and fears. Coexistence, therefore, becomes the issue. In my case, the brooding Tolstoyan rides forever beside the affable buyer for Walmart, fraternal twins on an existential bus tour (a seating arrangement Tolstoy himself would applaud, by the way), passing through deserts and forests, stopping at monuments and natural wonders and Atlantic City, incomprehensible to each other, but sharing a window, and occasionally a bag of barbecue-flavored potato chips, which neither of us likes, but they were two for one at the grocery store. A gift from my mother for the daughter she loves.

Naomi Shihab Nye

Thanksgiving Picnic

MY DREAM OF A PERFECT HOLIDAY is to bypass tradition, make
your own tradition. Gather the simplest picnic—apples, cheeses,
cucumbers, thick bread, the last arugula leaves plucked from the
garden and rinsed, maybe homemade oat cookies—a jug of cran-
berry lemonade on ice, a faded tablecloth, and make a short drive
(under two hours) to a town in which you have no relatives or
friends. Names like Shiner and Gonzales, Texas, come to mind.

On the way to this town, you find yourselves stopping at a We
Trust You to Pay vegetable stand where you stuff five bucks into
a tin container for a fistful of beets and some new potatoes. (This
can be dinner, when you get home.) You pause at the monument
for the hero Juan Seguín, which you never read before. You had
no idea he championed literacy. You discover a ruined mansion
tangled in vines.

In Cuero, a man and his son are standing on a corner trying
to sell a lawn mower. You talk about them for miles—why would
they be doing this right now, on this day? Desperation for a big

dinner? Are they sad? Meandering on back roads without traffic feels rich, involves no arguments, no replays of history, no obsessive planning, and no overeating.

You will be the only contender for the town's picnic table. Next to the river, in front of the old brewery, in the fat shade of an autumn tree, by the tombstones beyond the train tracks, spread out the cloth. Do this with your longtime darling and maybe your grown child, if he is available. Squirrels will come to stare at you. Birds dipping down. Two feral cats will creep through tall grasses, wait for a crust.

After your languid picnic, and some tasty talk, in which everything you've worried about for the last few months feels suddenly cleansed and simplified, you feed the cats and squirrels, fold the tablecloth, and wander the little streets of the town visiting with locals who are already out in their yards, dozing in hammocks to escape doing dishes, playing badminton, sullenly drinking beer after fighting with cousins and brothers. They are so ready to talk to anyone they have never seen before. They jump over to the fence to say, Hey. You can give the last cookies to the oldest man who lives alone, who is sitting in a rusty lawn chair in front of his hoarder's porch in the middle of his sidewalk. "I hate holidays," he says, when you ask how he is. "I refuse to go to anyone's home for a feast I don't like." When you offer the cookies, he says, "Now that I like. Were your hands clean when you made them?" These people tell you peculiar personal things because they will never see you again. They are relieved to have a new pair of listening ears. You have no expectations. They won't believe you came to their town on THAT DAY for no particular reason. They will stare at you hard, slightly jealous at your open-ended calm.

Joe Bonomo

The Blur Family

THE PHOTOGRAPH IS SO GRAINY it looks like a sand painting. A family of ten circling platters and plates of food at a Thanksgiving table, sometime in the early 1970s. The scene's poorly lit, the shot is poorly composed—I'm imagining mom used a cheap plastic camera that she purchased at Peoples Drugs—yet the dissolving faces are beaming in the low resolution, warm, a snug circle. What's odd is the angle of the lens; it tilts the scene forward so that everything threatens to spill out of the frame—one tip from behind and the table will go tumbling. In the small room the family's crowded together at one end (*so I can fit all of you in!*) as if they're holding on underneath, steadying the table, the tall candlesticks, the dinner plates. The faces are barely faces at all. Not bathed by a flash, the countenances glow anyway, pillowy masks, dreamy abstractions hovering gently over varying body types, the details of noses, eyes, teeth, hair obscured. The more we rub our eyes to see, the less distinct the world is. Blurred faces around a Thanksgiving table: an archetype rendered beyond archetype into a kind of found art.

I know this family. For many years they lived in the cul-de-sac behind us, in Wheaton, Maryland. When I was ten or eleven they moved to a new, larger home in a far-flung suburban town north of Wheaton. My parents would take me and my younger brother to parties there on St. Patrick's Day, where at night we'd swim in a heated outdoor pool. Moved away: we can do it physically, but the imagination calls us back to where we started. They'll always live in the cul-de-sac in Hippocampus, Everywhere, in an eternally messy house, nine kids banging around making noise and mayhem. The grainy photographs prove it.

RECENTLY THE SMALL, face-shaped smudge in the bottom right corner of the photo made contact with me on Facebook. A friend request after more than thirty years. His profile picture was blank, or, more accurately, generic, that mysterious silhouette that brands Facebook members who've yet to upload profile photos, a string of faceless thousands looming on walls and in message threads. I checked: he still hasn't uploaded a profile pic. He remains an outline into which I can paint my many drafts of him. I spotted among his online friends his younger sister (she's the tiny blur in the top left of the Thanksgiving photo, sitting on her oldest blur's lap), and dashed off to her a quick message, sharing my memories of riding bikes with her and with Silhouette Brother, playing bocce ball in the yard, darting through the expansive woods behind their house. She wrote back. We friended each other. I accessed her photos, recent ones, and saw a woman in her mid-forties resembling vaguely the skinny colt who pranced in front of me down the trails, on the sidewalks. She's smiling a lot now, which is nice. She seems well-adjusted, surrounded by family and friends.

The lens turned and focused. Her fuzzy outline at the table sharpened into a real face, from abstract to representational. That I have difficulty matching up the two versions of my former neighbor—the girl then, the woman now—is, of course, my problem, and a precious one at that. Why do I prefer her in the photo of her blurred family? In many ways the image is a comforting placeholder, a moment in time secured in youthful anti-knowledge of the future's complexity, a family of young people I recall as still young, still laughing, still wandering eagerly around the annual block parties on their cul-de-sac, bikes and Big Wheels, fireflies and dusk. But there's more: I *love* the photo of the Blur family, the timeless happenstance of a cheap camera and low lighting, a smear of particulars that somehow cheers me. Their eyes are gone, dimmed to nothing, but that's not creepy; their smiles are sullied, darkened dots-per-inch, but that's not melancholy. What I love about the photograph is what trendy nostalgia-mill digital applications such as Hipstamatic and Instagram cash in on: a tumble into the comfort of a gauzy, sentimentalized past paradoxically made softer by a Polaroid's harshness, scratchy film that nonetheless soothes in its promises of eternal adolescence and a vanishing point that never arrives.

"Instead of just recording reality, photographs have become the norm for the way things appear to us, thereby changing the very idea of reality and of realism."

That's Sontag. I think about this a lot in relation to memory's slide shows. More accurately: nostalgia, that gateway drug to solipsism and sentimentality. There's nothing static about a memory, and yet I stop and stare. I pretend that a memory remains as still and compliant as a photo, but a memory is not a photograph: a memory morphs, slipping undetected from one side of the brain to the other and back again, excising plot lines, adding characters, altering the personal politics of the figures. Though memories retell themselves at every opportunity, shape-shifters that can't be trusted, they do, after Sontag, become the norm for the way things appear. They do change the very idea of reality. What's real becomes *what-was* which becomes *what-is*. Try and frame that.

LOOKING AT RECENT IMAGES of my neighbor, her face lifted out from another decade, now strikingly contemporary and detailed, brought something else into focus. One afternoon, decades ago, her older brother and I took her into the woods behind her house where her brother yanked down her shorts and scrawled a word on her buttocks with a black Magic Marker. She squirmed and resisted, and dashed off crying after he'd (we'd) finished. A small childhood transgression that becomes eternal, its retelling shaming me with each half-remembered version, incriminating me in violence and bullying. I've thought about this incident often, naming the participants, implicating myself—but that was before I saw the girl, the woman, in her present life. Before, I had only the blur, the reassuring haze which erased her features, replaced her worrying cries with the whoops of playdates, her urgent escape from the woods with cartwheels into suburbia. Now she's looking at me from last week, not last century. I don't know if she remembers, or what reality her memories may have altered. Her brother who friended me on Facebook—he was the one with the Magic Marker—is still little more than a generic silhouette. And I'm relieved. If he ever updates his profile pic, I may turn the other way, preferring the blur to the clarity.

Judith Kitchen

Who

OH MY GOD, who is she? I want her for my own. I want her affinity with all those chickens, her lopsided leaning, her house all atilt. I want that tipping chimney and the angle of her neck as she lets one hen push its way into her heart, another pose as a hat. I want

that practical dress and the long black stockings, even the sensi-
ble shoes. The light that fattens itself on late-afternoon windows,
and the shadows that lengthen the yard. The chickens that peck at
their shadows, whittling away at their lives. Look at the way light
catches each shingle, each brick, each clapboard lining the side of
the house. Look at it fasten itself to the folds of her skirt.

This was a moment—the day of the chickens. But all days were
chickens, scattering feed, and gathering eggs. Off lens: the hen-
house with its strange, musty odors. Off lens: the rustle of worry
at the doorway, the nattering fuss as her fingers sift through straw.
Chore after chore. The lifetime that added more, and then more.

I want this moment, but not what it stands for. Want one minute of overlapping shadow, one slapdash second of light. Quick,
while she has a perch on pleasure. Quick, before her tiny breasts
grow bigger, before she lifts up her hand to lift down that feathery
weight.

Sonja Livingston

A Thousand Mary Doyles

THERE SHE IS, Mary Doyle, and another right beside her. Heads turned for one last view of land before the Cork coastline slips out of sight. Dishwater strands pushed behind her ears, yellow curls pulled up under a hat, dark frizz flying in the wind. She is seventeen. She is twenty-two. She is just yesterday turned twenty-nine. Look at her now, studying the sky in place of crying, trying to remember what everyone has said, begging Mary-the-most-holy-mother-of-God they might make it across the ocean alive.

She leaves behind her favorite cow and the kitchen garden she's been fighting for years. She leaves behind her mother's grave, her sister's face, her Uncle Timmo's way with the plow. She leaves behind the traveling priest, the Sunday Masses, and the words to every song she knows, my apple tree, my brightness, and oh ro, soon shall I see them, the pretty laments and the keening, and Mr. Byrne with the tin whistle, and here it comes now, her father's hand, swollen and cracked as it is, the way he held it to her, her father's hand, soft as old cloth against her cheek.

She leaves behind the big house on the hill and the splintered wheel leaning against Coughlan's cottage, will it oh will it ever get fixed? And the marsh violet and the burnet rose and the black-thorn too sometimes, the patchwork of fields, and the baby Lizzie with her dark eyes and funny ways—what will the little one be like as she grows? And the Abbey, of course, what times they had there, the slick moss and cold stone, and her best friend, Birdy, who swears upon her life she will write but both girls know how these things go, a few long letters at first, the distance between them widening as the world settles into the spaces made by those who leave until words are folded less often into envelopes, because if there's one thing everyone knows it's that when someone leaves Ballyhaunis, sure enough, she's gone for good.

Mary Doyle.

Come from Moycullen from Westmeath and Usher's Quay. Come from Poulnamuck, Gweesalia, and Tourmakeady. From Clongeen, Collooney, and Cahermacrea. From Kilkelly and Kilmeena, Ballina and Bonniconlon. From Portlaoise, Mount-shannon and Roscommon. From Donoughmore, Dún Laoghaire, and Drogheda.

That one there with the reddish hair, the tall one with the over-proud back, the one gone flat against the rail, trying her best to hide the sight of a broken shoe under her trunk, fan of fingers placed upon her brow. That one. And that one. And then again that one too. Sailed in 1851. Sailed in 1847. Left from Queenstown in 1869.

See her now, stepping from the gangway, swaying a bit as her feet reach solid land. That's her there, scanning the crowd for the sight of a familiar face. And here we are. We can't call out, yet she stands before us on a ship. Every girl bound for Boston, New York, and the upper St. Lawrence. Let us stop now and look into her face, if only in this moment, for she belongs to each of us does our girl Mary Doyle.

Josette Kubaszyk

Swing

WHAT GIRL BEFORE NEEDED a flat-board swing hanging in grey twisted braids from that towering red oak? The swing I first met when we came, even before we moved, on that day we came to see what would be our home. Up on the high ground, above the salamander wall, before I knew it was the salamander wall (*did she know about the salamander?*), where the three old oaks shadow the point of lawn between the highway and the road. It was that first day I met somebody else's swing, the first thing I remember. And all she ever left us.

She must have loved that suspended board like a stowaway would a steamer trunk. The swing where sometimes now I sway, swooping forward, falling back, swooping forward, falling back, humming the rhythm of the wind. A dusty bowl beneath the seat patters tales of bare feet and sweeping journeys to the sky, high above the nesting owls and clammy salamander rocks. I wonder if she traveled to China in that seat, over the Pacific Rim, around the Arctic Circle, into the land of Never Never.

I wonder if she laid her belly flat across the wooden board, draping like a boy's limp familiar cat and twisted, twisted, twisted the ropes in tiny circles around and around and around until her toes could barely touch and the ropes were tight as knots and then let go—spinning spinning spinning fast ponytails whipping horizontal branches sky and dusty earth and dizzy dizzy dizzy and the mossy blurring bark until her eyes and mind and breathless belly hollered *Stop!* When she'd had enough. But her world maintained its whirring, all the time going round and round and round and round.

Emily Holt

Hunger

Arklow, **An tInbhear Mór**, *The Great Estuary*

One never manages to determine the instant when a stimulus once seen is seen no longer.

—Maurice Merleau-Ponty.

ARKLOW—the beautiful word conceals, starting as it does with the soft *a* and ending open, evoking the bows of fiddle strings, windows to the sea.

Arklow—the squat white and pink houses at the edge of the prisoner's window. He's lined up pills on the windowsill. Not yet awake, he thinks he'll rise and see the sea, knowing, knowing it's only the River Avoca, *smothered river, battle-worn river, the meeting of the waters.*

Arklow—all word and image, but here, they're not the same. The language is in the mind, but the mind paints, used to telling itself a good story, waiting for the ship, the guard, the execution.

Image—what but memory? The moment before light enters the eye, we hope to be astonished, lie and say we want pattern.

Public—the white gothic arches of Shelton Abbey where prisoners raise cattle for Africa; a vale of two lakes, the one always hidden in fog; the pottery shop at the bottom of the town; men smoking in the old shipyard, huddled and cursing the coalfish, the rockling, the bare waters.

Private—the house on Main Street, Arklow, February 1996. Into the cease-fire, and does that matter here, where a child peers past a wisp of white hair to an ice-water bath? Does it matter when, still, there's the sense one could be made to freeze or drown, any minute? Door open to the yard, the smell of turf saying *Return*. Not *Go back* but *Come back*. Gate open to a street of sixteen pubs. Our pub—Kitty's, where the children go too. Beyond, the hills, the Wicklow Mountains. The Mottie Stone. Back down in the valley, The Orchard, blood in the lambing sheds. Beds that dip in the middle. A mother stationed in an armchair by a false fireplace. She announces to the room, 'The hall-door is crooked.' *Crooked*, she says, insistent. *Sober*, she says. Insistent, the sibilant *s* and clatter of *t*, the sounds of a scold, wind in silver firs.

Here, in Arklow, sound is everything, each word a veil for a thing too-fragile, raw at the edges. The session, the screaming. A drunken cousin cooing 'Hush Little Baby,' rocking the two-year-old niece she just met. Inventing lyrics that turn dirty, echo the grunts in the driveway below. A child whose mother, and father, will leave her. Others say, *drink*, *bipolar*. We're up to date, though our patterns persist. Headlights flash on the cemetery, below, where, if I lived here, I would be buried. The sound of a heel slipping on concrete, a gasp. Guttural. No sense to it. Rubbish.

Still, we're flush with speech. We try to choose, sort *illness* and *prison* from *come* and *yes*, cut *wait* from *leave*, listen for the unsaid edge: *suicide*. One that rises like bile, like whiskey, swiftly and inevitably. Act or accident? Climbing over a fence, a man leans on a gun. Where's the logic, the movement? Where are the wooden fences, in this country of wire? Where did the bullet enter? Hand, rib, stomach? Could he still feel his hunger then? Past and present, *hunger* infuses it all. Bread dipped in tea, beer batter licked off paper. Sexual hunger. Spiritual hunger. No specific word for satiation. Just, *Come back, please, come back.* Here, it's never just one place. Each one gnaws at your hand. Exile is built-in, desired as much as required. We're indirect, all possibilities running off in rivers that splinter the country, because who would want to choose just one river?

One river means one house means one cell means one grave. So many ways, so many rooms to keep passion from spilling over the walls. If river is town is prison, do we enter it to slow the suicide? Do we wear the town to slow the desire? Images cascade, converge, fall apart. And I'm left with one human life tucked away in the pubs, the shops, the petrol station. Arklow. At the top of the town—two housing estates divided by a field. A dumpster at the edge. Footprints that round out where green metal feet rise from the mud. Round marks—where knees could go.

Paul Lisicky

A Phone Call with My Father

"MAYBE THAT'S THE WAY TO GO," my father says. "All at once you're flat on your back and speechless, listening to your upstairs neighbor go on."

"What exactly did you say to her?" I say.

He pauses, as if he's trying to ground himself, before acting it out, as a storyteller would. "I said, 'Listen. Ethel. You're going to see your mother, your father, and your husband soon. Your older sister, and the cat you used to feed. Everyone you ever knew and missed.' And she gripped my hand as hard as she could and looked me straight in the eye.' And that was that. And wouldn't you know that's when the stupid ambulance pulls up."

"And you're sure she wanted to see these people? What if she couldn't stand her mother?"

But I should be quiet already. The truth is, I'm wondering where *he's* gone. Where's the father who used to insist that when you're dead you're dead, even as he took us, week after week, to church?

"What's religion have to do with it?"

"I'm just saying I think it's important that what you say in that kind of situation be exactly right. Not everyone believes in a Heaven."

"Okay, Mister You-Have-All-the-Answers. Who'd *you* want to see?"

And that stops me. Not because I can't begin to form the words I'd want to make, and not because I'm stumped (this face and that face come flying toward me like snow) but because she's right there with him in the next room, waiting for him to bring her a cup of something warm. But it isn't my father my mother wants, not the man she's lived with fifty-one years, but Lulu or Bernice, or whatever new name she'll give him tonight. And I'd be lying to you if my father and I don't shake our heads and laugh some about this, especially on a good day, when her neck isn't hurting, or when she isn't talking too much about her mother, and how she'd be able to see her if she just had the energy to walk to the other side of the road.

Is that how we want to go, with most of our memory scraped? Think of how it was to live just seconds after we entered the world. Our senses so raw, they couldn't get enough of things.

This is the day the Lord has made.

Now I wonder if I'd recognize her if I saw her again. I mean the old mother. Walking down the highway with suitcase in hand. Would she even stop to talk if I said hello?

Maybe we all made her up, that lady who shared our house, and put on red lipstick, and told us she was proud of us.

"Aside from her," my father says finally, quiet now, as if trying to make things simpler.

*

Sometime before the first life became the next life—though there were never really two lives, even as we talk about them like that—

my mother walked up to him with wonder and alarm in her eyes. "What is it, hon?" he said, startled, without the old impatience we'd grown so used to. "You look funny." And it was true: her green eyes looked clearer than they'd looked in weeks. Without even waiting for her reply, he knew she knew there was a stranger in her kitchen. And though she might have said, "Get out of my house," she reached for his hand and held it. They stood like that for a while, leaning into the refrigerator, nodding, as she pressed that hand to her side. And though I know not the details, and know not the new name she called him, I picture my father leading my mother down the hall past the place where the piano used to be. And the story of whatever happened inside the bedroom carried them together for a long, long time, even after things got worse, even after my mother started telling people in the lobby of her building, with an exhilarated hush, "A man has moved into our apartment and I think I really like him."

Fifty-one years of arguments: gone like that.

And Jesus appeared before him with his shining body: *Put your hand into my side if you believe.*

Dinah Lenney

Future Imperfect

Dinah

Comment [1]:
Other possible titles:
Future Past
Future Terrible
Fast Forward
Track Changes

HIGH SUMMER on a crowded beach in Massachusetts. A little girl, six or seven, in a red bathing suit, presses shells into the sides of an elaborate sand castle, while a man trudges up and back from the shoreline, a plastic pail in each hand, to fill their sizable moat. The girl has sand in her hair. Freckles on her nose. Her shoulders are sunburned, perhaps, and once the moat is full, likely as not the man orders her up the beach to put on a T-shirt. And yes, she can wear it in the water, why not? He removes his glasses then, puts them down on a towel, and races her to the waves.

*

Someone asks: *How do you remember?*
Answer: I concentrate! I hurl myself back; I wade in, I dive under—I use my imagination.
Someone else asks (looking to trip me up?): *How do you mean you use your "imagination"?*
Why—why, the focusing of the lens with language—

the fixing on an image and getting it right in a sentence—isn't that an act of imagination?

Someone scoffs, or teases, or is, perhaps, genuinely curious: *Why don't you just make it up?*

AS IF I'M NOT MAKING IT UP every day—as if that weren't the truth of how we live, isn't it? Aren't we making it up? Can I ever have been that young (was that really me?)? Although I don't much question the fact of my youth—not so much as I *will* anyway, so I'm told, when I'm *old*. Speaking of which, can I possibly be as old as I am (is *this* me?)?—and growing older all the time? (*This* I do think about: *How will it be?*)

> **Dinah**
>
> **Comment [2]:** Will I have had my knees replaced? If so—and this is good news—I'll be able to get down on the floor with my grandchildren, won't I? And we'll play pick-up sticks and Jacks. And I'll push them on the swings, two at a time. And I'll get distracted, remembering other swings, another park, and they'll have to call me back to the present (in the future).

NEVER MIND the things we take for granted (like making it all the way to tomorrow)—as if imagining isn't involuntary, doesn't begin even before I open my eyes: *I'll make the coffee, that's what I'll do*—. Whereas not much imagination required—no great-powers-of, I mean—to *ruin* a day before it starts: *Why did I say I would do x or y . . . How will I ever get everything done?* As if I don't delude myself on a regular basis—in the present, that is—in the moments when I suppose I intuit or understand (talk about imagination), only to find out (in the future) that I didn't know squat.

*

This is the truth of my imagining, okay? Here and now, eyes open, fingers on the keys: Three thousand miles away, he's nodding off in the middle of breakfast—*her* breakfast, that is. She's eating rye toast with Philadelphia cream cheese, which she buys by the tub; she's wearing her nightgown; she smells of sleep and yesterday's scent, dabbed behind her ears. And he: he's arranged a makeshift IV pole, a bag attached to a wire hanger and hooked over the top of the pantry door. He does all this all by himself, by the way (that is a *fact*): he opens two cans of something like baby formula, pours them into a plastic pouch, discreetly unbuttons his pajamas and attaches the tubing to the peg in his stomach. His hair is combed. His face is clean-shaven. He's determined to sit at this table three times a day as if they were sharing a meal. But his breathing is labored through the hole in his neck, and he cannot talk anymore, cannot croak more than three words at a time, since to speak requires him to put his index finger over the hole through which he breathes. And the tumor is growing. And growing.

SO THAT'S WHAT'S HAPPENING now, this morning. And tonight? I can imagine that, too. Having taken three hours to shower and dress, having worked at his desk (at what, Dad? What are you working at? How many times can a man arrange his papers?), having dozed off (for lack of oxygen) at least a dozen times— he will sit with my mother all over again, opposite her most carefully arranged single place setting (good china, wine glass, cloth napkin, salad fork), while she eats her chicken sauté and finishes supper with a tiny cup of Häagen-Dazs vanilla ice cream. She buys them—single servings of Häagen-Dazs—six at a time.

*

I know very well how to imagine—I'm an actor! I was trained to imagine! To imagine the worst, to imagine the best! To systematically kill off every member of my family, or to award myself kudos, prizes, lottery winnings—to indulge in my fantasies, good and bad. To *cultivate* them. Whatever it took to prepare for the scene. No such thing as a bad thought. No misunderstanding or inflating of my powers either. Superstitious as I am, and though I never pass up the opportunity, I don't actually believe in wishing on pennies or eyelashes. Therefore I'm not about to punish myself because I know he's dying; or for saying so out loud; or because I can't stop myself thinking about how it's going to end.

*

Useful quotes:

> *Acting is living truthfully under the given imaginary circumstances.*
>
> —Sanford Meisner

Dinah
Comment [3]: Some discussion of imagination here? As requisite to all genres?—also about remembering v. projecting—is there a difference? Other than tense?

Dinah
Comment [4]: Shall I tell my wish? (Why not: wishes don't come true because we wish them, after all.) I wish for a brilliant review in the NYT for my 5th book. See how crafty I am, having only written three so far?

Dinah
Comment [5]: Smoother transition here? More context?

AND FROM NEUROSCIENTIST Antonio Damasio—

> *[Human beings] live every moment, every*
> *second of our lives poised between the lived past*
> *and the anticipated future.*

AND, Damasio again:

> *Every time you think what you're going to do*
> *next weekend, you're going to put that in your*
> *memory, so you have a memory of the future*
> *that you hope to live.*

> **Dinah**
> **Comment [6]:** Does everyone
> know what this means?
> Should I show instead of tell?
> With a scene about him? In
> which he plans for planting
> his bulbs as if he will see the
> flowers next spring?

*

Reframe, says the therapist.
As if to pretend there's what? A *bright* side?

BUT THERE ISN'T. And I can't. What I can do: I can
imagine that I get to see him once more. That he tells
me he has loved me as his own. As if he has to tell me,
as if I don't know; as if I don't know he *won't* tell me,
that isn't his style. But hasn't he been my father from
very nearly the beginning? And shouldn't that be
enough? And if he cannot remember my birth—well,
neither can I.

BETTER FOR HIM, for my mother—much better—
let him die sooner than later.

THERE. I said it. Let him die today, tonight, tomorrow—that's what he wants, I'm certain it is. That's why he keeps eating—if you call that eating—not in order to *live*. What he wants, rather, is to beat death at its game. To die fully clothed and still able to wipe his own ass. That's why he won't surrender: to surrender now, however dignified a choice, is to surrender to losing the last of his dignity.

*

This here, no less the truth of my imagination, is a fiction: One of my own children has a baby. This would have to be five years from now—or seven, or ten. Old as he is by this time—pushing a hundred years (he was miraculously cured of the cancer after all)—he must be helped into a chair so he can hold the baby: which he does—he holds him or her under the arms, above its baby belly. The afternoon sun falls in a stripe, catches the top of his head, his hair, which is white, and still thick, though the part is wide and pink; and the baby in this admittedly fictional memory of the future (wearing yellow, so as to keep me from getting hung up on whether it's a girl or a boy) blinks and squints and blinks again. Dad holds on so tight—looks so happy and proud—but wait: is he crying? He is. He's crying and my mother is crying and I'm crying, too. Also, I'm laughing. The poor baby looks so uncomfortable—the expression on its face, it's just so funny—but not unhappy. She—he—*it*—would let us know if it were unhappy. That's what babies do.

> **Dinah**
>
> **Comment [7]:** Do I have to say again that this is fiction? *Is* it?

*

The phone rings. Once—twice—in the time it takes for me to pick up the receiver, just before the third ring, I've already received the news: He died in his sleep. He died peacefully. As soon as I get off the phone I'll call American, I ought to have plenty of miles—

HELLO, I say.

And it *is* my mother. But she only wants to tell me that they're driving to the country for the weekend. He wants to see his garden. He wants to check the fruit trees, which should be blooming by now.

*

Here's what else I imagine—here's what I hope: that I *don't* get to see him one last time.

> **Dinah**
>
> **Comment [8]:** Except I so much want to see him. But does he want to see me? This is a whole other kind of conjecture, to try to imagine what he's thinking and feeling and whether and what he dreams—

THAT A YEAR FROM now, the funeral behind us, I visit my mother. That she is well—not depressed, not unbearably lonely. That she has plans to travel in England or in France. And this I can count on—this I *know*: she will still be buying vats of Tide and crates of toilet paper and tubs of Philadelphia cream cheese—which was ridiculous when it was only the two of them, so why would she stop herself now?

> **Dinah**
> **Comment [9]:** But I've left out so much about the man he was—he is—

DO YOU KNOW what else I hope? I hope I dream of him. I hope, in the dreams, he advises me as he always has. Though knowing those kinds of dreams, and knowing myself, I'll forget his counsel before I wake.

IN OTHER DREAMS, I hope he'll take me to the beach, and we'll look for shells, and we'll make a castle, and we'll go into the water again and again. And each time he'll hold my hand till we get past the breaking surf. And at the end of the day, he'll let me ride on his shoulders to the car. Except even if I'm able to dream him as he was, to summon him in sleep, chances are in the dream, I'll be as old as I am. Too old to ride—older than the man, who won't know me, will he? He won't recognize the future, not as it happened—not outside the scope of his imaginings. Even if I call to him: *Dad. It's me. Stay a minute. Stay with me as you are. As you were. Do you remember, Dad?*

DID IT HAPPEN that way? That day on the beach? If so, if not, might it happen in just that way in my dreams? How to insure the future, real or imagined? How to make it true? And what will I remember—in the future, about the future—that I don't remember now?

Julian Barnes

Grief

WE GO DOWN in dreams, and we go down in memory. And yes, it is true, the memory of earlier times does return, but in the meanwhile we have been made fearful, and I am not sure it is the same memory that returns. How could it be, because it can no longer be corroborated by the one who was there at the time. What we did, where we went, whom we met, how we felt. How we were together. All that. "We" are now watered down to "I." Binocular memory has become monocular. There is no longer the possibility of assembling from two uncertain memories of the same event a surer, single one, by triangulation, by aerial surveying. And so that memory, now in the first-person singular, changes. Less the memory of an event than the memory of a photograph of the event. And nowadays—having lost height, precision, focus—we are no longer sure we trust photography as we once did. Those old familiar snaps of happier times have come to seem less primal, less like photographs of life itself, more like photographs of photographs.

Wayne Koestenbaum

The Desire to Write About **The Green Line**

A GREEN line bisects the face of Matisse's wife, in a painting
Henri made in 1905, and so we call the painting *The Green Line*;
the line's unreasonable presence overshadows the woman it
besmirches. Or does the line have nothing to do with the woman?
Should we leave her out of it? Before I felt the desire to write about
The Green Line, I felt an overwhelming desire to write about a
1922 Man Ray photograph of Alice B. Toklas entering the atelier she shared with Gertrude Stein: Alice hovers in the doorway,
maybe entering, or maybe standing frozen, commanded by Man
Ray to strike a characteristic pose; I felt a desire to write about
Alice's threshold status, her occupation of an ambiguous point
between arrival and departure, but I felt a stab of remorse when I
realized that Toklas reminded me of a friend whose husband had
died a decade ago of heart disease.

Though I was not responsible for this man's death, and though
I would be doing no damage to his widow by writing about Alice
entering the atelier, nonetheless their resemblance chastened me
and made the prospect of writing about the Man Ray photograph
seem an act of premeditated violence; to write honestly about this

photograph, I would need to write about the widow, and to write honestly about the widow, I would need to describe the outline of Toklas's breasts beneath her dress, a smock that modestly veiled her body but allowed the breasts to declare their existence with an unembarrassed directness that corresponded to the steady, large grace of Gertrude Stein seated (in that same photograph) at her desk. Stein's blouse, tucked into her skirt, bunched in the back; this bunched place, a site of pressure and crowding, underlined Stein's physical amplitude, her regal comfort on her writing throne, a seat she occupied in a suspended present she would have called a continuous present. Permissive, unbroken, the time of writing (and the time of reading) didn't stop at the gate to pay a subservient toll but stretched into the past and future with a lazy (and secretly splenetic?) unfetteredness. If I were to write honestly about Stein's body and about her writing process, and if I were to write honestly about the visible implication of Toklas's breasts within her floral dress, then I would also need to describe the body of my friend whose husband died a decade ago of heart disease, and I would be trespassing on her body by mentioning it; to write about her body, I'd need to describe my torpor, as if I were drowsing in a Florida room whose jalousies admitted a variegated light, like the operating theater in *Suddenly, Last Summer*, or the ward where Tennessee Williams's sister Rose received a lobotomy. Afternoon torpor, redolent of jalousies and lobotomies, overtook me when I considered writing about Toklas entering a room suffused with a fine dust; and so I decided to write instead about Matisse's portrait of his wife, a portrait subtitled *The Green Line*. By defecting from Toklas, and hiding behind *The Green Line*, I felt cowardly—guilty of shirking my vocation's duties and cowering behind abstraction (the green line) as a way to avoid the hard work of describing ambivalence, destructiveness, guilt, and fatigue. The green line attracted me because it permitted a face to say two things at the same time. The green line permitted one half of the subject's face to be burdened (or heightened) by flesh-pink brushstrokes, wedges of conspicuous paint that offered a pressured statement, a demand, an exhibition; the other side of the face, yellow and flat, unenhanced by thick paint or emphatic brushwork, nonetheless borrowed enough green to cloak the eye-socket. Thus the face's downtrodden side flourished, albeit in a mephitic, doomed fashion, a dignity composed of too much green. Matisse's abundant green signifies a luxury that, for a writer, can only be approximated by the silence that follows an act of composition: the ordeal of sequential language, word following word, has been surmounted, and now the complicated respite of green, an indescribable green, can begin.

Lawrence Weschler

Motes in the Light

[2004]

ONE BALMY EVENING late in summer, my friend John and I drove over to the St. Ann's Warehouse performance space, slotted snug under the Brooklyn Bridge overpass on the Brooklyn side of the East River waterfront, to see a screening of Bill Morrison's *Decasia* the way it was meant to be seen. Which is to say with Michael Gordon's astonishing symphonic score being performed live by an orchestra ranged on scaffolds, one row of instrumentalists atop the next, behind three translucent screens that had in turn been arrayed in a sort of triangle, the audience seated on the floor inside, watching as three separate versions of the film were being projected onto the three screens in slightly staggered fashion—their intersecting cones of light expanding through the smoky air above us—while a conductor energetically directed the proceedings from her precarious perch on a sort of gangplank thrust out above it all. Morrison has fashioned his film entirely out of snippets of severely distressed and heartrendingly decomposed nitrate film stock: decades-old mouldering footage of geishas and desertscapes, waves breaking and clouds racing, dervishes whirling and boxers training, children playing and cells dividing—a mottled pullulating mass (the frenzy of moths at twi-light). And with Gordon's smearily decomposing score lashing the images along, the players arrayed behind the sweltering screens progressively stripping out of their clothes—the violinists down to their bras, the hairy-chested tuba player wrapped Laocoön-like in his instrument, the percussionists spraying sweat off their gleaming torsos—the whole thing packed an incredible wallop.

So anyway, afterward, you can imagine the spent exhilaration with which we left the theater and broached the warm night air, and the sense of baffled slippage with which we now spied another cone of light, this one spreading straight up vertically, high into the sky, from some mysterious source behind and beyond the dilapidated storage buildings between us and the river. We ambled down the block toward the waterfront to get a better view, and suddenly the entire downtown sweep of Manhattan opened before us, with two beams of light shooting out from its pain-fully stunted skyline. At which point we remembered, ah yes, we remembered, this was September 10, the eve of the anniversary of the disaster.

We joined a small throng gathered there on the waterfront, taking it all in, those two clean beams of light defiantly splitting the night sky. Several individuals were busy taking pictures (and several of them, improbably, were using flashes). It took a while for our eyes to adjust, but then things really began to get strange.

Because within the expanding cones of light, tiny specks of light seemed to be floating, suspended, like the spangle in an upturned snowglobe—flecks, though, of what? Confetti? Ashes? Souls? At first the swirl of motes seemed random and limited to the base of the light cones, maybe the first hundred feet above the upturned searchlights. It was hard to tell exactly from all those miles away. But the more we gazed, the more somehow volitional their movements came to seem—float, slide, wobble, but then dart and dash. Near collisions narrowly averted, sudden surges straight up. What could they possibly be? Birds? The scale was all wrong, confoundingly so, and there were thousands of them, tens of thousands, and the closer we looked, the higher they seemed to rise, hundreds of yards, all the way up, seemingly miles.

John and I decided to hop into his car, a convertible, to go investigate. We lowered the roof and negotiated the cloverleaf onto the bridge, the same bridge across which all those stunned and shell-shocked crowds had trod, in the opposite direction, that skybright morning just short of three years ago . . . (Oh, and by the way, can I just interject here, that Christo's curtain gates in Central Park this past winter were okay, I suppose, but they had nothing on the thrillingly majestic cavalcade of flexing lines you can experience any day or night of the year on the traverse across the Brooklyn Bridge?) Anyway, the brilliant motes, carnivaling about in the lightbeams beyond the bridge cables, seemed no more decipherable the closer we came. Surely they had to be alive, but then how could they be soaring like that so high into the sky, and were they huge or tiny or what? Traffic began to bunch up, and it took a good hour on the other side of the bridge to wend our way the last mile toward the bank of searchlights; we had our necks craned the entire while, the solution to the mote puzzle no more apparent. Eventually we parked and trod the last few blocks toward ground zero. Whereupon, rounding the corner, into that veritable blast of white light, we finally managed to figure it all out.

The motes were moths. Hundreds of thousands, millions of moths, rising thousands of feet into the air. Surely, it seemed, every single moth on the Eastern Seaboard had come to pay their respects that gleaming anniversary night.

Patricia Hampl

Reading

I HAVE A FRIEND who begins each day by reading a page of Proust, an intent literary mouse nibbling at the magnificent cheese. This has been going on for over ten years, and she is well beyond making showy references to the tea-drenched madeleine in volume one of *Swann's Way*. Another woman I know ends her day in bed reading Latin—"Greek would keep me awake," she once told me with an unfeigned modesty that took my breath away.

Both of these women are writers which is to say they are born and bred readers, people who begin and end the day with words streaming before them on the page, on the screen, moving from gutter to margin, back and forth in the sublime rhythm of that most intimate of relations: writer's mind to reader's mind. I read, therefore I am. But more than that: I read, therefore I am . . . *happy*.

You can see this happiness, the contentment of absolute independence of mind, on the subway, people performing this bravura act of interiority in public, reading their way past the uncaring crush of strangers, into the mysterious liberation they achieve in those secret pages. It's the privacy of reading that amazes. The writer's audience is always just one sequestered soul at a time.

But what about me at the end of the day, the first and only

time, really, that I can choose entirely what I want to read? The rest of the day is given over to reading too, but how much of it is devoted to tasks—to reviewing or blurbing (that justly ugly verb), to marking student papers, to re-reading texts for teaching? The lion's share, truth be told. On my passport it says "Writer" under Occupation, but really I'm a hired reader much of the time, tucking into words like a piggy at a smorgasbord, grabbing and tasting, nibbling an essay, pecking at a poem, a morsel of memoir, the great joint of a novel, a student's thickened thesis.

So here I am finally, tucked up for the night, as free as those subway readers I've always envied, heads bowed to their books. The stack on my nightstand is tottering—a new novel someone has sent me, a slim volume of poems by an Eastern European émigré, three recent (but not *that* recent) issues of the *New York Review of Books*, a couple *New Yorkers* squashed under a fat new biography of Emily Dickinson that I overheard someone at a dinner party say *really* settles the hash on her romantic life.

But I reach beyond all these. I grip—I'm gripped by—the latest Williams-Sonoma catalogue. It's devoted to summer, special emphasis on grilling. I don't have a grill and I've read somewhere that charred food is to be avoided, but I'm all attention. The grill accessories, especially the (*Exclusive!*) jalapeño pepper roaster and the meatball grill basket, captivate me by their blatant superfluity. The reader reviews give each of them four and a half stars (out of a possible five). A jalapeño pepper roaster—imagine *needing* one. I feel the flicker of desire spark and die. I turn the page. A full set of matching kitchen knives presents itself, including poultry shears, bread knife, boning knife, something called a slicer. The price is stratospheric. I read the accompanying text that includes testimony from a famous chef: if his house were on fire, he would snatch his cat and this set of knives as he runs for his life.

I move on to J.Crew. "For our latest collection," the text

reads, "we explored the crumbling colonial architecture and sun-drenched streets of La Antigua, Guatemala. Unearth your own summer wardrobe—and learn a bit about our shoot location while you're at it." Two louche young gringos in their light-gauge cashmeres and witty straw hats are leading a burro down one of the sun-drenched streets. I cringe and let it drop to the floor. But never mind—here's Lands' End and its refreshingly earnest Mid-western prose smoothing the flab of fashion with a promise of adequate swimsuit coverage.

The stack of catalogues goes back to winter, even to the fall before that, each season an occasion for the fevered poetics of retail. Fashion from "outerwear" to "intimate," home furnishings, bed frames and window treatments, electronics and gadgets, table linens, 600-thread-count Egyptian cotton sheets, jams and jellies, serrano hams and Himalayan rose salt, flowering bulbs, choco-lates, and sponge cakes—on and on through the endless narra-tives of avidity I go, night after night. Sometimes I cull the stack, pare my way back from winter to summer, ditch the chutney cata-logue and get real about imported Irish woolens.

But I cannot seem to give up entirely the literature of imag-inary consumption, the lift-off of paging through perfection. I almost never buy anything. There was a time when I circled choices, racking up scary totals on the catalogue order forms. But now I wing my way over the throw pillows and wicker sets of Pot-tery Barn in their "Coastal Styles" feature (which, next catalogue, will become "Mountain Ranges" or "Prairie Fire"). I give over to the frilly prose and vintage dresses of the J. Peterman catalogue with the cunning drawings (no photographs), all the better to encourage greater fantasy: "Newport Eyelet Dress . . . Light, airy, 100% cotton eyelet . . . For whatever your day may bring—a pool party, a long romantic walk, crashing society. Or creating a society of your own."

It wouldn't occur to me to order the dress. I've become a meta-shopper. I'm nothing but a reader now.

It started with cookbooks, the reading I instinctively turned to as a soporific for my insomnia. Nothing like reading your way through a recipe for boeuf bourguignon to slow the speeding mind. Elizabeth David, Richard Olney, Patricia Wells—all the Anglophones with their born-again discovery of French food made me forget whatever it was that had my mind buzzing with fret and worry. In a way, the catalogues are the CliffsNotes of sleep inducement, a sad replacement for the glory days of my cookery reading before bed.

Here, under the heading "Chopping" in *Simple French Food*, is that stern master Richard Olney in a prose unrivaled for its delicious archness: "I have tried a number of alternatives to hand-chopping, but I can only say this: Mechanical chopping will produce good results . . . and, I confess, some of my guests have been unable to discern the difference; the difference is, nonetheless, very marked. It is a question of whether you, the reader, will be satisfied with a decent product or whether you prefer something sublime."

I can only say this: believe me—I, the reader, *do* prefer something sublime. I do. I think I've proved that all these nights, flipping the slick pages, carried forward (and backward—those retro Peterman catalogues) by longing, by a desire too fine ever to be satisfied by the trivial purchase of a "decent product." Long ago I put my faith in the unreal estate of words (and pictures), the paradisal realm inhabited only by those who, like me, keep turning the pages in the night until the book slips from our hands, and the light of the ardent mind goes dark.

Marvin Bell

The Revolution Needs a Song

WHEN EVENTS OCCUR for which there are only insufficient words, when movement is forbidden, when there is only an odor of ash in darkness, when every sense has been stifled, when we wake in chains, there remains a simmering of song, a residue in which a microscopic ferment has already begun. Take two chopsticks on a countertop, a comb between two scraps of paper, two spoons to slap against a knee, a length of vinyl hose into which one has wedged a mouthpiece. If it causes you to sing or dance, if it pumps your heart or fills your lungs or rattles your spine, then you are, for the nonce, in the realm of the infinite no-mind, carried by a progression of changes. Now anything can happen. Never mind the key sign, the metronome, the trumpet players counting rests while the strings fill the hall. Never mind the danger to the longtime oboist, the bruised lips of the brass players, the stiffening fingers of the pianists. Forget that the players make music at a high personal cost. That's the profession. I am speaking here of the nature of rhythm, pitch, melody, phrasing, and harmony. The five food groups of the soul. Take a tingly triangle, a horsey woodblock, bowls full of tympani, the simplicity of a pipe with valves, the sonorous metalwork of a steel drum, a fretless washtub bass. The barest rhythm or tune can imprison or free us, and the words of songs, like dreams, are incontestable. Music always wins.

Alphabetical Table of Contents

Appendix: List of Themes

NOTE: Writers have concerns: readers find themes. At the risk of being reductive, we've listed several of the dominant ideas or images that we noticed while compiling these shorts, along with the pieces in which those concerns are evident.

Adolescence/Youth: Anastas, 127; K. Barnes, 123; Borich, 261; Boylan, 112; Capossere, 137; de Gutes, 263; Gay, 120; Gerstler, 195; Goldberg, 186; Houston, 166; Hurd, 75; Kitchen, 286; Kothari, 29; Krusoe, 230; Kubaszyk, 291; Lenney, 299; Lopate, 78; Martone, 213; McClanahan, 132; Miller, 253; Sandor, 220; Schwartz, 101; Sukrungruang, 57; Talbot, 130; Ulin, 106; Wickersham, 270; Wilson, 181

Aging: Auster, 240; Glazner, 174; Krusoe, 230; Lenney, 299; Lisicky, 296

Animal(s)/Pets: Goldberg, 186; Harvey, 110; Houston, 166; Iyer, 42; Kitchen, 286; Martone, 213; Merrill, 156; Montemarano, 85; Nadelson, 92; Oaks, 135; Philip, 259; Purpura, 68; Stephens, 160; Thomas, 210

Art/Artists: Borich, 261; Daley, 98; Daum, 115; Geyer, 151; Iuppa, 172; Koestenbaum, 308; Lopate, 78; Parms, 144; Rapp, 202; Ulin, 106; Weschler, 311

Chance/Luck: Cooper, 193; Glazner, 174; Hurd, 75; Kothari, 29; Madden, 33; Nadelson, 92; Sandor, 220

Clothing: Berne, 275; de Gutes, 263; Hampl, 314; Shumaker, 247; Wickersham, 270

Color(s): Birkerts, 38; Borich, 261; Boylan, 112; Fletcher, 62; Geyer, 151; Houston, 166; Koestenbaum, 308; Parms, 144

Bios

Hilton Als is a staff writer for the *New Yorker* whose cultural criticism weaves analyses of literature, art, and music with insights on race, gender, and history. His most recent book, *White Girls*, is a mixture of critique and meditation, fiction and nonfiction. He is the recipient of a Guggenheim fellowship and the 2002–03 George Jean Nathan Award for Dramatic Criticism.

Benjamin Anastas is the author of two novels and a memoir, *Too Good to Be True*. His work has appeared in the *Paris Review*, *Harper's*, the *New York Times Magazine*, *Bookforum*, the *Yale Review*, and *The Best American Essays*. He teaches at Bennington College and is also on the core faculty of the Bennington Writing Seminars. www.benjaminanastas.com.

Paul Auster is the author of fourteen novels and six works of nonfiction, most recently *Winter Journal*. The NPR anthology he edited, *I Thought My Father Was God*, was a national bestseller. He is a member of the American Academy of Arts and Letters, the American Academy of Arts and Sciences, and a Commandeur de l'Ordre des Arts et des Lettres. He lives in Brooklyn, New York.

Julian Barnes is the author of several books of stories, essays, and numerous novels. His recent publications include *The Sense of an Ending*, winner of the 2011 Man Booker Prize, and *Levels of Life*, described as a "triptych of history, fiction, and memoir." His honors include the Somerset Maugham

Award, the Geoffrey Faber Memorial Prize, and the E. M. Forster Award from the American Academy and Institute of Arts and Letters. He lives in London.

Kim Barnes is the author of two memoirs, including *In the Wilderness: Coming of Age in Unknown Country*, and three novels, most recently *In the Kingdom of Men*. Her work has been nominated for the Pulitzer Prize, won the PNBA Award for Nonfiction, and awarded the PEN USA Award for Literary Fiction. Barnes teaches writing at the University of Idaho. www.kimbarnes.com.

Marvin Bell's twenty-three books include *Vertigo: The Living Dead Man Poems*, *Mars Being Red*, and *Nightworks: Poems 1962–2000*. His poetic dialogue with Christopher Merrill will be published by White Pine Press in 2016. He divides his time between Port Townsend, Washington, and Iowa City, Iowa.

Suzanne Berne is the author of four novels, including *The Ghost at the Table*, *A Crime in the Neighborhood*, and, most recently, *The Dogs of Littlefield*. Her book of nonfiction is *Missing Lucile*. She lives outside of Boston. www.suzanneberne.net.

Sven Birkerts is director of the Bennington Writing Seminars. He edits the journal *AGNI* at Boston University. His books include *The Other Walk: Essays* and *The Gutenberg Elegies*. His next collection of essays, as yet untitled, will be published by Graywolf Press in 2015.

Joe Bonomo is the author of *Sweat: The Story of the Fleshtones, America's Garage Band*; *Jerry Lee Lewis: Lost and Found*; and, most recently, *This Must Be Where My Obsession with Infinity Began*. He is an associate professor of English at Northern Illinois University and the music columnist at the Normal School, and he appears online at www.nosuchthingaswas.com.

Barrie Jean Borich's *Body Geographic* won a Lambda Literary Award, an IPPY Gold Medal in Nonfiction, and an IndieFab Bronze Award for Essays. Her previous book, *My Lesbian Husband*, won the Stonewall Book Award. She's a faculty member at DePaul University in Chicago, where she edits the nonfiction journal *Slag Glass City*. www.barriejeanborich.com.

Jennifer Finney Boylan is the author of thirteen books, including the memoirs *She's Not There*, *I'm Looking Through You*, and *Stuck in the Middle* *with You.* She is the Anna Quindlen Writer in Residence at Barnard College of Columbia University. A resident of Maine and New York City, she has served on the board of directors of GLAAD; the Kinsey Institute for Research on Sex, Gender, and Reproduction; and is a contributing opinion writer for the *New York Times.* www.jenniferboylan.net.

Jane Brox is the author of four books, including *Brilliant: The Evolution of Artificial Light* and *Five Thousand Days Like This One: An American Family History.* Her work has been selected for *The Best American Essays* and *The Pushcart Prize Anthology.* She is the recipient of grants from the Guggenheim Foundation and the National Endowment for the Arts. She lives in Maine and teaches in the Lesley University Low-Residency MFA Program. www.janebrox.com.

Bill Capossere's fiction and nonfiction have appeared in the anthologies *Man in the Moon, Short Takes,* and *In Short,* as well as in several journals/magazines, including *Harper's,* the *Colorado Review,* and *Alaska Quarterly Review.* He lives in Rochester, New York.

Martha Cooley is the author of two novels, *The Archivist* (a national bestseller also published in a dozen foreign markets) and *Thirty-Three Swoons.* Her short fiction, essays, and translations have appeared in numerous literary journals. She is an associate professor of English at Adelphi University.

Bernard Cooper is the recipient of the PEN/USA Ernest Hemingway Award, an O. Henry Prize, a Guggenheim grant, and an NEA fellowship in literature. His most recent book is *My Avant-Garde Education.* His work has appeared in many anthologies, including *The Best American Essays.* For six years he wrote monthly features as the art critic for *Los Angeles* magazine. www.bernardcooper.net.

Jennifer Culkin is the author of *A Final Arc of Sky.* A winner of the 2008 Rona Jaffe Foundation Writers' Award, she is also a registered nurse whose career has encompassed neonatal, pediatric, and adult critical care, as well as emergency air transport. www.jenniferculkin.com.

Chris Daley's work has appeared in the *Los Angeles Times,* the *Los Angeles Review of Books,* and the *Collagist.* She teaches academic writing at the California Institute of Technology and, as codirector of Writing Workshops Los

Angeles, offers creative nonfiction workshops for students at all levels. www
.chrisdaley.com.

Tracy Daugherty is the author of four novels and five short story collections, including *Hiding Man, Just One Catch*, and *The Last Love Song*. He is also the author of a book of personal essays, *Five Shades of Shadow*, as well as biographies of Donald Barthelme, Joseph Heller, and Joan Didion. He has received fellowships from the Guggenheim Foundation and the National Endowment for the Arts. He lives in Oregon. www.tracydaugherty.com.

Meghan Daum is the author of four books, most recently *The Unspeakable . . . And Other Subjects of Discussion*. An opinion columnist for the *Los Angeles Times* since 2005, she has contributed to publications such as the *New Yorker, Harper's*, and *Vogue*, and is the editor of the anthology *Selfish, Shallow, and Self-Absorbed: Sixteen Writers on the Decision Not to Have Kids*. www
.meghandaum.com.

Kate Carroll de Gutes writes on a wide range of topics, but her obsession seems to focus on sexuality and gender presentation. Some of her favorite publication credits include *Brevity, Fourth Genre*, the *Los Angeles Review, PANK*, and the *Seattle Review*. Kate lives, writes, and rides her bikes in Portland, Oregon. katecarrolldegutes.com.

Stuart Dybek's most recent books of fiction, *Ecstatic Cahoots* and *Paper Lantern*, were published simultaneously in 2014. He is the author of three other books of fiction and two books of poetry. His work has received numerous awards, including a MacArthur Fellowship. He is the distinguished writer in residence at Northwestern University.

Anika Fajardo was born in Colombia and raised in Minnesota. Her work has appeared in various publications, including *Creative Nonfiction, McSweeney's Internet Tendency, Hippocampus* magazine, and others. "What Didn't Happen" is an excerpt from her memoir entitled *Magical Realism for Non-Believers*. www.anikafajardo.com.

Harrison Candelaria Fletcher is the author of *Descanso for My Father: Fragments of a Life*, winner of the Colorado Book Award for Creative Nonfiction and International Book Award for Best New Nonfiction. He teaches in the Virginia Commonwealth University MFA in Writing Program. www
.harrisoncandelariafletcher.com.

Eduardo Galeano, one of Latin America's most distinguished writers, is the author of the three-volume *Memory of Fire*, *Open Veins of Latin America*, *Mirrors*, and *Children of the Days*, among others. He was the recipient of many prizes, including the Lannan Prize for Cultural Freedom. He lives in Montevideo, Uruguay. Mark Fried is the translator of seven books by Eduardo Galeano. He lives in Ottawa, Canada.

J. Malcolm Garcia is the author of *What I Leave Behind: The Faceless and the Forgotten*. Other books include *Riding Through Katrina with the Red Baron's Ghost* and *The Khaarijee: A Chronicle of Friendship and War in Kabul*. His articles have been featured in *The Best American Travel Writing* and *The Best American Nonrequired Reading*. He has received the Studs Terkel Prize and the Sigma Delta Chi award for excellence in journalism. www.malcolmgarcia.com.

Roxane Gay's writing has appeared in *The Best American Mystery Stories*, *The Best American Short Stories*, *McSweeney's*, *Tin House*, *West Branch*, *Virginia Quarterly Review*, the *New York Times*, the *Los Angeles Times*, the *Nation*, and others. She is the co-editor of *PANK*. She is also the author of *An Untamed State*, *Bad Feminist*, and *Hunger*, forthcoming from Harper in 2016. She teaches at Purdue University. www.roxanegay.com.

Amy Gerstler is the author of *Dearest Creature*, *Ghost Girl*, and *Medicine*, among other titles. She is a professor of English in the MFA Programs in Writing (Poetry) at the University of California at Irvine.

Nancy Geyer is an essayist and the art editor for *Terrain.org: A Journal of the Built + Natural Environments*. Her work has appeared in *Alaska Quarterly Review*, the *Georgia Review*, *Gulf Coast*, and the *Iowa Review*, among other journals, and in *Pushcart Prize XXXIX: Best of the Small Presses*. She lives in Washington, D.C.

Greg Glazner's books of poetry are *From the Iron Chair*, which won the Walt Whitman Award, and *Singularity*. His recently completed novel is *Opening the World*. Also an electric guitarist, he reads and performs with his band Professor Len and the Big Night. He teaches at UC Davis. www.gregglazner.com.

Tod Goldberg is the author of the novel *Gangsterland*, the story collection *Other Resort Cities*, and the popular *Burn Notice* series. His nonfiction has appeared in the *Los Angeles Times*, the *Wall Street Journal*, and *The Best American Essays*. He lives in Indio, California, where he directs the Low-Residency MFA in Creative Writing at UC Riverside. www.todgoldberg.com.

Patricia Hampl is the recipient of a Guggenheim Foundation Fellowship and a MacArthur Fellowship. An American memoirist, writer, lecturer, and educator, she teaches in the MFA program at the University of Minnesota at Minneapolis and is one of the founding members of the Loft Literary Center. Her books include *The Florist's Daughter* and *A Romantic Education*; a new book, *The Art of the Wasted Day*, will be published in 2016.

Steven Harvey is the author of four books of essays, most recently *The Book of Knowledge and Wonder*. His work has appeared in *Harper's*, the *Georgia Review*, *River Teeth*, *Fourth Genre*, and the *Oxford American*. An emeritus professor of English at Young Harris College as well as a member of the faculty in the Ashland University MFA Program in Creative Writing, he now serves as a senior editor for *River Teeth* magazine. www.the-humble-essayist .com.

Emily Holt lives in Seattle, Washington, where she facilitates writing with youth in juvenile detention and psychiatric care. She will receive her MFA from the Rainier Writing Workshop in 2016. Her essay in this book is her first major publication.

Pam Houston is the author of the story collections *Cowboys Are My Weakness* and *Waltzing the Cat*, the novels *Contents May Have Shifted* and *Sight Hound*, and a collection of essays, *A Little More About Me*. She is the winner of the Western States Book Award. She is a professor of English at UC Davis, directs the literary nonprofit Writing by Writers, and teaches in the Pacific University low-residency MFA program. www.pamhouston .wordpress.com.

Barbara Hurd is the author of four books of creative nonfiction, including the forthcoming *Putting an Ear to the Ground*. Winner of the Sierra Club's Nature Writing Contest, an NEA Fellowship, and five Maryland State Arts Council grants, she teaches in the Vermont College of Fine Arts MFA in Writing Program.

M. J. Iuppa lives on a farm near the shores of Lake Ontario. *Between Worlds* is her most recent chapbook, featuring lyric essays, flash fiction, and prose poems. She is director of the Visual and Performing Arts Minor Program at St. John Fisher College in Rochester, New York. Her musings on writing and sustainability on Red Rooster Farm can be found on www.mjiuppa .blogspot.com.

Pico Iyer is the author of two novels and eight works of nonfiction, including *Video Night in Kathmandu*, *The Lady and the Monk*, *The Global Soul*, and *The Man Within My Head*. Much of his writing is about travel, much is about stillness. www.picoiyerjourneys.com.

Leslie Jamison is the author of *The Empathy Exams*, an essay collection, and a novel, *The Gin Closet*, a finalist for the *Los Angeles Times* First Fiction Award. Her work has appeared in *Harper's*, *Oxford American*, *A Public Space*, *Boston Review*, *Virginia Quarterly Review*, the *Believer*, and the *New York Times*, where she is a regular columnist for the *Sunday Book Review*. www .lesliejamison.com; @lsjamison.

Judith Kitchen authored four collections of essays, most recently *The Circus Train* (essays) and *What Persists*, a selection of her essay reviews of poetry. She edited or co-edited four anthologies of brief nonfiction for W. W. Norton. Until her death in November 2014, she lived and wrote in Port Townsend, Washington. www.ovenbirdbooks.org; judithkitchen.com.

Wayne Koestenbaum is an American poet and cultural critic. His books include *My 1980s and Other Essays*, *Humiliation*, and *The Queen's Throat: Opera, Homosexuality, and the Mystery of Desire*. Currently he lives in New York City, where he is distinguished professor of English at the City University of New York Graduate Center.

Geeta Kothari is the nonfiction editor of the *Kenyon Review*. Her fiction and nonfiction have appeared in various journals and anthologies, including the *Kenyon Review*, the *Massachusetts Review*, *Fourth Genre*, and *The Best American Essays*. She teaches at the University of Pittsburgh.

Jim Krusoe is the author of six novels, the most recent being *Parsifal*. He has also written two books of stories, five books of poems, and is the founding editor of the *Santa Monica Review*. He teaches at Santa Monica College and in the Graduate Writing Program at Antioch University.

Josette Kubaszyk's poetry and essays have appeared in *Marco Polo Arts* magazine, *Riverbend*, the *Noun*, and *Storm Cellar*. She writes literary reviews for *River Teeth: A Journal of Creative Nonfiction* and teaches part-time at Purdue University's north-central campus. She lives with her family in La Porte, Indiana. www.josettekubaszyk.com.

Lance Larsen, poet laureate of Utah, has published four poetry collections, most recently *Genius Loci*. His nonfiction has appeared in *Southern Review*, *Brevity*, *Kenyon Review Online*, and elsewhere. His awards include an NEA grant and a Pushcart Prize. His new collection of essays is titled *Seventeen Ways to Float*. He teaches at Brigham Young University.

Dinah Lenney is the author of *Bigger than Life: A Murder, a Memoir*, and *The Object Parade*, and co-edited *Brief Encounters* with the late Judith Kitchen. She serves as core faculty in the Bennington Writing Seminars and in the Rainier Writing Workshop, and as the senior nonfiction editor for the *Los Angeles Review of Books*. www.dinahlenney.com.

Paul Lisicky is the author of *The Narrow Door*, *Unbuilt Projects*, *The Burning House*, and two other books. He teaches in the MFA program at Rutgers-Camden and serves as editor of *StoryQuarterly*. www.paullisicky.com.

Sonja Livingston's first book, *Ghostbread*, won the AWP Prize for Nonfiction. Her essays have been honored with an *Iowa Review* Award, a Susan Atefat Prize, and fellowships from New York Foundation for the Arts, the Vermont Studio Center, and the Deming Fund for Women. She splits her time between New York State and Tennessee, where she teaches in the MFA program at the University of Memphis. www.sonjalivingston.com.

Phillip Lopate is the author of over a dozen books—novels, poetry, and essay collections—and the editor of the anthology *Art of the Personal Essay*. His own titles include, most recently, *Portrait Inside My Head* and *To Show and to Tell: The Craft of Literary Nonfiction*. He directs the MFA nonfiction program at Columbia University and lives in Brooklyn, New York, with his wife and daughter. www.philliplopate.com.

Joe Mackall is the author of *Plain Secrets: An Outsider Among the Amish*, and the memoir *The Last Street Before Cleveland*. He is the cofounder and co-editor of *River Teeth: A Journal of Nonfiction Narrative*. His essays have appeared in the *New York Times*, the *Washington Post*, and on NPR's *Morning Edition*. He teaches in the MFA program at Ashland University.

Patrick Madden is the author of *Quotidiana* and *Sublime Physick*, and co-editor of *After Montaigne: Contemporary Essayists Cover the Essays*. His essays have been selected for *Best American Spiritual Writing* and *Best Creative Nonfiction*. He teaches at Brigham Young University and the Vermont College of Fine Arts, and has twice been a Fulbright fellow in Uruguay. www.quotidiana.org.

Michael Martone was born in Fort Wayne, Indiana, and is the author of *Michael Martone*, a memoir done in contributor's notes like this one. His other books include *The Flatness and Other Landscapes*, *Unconventions*, and *Racing in Place*. He lives below the bugline, in Tuscaloosa, Alabama, where he teaches writing at the University of Alabama.

Rebecca McClanahan's tenth book is *The Tribal Knot: A Memoir of Family, Community, and a Century of Change*. Her text *Word Painting: The Fine Art of Writing Descriptively* was published by Writer's Digest Books. Recipient of the Glasgow Award in nonfiction, the Wood Prize from *Poetry*, and a Pushcart Prize, she teaches in the MFA programs of Queens University and the Rainier Writing Workshop. www.mcolanmuse.co.

Cheryl Merrill's essays have appeared in such journals as *Fourth Genre*, *Brevity*, *Alaska Quarterly Review*, and *Isotope*. Her essay "Singing Like Yma Sumac" was selected for the *Best of Brevity* 2005 and included in *Creative Nonfiction* #27 as well as *Short Takes: Model Essays for Composition*, Tenth Edition. She is currently working on a book about elephants, *Larger than Life: Living in the Shadows of Elephants*. www.cherylmerrill.com.

Brenda Miller is the author of *Who You Will Become*, *Listening Against the Stone*, *Blessing of the Animals*, and *Season of the Body*. She co-authored *Tell it Slant: Creating, Refining, and Publishing Creative Nonfiction* and *The Pen and the Bell: Mindful Writing in a Busy World*. Her work has received six Pushcart Prizes. She is a professor of English in Western Washington University's MFA program. www.brendamillerwriter.com.

Nicholas Montemarano is the author of three books, most recently the novel *The Book of Why*. His stories have appeared widely in places such as *Esquire*, *Tin House*, *Zoetrope: All-Story*, and *DoubleTake*. He has won a Pushcart Prize in fiction and an NEA grant. He teaches at Franklin & Marshall College. www.nicholasmontemarano.com.

Dinty W. Moore is author of the collection *Dear Mister Essay Writer Guy: Curious Meditations on Life, Love, Cannibals, and the Imminent Polar Bear Apocalypse*, as well as the memoir *Between Panic & Desire*, winner of the Grub Street Nonfiction Book Prize. A professor of nonfiction writing at Ohio University, Moore lives in Athens, Ohio, where he grows heirloom tomatoes, lemon cucumbers, and edible dandelions. www.dintywmoore.com.

Scott Nadelson is the author of three story collections, most recently *Aftermath*, and a memoir, *The Next Scott Nadelson: A Life in Progress*. Winner of an Oregon Book Award, the Great Lakes Colleges Association New Writers Award, and the Reform Judaism Fiction Prize, he teaches at Willamette University and in the MFA Program at Pacific Lutheran University. www.scottnadelson.com.

Naomi Shihab Nye's most recent books are *The Turtle of Oman* and *Transfer*. She has edited eight prizewinning anthologies of poetry and is a chancellor of the Academy of American Poets. Website: www.barclayagency.com/nye.html.

Jeff Oaks is the author of four chapbooks, most recently *Mistakes with Strangers*. His poems and essays have appeared in *Field*, *Mid-American Review*, *Creative Nonfiction*, *At Length*, and *Assaracus*. The recipient of three fellowships from the Pennsylvania Council on the Arts, he teaches writing at the University of Pittsburgh and blogs at www.jeffoaks.wordpress.com.

Jericho Parms is an essayist whose work has appeared in *Hotel Amerika*, *American Literary Review*, *Bellingham Review*, *Sonora Review*, and elsewhere. Her writing has received support from the Vermont Arts Council and National Endowment for the Arts. She earned her MFA at Vermont College of Fine Arts, and is a nonfiction editor at *Hunger Mountain*.

Leila Philip is the author of *The Road Through Miyama*, for which she received the 1990 PEN Martha Albrand Special Citation for Nonfiction; and the memoir *A Family Place: A Hudson Valley Farm, Three Centuries, Five Wars, One Family*. She has received fellowships from the NEA and NEH, as well as the John Simon Guggenheim Foundation. She is a professor in the English Department at the College of the Holy Cross. Her new book, *Water Rising*, is available from New Rivers Press. www.leilaphilip.com.

Lia Purpura is the author of eight collections, including *Rough Likeness* and *On Looking* (essays), a finalist for the National Book Critics Circle Award. Her work has been awarded Guggenheim, Fulbright, and NEA fellowships as well as three Pushcart Prizes. She is writer in residence at the University of Maryland, Baltimore County, and a member of the core faculty of the Rainier Writing Workshop. www.liapurpura.com.

Claudia Rankine is the author of *Citizen* and *Don't Let Me Be Lonely*. She is co-editor of the *American Women Poets in the Twenty-First Century* series for Wesleyan University Press. Forthcoming is *The Racial Imaginary* with Fence Books and *Oft*, co-authored with Karen Green, with Omnidawn. A recipient of the Jackson Prize and fellowships from the Academy of American Poets and the National Endowments for the Arts, she teaches at Pomona College. www.claudiarankine.com.

Emily Rapp is the author of *The Still Point of the Turning World* and *Poster Child*. Her work has appeared in the *New York Times*, the *Boston Globe*, *Slate*, *Salon*, *Vogue*, *Redbook*, the *Sun*, *O the Oprah Magazine*, and many other publications. She teaches writing in the University of California-Riverside Palm Desert MFA program and at the University of New Mexico as the Joseph M. Russo Endowed Chair of Creative Writing.

James Richardson's most recent collections are *Theory of Everything*, *By the Numbers: Poems and Aphorisms*, which was a finalist for the National Book Award, and *Interglacial*, which was a finalist for the National Book Critics Circle Award. He teaches at Princeton University.

Marjorie Sandor is the author of four books, most recently *The Late Interiors: A Life Under Construction*. Her story collection *Portrait of My Mother, Who Posed Nude in Wartime* won the 2004 National Jewish Book Award in Fiction, and *The Night Gardener: A Search for Home* won a 2000 Oregon Book Award. She is the editor of a new anthology, *The Uncanny Reader*, and teaches in the MFA program at Oregon State University. www.marjoriesandor.com.

Lynne Sharon Schwartz is the author of the novels *Leaving Brooklyn*, *The Writing on the Wall*, and *Disturbances in the Field*; the memoir *Ruined by Reading*; and the essay collections *Face to Face* and *This Is Where We Came In*.

She has received awards from the Guggenheim Foundation, the NEA, and the New York State Foundation for the Arts. She is on the faculty of the Bennington Writing Seminars and also teaches at the Columbia University School of the Arts. www.lynnesharonschwartz.com.

Peggy Shumaker, Alaska State Writer Laureate for 2010–12, is the author of seven books of poetry, most recently *Toucan Nest: Poems of Costa Rica*. Her memoir is *Just Breathe Normally*. Professor emerita from University of Alaska, Fairbanks, she now teaches in the Rainier Writing Workshop. She is founding editor of Boreal Books and edits the Alaska Literary Series at University of Alaska Press. She was the Rasmuson Foundation's Distinguished Artist for 2014. www.peggyshumaker.com.

Liz Stephens is the author of a memoir, *The Days Are Gods*. She has work in other anthologies, including *Dirt: A Love Story* from University of New England Press and *Westering Women*, edited by Mary Clearman Blew. Previous work can be found in *Fourth Genre* and *Brevity*. She is at work on her second book, called *American Animal*. www.thedaysaregods.com.

Ira Sukrungruang is the author of the memoirs *Talk Thai: The Adventures of Buddhist Boy* and *Southside Buddhist*. He is the co-editor of *What Are You Looking At? The First Fat Fiction Anthology* and *Scoot Over, Skinny: The Fat Nonfiction Anthology*. One of the founding editors of *Sweet: A Literary Confection*, he teaches in the MFA program at University of South Florida and the low-residency MFA program at City University in Hong Kong. www.buddhistboy.com.

Jill Talbot is the author of *The Way We Weren't* and *Loaded: Women and Addiction*, the co-editor of *The Art of Friction: Where (Non)Fictions Come Together*, and the editor of *Metawritings: Toward a Theory of Nonfiction*. Her essays have appeared in *Brevity*, *DIAGRAM*, *Ecotone*, *Passages North*, the *Paris Review Daily*, the *Pinch*, the *Rumpus*, *Seneca Review*, and more. www.jilltalbot.net.

Abigail Thomas's memoir *A Three Dog Life* was named one of the best books of 2006 by the *Los Angeles Times* and the *Washington Post*. Other books include *Safekeeping*, a memoir, and *Thinking About Memoir*. She is the mother of four children and the grandmother of twelve. When Thomas can't write, she paints on glass. She lives with her four dogs in Woodstock, New York. www.abigailthomas.net.

David L. Ulin is the author of the novella *Labyrinth*. His other books include *The Lost Art of Reading: Why Books Matter in a Distracted Time*, *The Myth of Solid Ground: Earthquakes, Prediction, and the Fault Line Between Reason and Faith*, and *Writing Los Angeles: A Literary Anthology*, which won a California Book Award. He teaches at USC and in the low-residency MFA in creative writing program at UC Riverside. He is book critic of the *Los Angeles Times*.

Lawrence Weschler, for twenty years a staff writer at the *New Yorker*, is the author of *Uncanny Valley: Adventures in the Narrative*, *Vermeer in Bosnia*, *Mr. Wilson's Cabinet of Wonder*, and *Everything That Rises: A Book of Convergences*, among others. He has been a contributing editor at *McSweeney's*, *Wholphin*, the *Virginia Quarterly Review*, and the *Threepenny Review*. From 2001 to 2013, he was director of the New York Institute for the Humanities at NYU. www.lawrenceweschler.com.

Joan Wickersham's most recent book, *The News from Spain*, was named one of the year's best fiction picks by NPR, *Kirkus Reviews*, and the *San Francisco Chronicle*. Her memoir *The Suicide Index* was a National Book Award Finalist. Her short fiction and essays have appeared in *The Best American Short Stories* and *The Best American Nonrequired Reading*. She writes a regular op-ed column for the *Boston Globe*. www.joanwickersham.com.

Jonathan Wilson is the author of eight books, including the novels *The Hiding Room* and *A Palestine Affair*, as well as *Kick and Run*, a memoir. His work has appeared in the *New Yorker*, *Esquire*, and the *New York Times Magazine*. Recipient of a John Simon Guggenheim Fellowship, Wilson lives in Massachusetts, where he is Fletcher Professor of Rhetoric and Debate and director of the Center for the Humanities at Tufts University. www.jonathanmwilson.com.

S. L. Wisenberg is the author of three prose books, *The Sweetheart Is In*, *Holocaust Girls: History, Memory & Other Obsessions*, and *The Adventures of Cancer Bitch*. She has received grants and awards from the Fine Arts Work Center in Provincetown, the Illinois Arts Council, and the National Endowment for the Humanities. She grew up in Texas and lives in Chicago. www.slwisenberg.blogspot.com.

Photo Credits

Permissions

Sonja Livingston, "A Thousand Mary Doyles," first published in *Brevity*/brevitymag.com. Printed by permission of the author.

Phillip Lopate, "Max and Minna." Printed by permission of the author.

Joe Mackall, "When You Write About Murder," first published in *Solstice Review*/ solsticelitmag.org. Printed by permission of the author.

Patrick Madden, "Dispatch from Montevideo, in which the Madden family flies to Uruguay and plays the lottery," from "Dispatches from Montevideo," first published in *McSweeney's*/www.mcsweeneys.net. Printed by permission of the author.

Michael Martone, "Brooding" first published in *bending genre*/bendinggenre.com. Translations, original. Printed by permission of the author.

Rebecca McClanahan, "Things Gone the Way of Time," first published in *Brevity*/brevitymag.com. Printed by permission of the author.

Cheryl Merrill, "Wild Life." Printed by permission of the author.

Brenda Miller, "Swerve," first published in *Brevity*/brevitymag.com, from *Who You Will Become*, Shebooks, 2014. Printed by permission of the author.

Nicholas Montemarano, "No Results Found." Printed by permission of the author.

Dinty W. Moore, "If Mr. Clean Had Been My Father," first published in *Fourth Genre: Explorations in Nonfiction*, Fall 2003. Printed by permission of the author.

Scott Nadelson, "Parental Pride." Printed by permission of the author.

Naomi Shihab Nye, "Thanksgiving Picnic." Printed by permission of the author.

Jeff Oaks, "4 for Easter," from a blog/jeffoaks.wordpress.com. Printed by permission of the author.

Jericho Parms, "Red," excerpt from "Red," first published in *Hotel Amerika*. Printed by permission of the author.

Leila Philip, "Water Rising," first published in *River Teeth*. Printed by permission of the author.

Lia Purpura, "Brief Treatise Against Irony," first published in *AGNI* magazine. Printed by permission of the author.

Claudia Rankine, "Excerpt from *Don't Let Me Be Lonely*." Claudine Rankin, *Don't Let Me Be Lonely: An American Lyric*. Copyright © 2004 by Claudia Rankine. Reprinted with the permission of The Permissions Company, Inc., on behalf of Graywolf Press/www.graywolfpress.org.